EFFECTIVENESS OF PROGRAMMED INSTRUCTION

EFFECTIVENESS OF PROGRAMMED INSTRUCTION

By

Dr. Mallikarjun C. Kankatte

M.Sc., M.Ed., M.Phil. Ph.D.
Principal
Sahil College of Education
Bidar, (Karnataka) (India)

Editor

Dr. Digumarti Bhaskara Rao

M.Sc., M.A., M.A., M.Ed., Ph.D.
Principal & Professor
R.V.R. College of Education
D-43 (277) S.V.N. Colony
Guntur - 522 006 (India)
&
Member, Board of Studies in Education
Acharya Nagarjuna University
digumartibhaskararao@rediffmail.com

DISCOVERY PUBLISHING HOUSE PVT. LTD.
NEW DELHI-110 002

Published by:
Tilak Wasan
DISCOVERY PUBLISHING HOUSE PVT. LTD.
4383/4B, Ansari Road, Darya Ganj
New Delhi-110 002 (India)
Phone : +91-11-23279245, 43596064-65
Fax : +91-11-23253475
E-mail : discoverypublishinghouse@gmail.com
sales@discoverypublishinggroup.com
parul.wasan@gmail.com
web : www.discoverypublishinggroup.com

***First Edition:* 2013**

ISBN: 978-93-5056-258-1

Effectiveness of Programmed Instruction

Printed at:
Dynamic Printers
Delhi

Dedicated

to

Lord Sri Venkateswara Swamy

Foreword

Science is considered as one of those human activities that man has created to satisfy his needs and desires. The systematized store of human knowledge gained after generalizing and inter-relating the various isolated facts is known as science. Science is a cumulative and endless series of empirical observations, which result in the formation of concepts and theories, with both concepts and theories being subject to modification in the light of further empirical (practical) observations. Science is both a body of knowledge and the process of acquiring it. Science is accumulated and systematized learning in general usage restricted to natural phenomenon. The progress of science is not marked not only by an accumulation of fact, but by the emergence of scientific method and of the scientific attitude.

The purpose of physical science teaching in secondary schools is to enable the students to grasp systematically the basic knowledge of physical science needed for the further study of modern science and technology and to understand its applications. In addition, it should help them to acquire experiment skills, develop the ability to think and to use mathematics to solve physical problems, cultivate a dialectical material First view point and make them aware of need to study haul and to struggle for the modernization, along socialist lines, of industry, agriculture, national defense and science and technology. For teaching physical science more effectively, we need more advanced teaching strategies along with the traditional ones. One such is programmed instruction.

Programmed instruction is the process of arranging the material to be learned into a series of sequential steps, usually it moves the student from a familiar background into a complex and new set of concepts, principles and understanding (Smith and More, 1962). A programme is a sequence of small steps of institutional material (called frames), most of which requires a response to be made by completing a blank space in a sentence. To ensure that required responses are given, a system of cuing is applied, and each response is verified by the provision of immediate knowledge of results. Such a sequence is intended to be worked at the learners 'own pace as individualized self-instruction (Leith, 1966). Programmed learning is the first application of laboratory technique utilized in the study of the learning process to the practical problems of education (Skinner, 1954). Programmed learning as popularly understood as a method of giving individualized instruction, in which the student is active and proceeds at his own pace and is provided with immediate knowledge of results. The teacher is not physically pre-sent (Gulati and Gulati, 1976). The programmer, while developing programmed material has to follow the laws of behaviour and validate his strategy in terms of student learning.

Identifying the role of the effectiveness of programmed instruction as an instructional strategy in teaching physical science, the present has been undertaken for a detailed study. The findings of the study were stated below.

The post-test scores of academic achievement in physical science of secondary school students are high as compared to pre-test of academic achievement in physical science experimental group students. The post-test academic achievement in physical science of secondary school students is high as compared to pre-test academic achievement in physical science of secondary school conventional group students. The post-test academic achievement in physical science of secondary school students is high as compared to pre-test of academic achievement in physical science of secondary school experimental group boys. The post-test academic achievement in physical science of secondary school boys is high as compared to pre-test academic achievement in physical science of secondary school conventional group students. The post-test academic achievement in physical science of secondary school students is high as compared to pre-test academic achievement in physical science of secondary school experimental group girls. The post-test academic achievement in physical science of secondary school girls is high as compared to pre-test academic achievement in physical science of secondary school conventional group students. The post-test academic achievement in physical science of secondary school students is high in experimental group as compared to conventional group. The gain of pre- and post-test of academic achievement in physical science of secondary school students is high in experimental group as compared to conventional group. The post-test of academic achievement in physical science of secondary school students is high in experimental group as compared to conventional group. The gain of pre- and post-test of academic achievement in physical science of secondary school students is high in experimental group as compared to conventional group. The pre-test of academic achievement in physical science of secondary school boys is high in experimental group as compared to conventional group. The post-test of academic achievement in physical science of secondary school boys is high in experimental group as compared to conventional group. The gain of pre- and post-test of academic achievement in physical science of secondary school boys is high in experimental group as compared to conventional group. The pre-test of academic achievement in physical science of secondary school girls is high in experimental group as compared to conventional group. The post-test of academic achievement in physical science of secondary school girls is high in experimental group as compared to conventional group. The attitude towards physical science of secondary school students is high in experimental group as compared to conventional group. The attitude towards programmed instruction of secondary school students is high in experimental group as compared to conventional group. The achievement motivation of secondary school students is high in experimental group as compared to conventional group. The achievement motivation of secondary school girls is high in experimental group as compared to conventional group. The secondary school boys are high in post-test academic achievements in physical science as compared to girls of secondary schools. The secondary school boys have high in post-test academic achievements in physical science as compared to secondary school girls in experimental group. The urban and rural secondary school students have different post-test academic achievements in physical science. The urban and rural secondary school experimental group students have different post-test academic achievements in physical science. The urban secondary school conventional group students have high in post-test academic achievement in physical science than the post-test academic achievement in physical science. The urban and rural secondary school conventional group students have different gain of pre-test and post-test academic achievements in physical science. The urban and rural secondary school students have different levels attitude towards physical science. The urban and rural secondary school students have different levels of attitude towards programmed instruction. The urban and rural secondary school students have different levels of achievement motivation. The urban secondary school experiment group students have high on attitude towards physical science when compared to rural secondary school students. The urban secondary school experiment group students have high on attitude towards programmed instruction when compared to rural secondary school students. The urban secondary school students have high on attitude towards programmed instruction in conventional group when compared to rural secondary school students. The urban secondary school conventional group students have high achievement motivation as compared to rural secondary school students. The students of aided secondary schools have high academic achievement in physical sciences in post-test as compared to unaided and government school students. The students of aided secondary schools have high gain in academic achievement in pre-and post-tests in physical sciences as compared to unaided and government school students. The students of aided secondary schools have high in academic achievement in physical sciences in post-test as compared to unaided and government school conventional group students. The students of aided secondary schools have high gain academic achievement in pre- and post-tests in physical sciences as compared to unaided and government schools conventional group students. The students of aided secondary schools have high attitude towards physical science as compared to unaided and government school students. The students of aided secondary schools have high attitude towards programmed instruction as compared to unaided and government school students. The students of aided secondary schools have high in achievement motivation as compared to unaided and government school students. The students of aided secondary schools have high attitude towards physical science as compared to unaided and government school conventional group students. The students of aided secondary schools have high in attitude towards programmed instruction as compared to unaided and government school conventional group students. The students of aided secondary schools have high in achievement motivation as compared to unaided and government school conventional group students. The secondary school students belonging to high achievement motivation have high academic achievement in physical science in pre-test as compared to secondary school students in achievement motivation. The secondary school students belonging to high achievement motivation have high academic achievement in physical science in post-test as compared to secondary school students having lower academic achievement. The secondary school students of belonging to high achievement motivation have high gain of pre- and post-test of academic achievement in physical science as compared to secondary school students with low achievement motivation. The secondary school students belonging to high achievement motivation have high attitude towards physical science as compared to secondary school students with low achievement motivation. The secondary school students belonging to high achievement motivation have high attitude towards programmed instruction as compared to secondary school students with low achievement motivation. The secondary school students belonging to high achievement motivation have high academic achievement in physical science in pre-test as compared to secondary school experiment group students with low achievement motivation. The secondary school students belonging to high achievement motivation have high academic achievement in physical science in post-test as compared to secondary school experimental group students with low achievement motivation. The secondary school students belonging to high achievement motivation have high gain in academic achievement in physical science in pre-- and post-test as compared to secondary school experimental group students with low achievement motivation. The secondary school students belonging to high achievement motivation have high attitude towards physical science as compared to secondary school experimental group students with low achievement motivation. The secondary school students belonging to high achievement motivation have high attitude towards programmed instruction as compared to secondary school experimental group student with low achievement motivation. The secondary school students belonging to high achievement motivation have high post-test academic achievement in physical science as compared to secondary school conventional group students with low achievement motivation. The secondary school students belonging to high achievement motivation have high attitude towards physical science as compared to secondary school conventional group students with low achievement motivation. The secondary school students belonging to high achievement motivation have high attitude towards programmed instruction as compared to secondary school conventional group students with achievement motivation.

Increase in attitude towards physical science increases their academic achievement in physical science of secondary school students as a whole. Increase in the attitude towards programmed instruction increases their academic achievement in physical science of secondary school students as a whole. Increase in the achievement motivation increases their academic achievement in physical science of secondary school students as a whole. Increase in the attitude towards physical science increases their academic achievement in physical science of secondary school conventional group students. Increase in the attitude towards programmed instruction increases their academic achievement in physical science of secondary schools conventional group students. Increase in the achievement motivation increases their academic achievement in physical science of secondary school conventional group students. Increase in the achievement motivation increases their academic achievement in physical science of secondary school conventional group boys. Increase in the attitude towards physical science increases their academic achievement in physical science of secondary school conventional group girls. Increase in the attitude towards programmed instruction increases their academic achievement in physical science of secondary school conventional group girls. Increase in the achievement motivation increases their academic achievement in physical science of secondary school conventional group girls. Increase in the attitude towards physical science increases their academic achievement in physical science of secondary school experimental group students. Increase in the attitude towards programmed instruction increases or decreases with increase in physical science of secondary school experimental group students. Increase in the achievement motivation increases their academic achievement in physical science of secondary school experimental group students. Increase in the attitude towards physical science increases their academic achievement in physical science of secondary school experimental group boys. Increase in the attitude towards programmed instruction increases their academic achievement in physical science of secondary school experimental group boys. Increase in the achievement motivation increases their academic achievement in physical science of secondary school experimental group boys. Increase in the attitude towards physical science increases their academic achievement in physical science of secondary school experimental group girls. Increase in the attitude towards programmed instruction increases their academic achievement in physical science of secondary school experimental group girls. Increase in the achievement motivation increases their academic achievement in physical science of secondary school experimental group girls. Increase in the attitude towards physical science increases their academic achievement in physical science of secondary school boys. Increase in the attitude towards programmed instruction increases their academic achievement in physical science of secondary school boys. Increase in the achievement motivation increases in their academic achievement in physical science of secondary school boys. Increase in the attitude towards physical science increases their academic achievement in physical science of girls. Increase in the attitude towards programmed instruction increases their academic achievement in physical science of secondary school girls. Increase in the achievement motivation increases their academic achievement in physical science of secondary school girls. Increase in the attitude towards physical science increases their academic achievement in physical science of urban secondary school students. Increase in the attitude towards programmed instruction increases their academic achievement in physical science of urban secondary school students. Increase in the achievement motivation increases their academic achievement in physical science of urban secondary school students. Increase in the attitude towards physical science increases their academic achievement in physical science of rural secondary school students. Increase in the attitude towards programmed instruction increases their academic achievement in physical science of rural secondary school students. Increase in the achievement motivation increases their academic achievement in physical science of rural secondary school students.

The variable attitude towards physical science contributes maximum followed by others. The variable achievement motivation contributes maximum followed by others. The variable attitude towards physical science contributes maximum followed by others.

The dependent and independent variables and achievement of secondary school students in physical science have significant interrelations. The direct effect of attitude towards physical science and achievement motivation on achievement of secondary school students in physical science is found to be significant as a total. The indirect effect of attitude towards physical science through attitude towards programmed instruction and achievement motivation on achievement of secondary school students in physical science is found to be significant as a total. The indirect effect of attitude towards programmed instruction through attitude towards physical science and achievement motivation on achievement of secondary school students in physical science is found to be significant as a whole. The indirect effect of achievement motivation through attitude towards physical science and attitude towards programmed instruction on achievement of secondary school students in physical science is found to be significant as a whole. The direct effect of attitude towards physical science and achievement motivation on achievement of secondary school students in physical science is found to be significant in conventional group. The direct effect of attitude towards physical science through attitude towards programmed instruction and achievement motivation on achievement of secondary school students in physical science is found to be significant in conventional group. The indirect effect of attitude towards programmed instruction through attitude towards physical science on achievement of secondary school students in physical science is found to be significant in conventional group. The indirect effect of achievement motivation through attitude towards physical science on achievement of secondary school students in physical science is found to be significant in conventional group. The direct effect of attitude towards physical science, attitude towards programmed instruction and achievement motivation on achievement of secondary school students in physical science is found to be significant in experimental group. The direct effect of attitude towards physical science through attitude towards programmed instruction and achievement motivation on achievement of secondary school students in physical science is found to be significant in experimental group. The indirect effect of attitude towards programmed instruction through attitude towards physical science and achievement motivation on achievement of secondary school students in physical science is found to be significant in experimental group. The indirect effect of achievement motivation through attitude towards physical science and achievement motivation on achievement of secondary school students in physical science is found to be significant in experimental group. The direct effect of attitude towards physical science and achievement motivation on achievement of secondary school boys in physical science is found to be significant in conventional group. The direct effect of attitude towards physical science through Attitude towards programmed instruction and achievement motivation on achievement of secondary school boys in physical science is found to be significant in conventional group. The indirect effect of attitude towards programmed instruction through attitude towards physical science on achievement of secondary school boys in physical science is found to be significant in conventional group. The indirect effect of achievement motivation through attitude towards physical science on achievement of secondary school boys in physical science is found to be significant in conventional group. The direct effect of attitude towards physical science, attitude towards programmed instruction and achievement motivation on achievement of secondary school girls in physical science is found to be significant in conventional group. The direct effect of attitude towards physical science through attitude towards programmed instruction and achievement motivation on achievement of secondary school girls in physical science is found to be significant in conventional group. The indirect effect of attitude towards programmed instruction through attitude towards physical science on achievement of secondary school girls in physical science is found to be significant in conventional group. The indirect effect of achievement motivation through attitude towards physical science on achievement of secondary school girls in physical science is found to be significant in conventional group. The direct effect of attitude towards programmed instruction and achievement motivation on achievement of secondary school boys in physical science is found to be significant in experimental group. The direct effect of attitude towards physical science through attitude towards programmed instruction and achievement motivation on achievement of secondary school boys in physical science is found to be significant in experimental group. The indirect effect of attitude towards programmed instruction through attitude towards physical science on achievement of secondary school boys in physical science is found to be significant in experimental group. The indirect effect of achievement motivation through attitude towards physical science on achievement of secondary school boys in physical science is found to be significant in experimental group. The direct effect of attitude towards physical science, attitude towards programmed instruction and achievement motivation on achievement of secondary school girls in physical science is found to be significant in experimental group. The direct effect of attitude towards physical science through attitude towards programmed instruction and achievement motivation on achievement of secondary school girls in physical science is found to be significant in experimental group. The indirect effect of attitude towards programmed instruction through attitude towards physical science on achievement of secondary school girls in physical science is found to be significant in experimental group. The indirect effect of achievement motivation through attitude towards physical science on achievement of secondary school girls in physical science is found to be significant in experimental group.

The educational implications of the present study were: Research evidence suggests that the Programmed Instruction (PI) improves the student performance in physical sciences, particularly if used in combination with the other techniques. Immediate feedback helps the students verify their learning. Self-pacing is possible, if the tutorial mode is used. The higher cognitive abilities are achievable with the right mode. Programmed instruction is more successful in critical sagacity of the logic of various subjects and inspires the student in creative thinking and judgment making. Good teachers are freed from the humdrum of routine class-room activity and they are in a position to devote their time to more creative activities. Some educationists fear that the programmed instruction will deteriorate the quality of instruction. On the other hand, the use of it has improved the quality of education in general. The use of programmed instruction has brought a revolution in the social setting of the classroom. Many emotional and social problems have been eliminated and problems of discipline have been automatically solved. Programmed instruction is a great thrust in the direction of individualized instruction. A well-organized programmed instructional device is tailored to cater to the needs of individual students of the class. Programmed instruction helps the teacher to diagnose the problems of the individual learner. By presenting the material in small segments of information (i.e., in small frames), it makes the learning as an interesting game in which the learner is challenged by his own capabilities.

Dr. Digumarti Bhaskara Rao
digumartibhaskararao@rediffmail.com
Tele-mobile +91 949 3333 555

Contents

CHAPTER 1

Introduction

The speculations on the operant conditioning theory of learning, the experimentation and ensuring controversy resulted in the proof that competent and complete teaching is based on the principle of reinforcement. The epoch making discoveries of Skinner (1968) laid the foundations of programmed instruction in the later part of the 19th century. Since then investigations on programmed instruction were carried all over the world and various techniques were discovered. This technological revolution was found to be multi-disciplinary in its application in various subjects like Biology, Mathematics, Physics, Chemistry, Geography, History etc. Programmed is an instruction an innovative step that has been proved effective utilization in correspondence education, and is drawing the attention of researchers towards automation and individualization of instruction in classroom situation.

Science

Today everybody says that we are living in the age of science and technology, computer age, age of information, atomic age etc. 1. What is age of scientific living? 2. What is the age of science and technology? What is that atomic age? What is the age of information science and technology? The answer is that these are all the fruits of progress in science. As we are the students of science we are much interested to understand what science is? How does it grow? What are the benefits we have by studying science? To have to answer for all these questions primarily our duty is to understand the nature and scope of science. The embryo of civilization began with the curiosity of man to know about the things around him. This curiosity led him to know about nature and unveil its mysteries. Unveiling of mysteries led to the establishment of certain knowledge which is based upon facts. These facts are used by him for his daily life. So science has been considered is one of those human activities that man has created to satisfy his needs and desires. Before we go deep into the nature of science, let us discuss about the definitions of science and its origin.

The term 'Science' originated from the Latin word 'Scientia', it means 'Knowledge', all that, there is that, anybody can know. There is no single definition, which is universally accepted. We have many definitions of science as many as we have scientists. To clear ourselves with the nature of science let us discuss some of the definitions quoted by our scientists. "Science is the attempt to make the chaotic discovery of our sense, and experiences correspond to a logically uniform system of thought." According to a scientist, science is a sincere attempt of an individual to discover the miracle of nature, which is experienced by his sensory organs, but it should be corresponded with uniformity of thoughts based on logic. Sharma (1978) According to Einsten (1905), "Science is not just collection of laws a catalogue of facts. It is a creation of human mind with its freely invented ideas and concepts".

Science is not just mere collection of facts and laws. These facts and laws are based on the free intervention or interactions of an individual with the nature. So science is the interpretation of nature and man is the interpreter. Science is a cumulative and endless series of empirical observations, which result in the formation of concepts and theories, with both concepts and theories being subject to modification in the light of further empirical (Practical) observations. Science is both a body of knowledge and the process of acquiring it.

Science is accumulated and systematized learning in general usage restricted to natural phenomenon. The progress of science is not marked not only by an accumulation of fact, but by the emergence of scientific method and of the scientific attitude.

The nature of science is basically standing on three principles. These are: 1. Science is an accumulated and systematized body of knowledge, 2. The scientific method of inquiry, and 3. The scientific attitude.

From these principles, we can say Science is both a product and process, because the first principle emphasizes on the product of science, while 2nd and 3rd principles emphasizes on the process. (R.C. Sharma)

The true nature of science is revealed more in the way it is sought rather than in what is found, although the two efforts cannot be truly separated. In another way, it could be said that Science is more a verb than it is a noun.

Science answers to many questions like, what is in the universe. How many? How much? How long? How frequently? Where? When? What circumstances? But it fails to answer why? The aim of science is to find out the laws of nature. The following diagram gives a clear idea of the relationships between observation and experimentation on which laws are based.

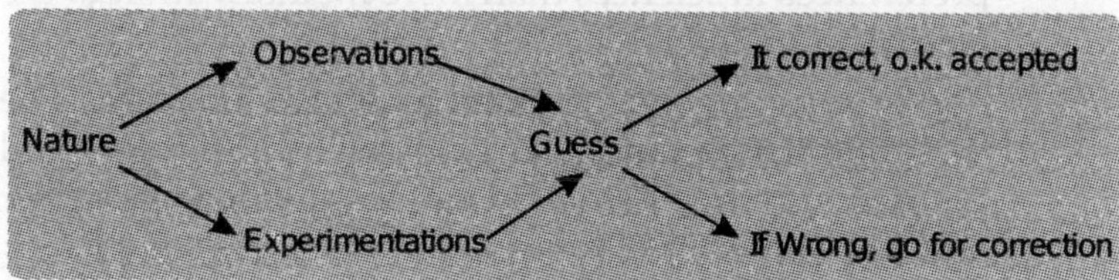

Fig. 1.1 : Explains the relationship between Observation and Experimentation

Characteristics of the Process of Science

National Science Teacher's Association, Washington advocates the following major items in the process of science.

1. Science proceeds on the assumption, based on centuries of experiences, that the universe is not capricious.

2. Science knowledge is based on observations of samples of matter that are accessible to public investigations in contrast to purely private inspections.
3. Science proceeds in a piecemeal manner, even though it also aims at achieving a systematic and comprehensive understanding of various sectors or aspects of nature.
4. Science is not, and probably never will be, a finished enterprise, and there remains very much more to be discovered about how things in universe behave and how they are interrelated.
5. Measurement is an important feature of most branches of modern science because the formations as well as the establishment of laws are facilitated through the development of quantitative distinctions.

From the discussion it can be summarized as follows.

1. Science is a process as well as product of that process. In process form it suggests the ways and means of exploring truth and in its product form it presents a systematic and organized body of knowledge.
2. The process form of knowledge is more important than its product form as the way of exploring truth and acquiring knowledge is always given more preferences in sciences than mere memorization of the factual knowledge.
3. The science always remains in search of truth. The Scientific truths can never be taken as absolutely and permanently true. Thus by nature science is dynamic and not static.
4. The methodology or process followed by science in the explanation of truth is quite unique and distinct from the methods adopted in such a study by other subjects. It is known as scientific method. A scientific method is characterized by such qualities as soundness, validity, reliability, consistency, impartiality, objectivity, etc.

5. By studying science it brings a typical change in the attitude of learner and development of such attitude is known as scientific attitude. The person with scientific attitude is found to have love for the explanation and believing in results of such true findings.
6. In the school science subjects includes physiological sciences and physical science. The present study is about Physical science.

Place of Science in School Curriculum

Science is considered as an important subject in school curriculum because the man's future depends to a large extent on scientific advances and development of productive activity. There is great feeling to teach science.

The International Congress on Science and Technology Education convened by UNESCO in 1981 made numerous recommendations for UNESCO's future role in this broad field of activity.

With the funds provided by UNESCO studies were carried out regarding the place of science in curriculum in various countries.

Kothari Commission was given the task of suggesting necessary improvements in educational system of the country. It worked during the years 1964-1966 and made a detailed study of educational system in India. It suggested various changes for improvement of education in India. Here we concentrate on the suggestions made by the commission about the science education. The commission suggested that great emphasis be laid on science education and that science be made a compulsory object of the school curriculum. Following lines from the commission report make the point clear: "We lay great emphasis on making science an important element in the school curriculum. We, therefore, recommend that science and mathematics should be taught on compulsory basis to all pupil as a part of general education during the first ten years of schooling. In addition there should be provision of special course in these subjects at the secondary stage, for students of more than average ability."

The recommendations made by UNESCO's International Commission in (1972) about the teaching of science and technology are as under:

> "Science and Technology must become essential components in any educational enterprise; they must be incorporated into all educational activity intended for children, young people and adults, in order to help the individual to control social energies as well as natural and productive ones – thereby achieving mastery over himself, his choices and actions – and finally, they must help man to acquire a scientific turn of mind so that he becomes able to promote science without being enslaved by it."
>
> "The natural science will one day incorporate the science of man, just as a science of man will incorporate the natural science, there will be single sciences."

Teaching of Physical Sciences

In order to accomplish the task of teaching physical science, it is essential for us to understand clearly the purpose of teaching physical science. This clarity of purpose could be helpful to teach any prescribed course and also in measuring the effectiveness of teaching that course. Many educational reform committees have emphasized spelling out aims and objectives of teaching a particular subject.

The purpose of physical science teaching in secondary schools is to enable students to grasp systematically the basic knowledge of physical science needed for the further study of modern science and technology and to understand its applications. In addition, it should help them to acquire experiment skills, develop the ability to think and to use mathematics to solve physical problems, cultivate a dialectical material First view point and make them aware of need to study haul and to struggle for the modernization, along socialist lines, of industry, agriculture, national defense and science and technology. For clarity of purpose of physical science teaching an emphasis has been placed by many educational reform committees to spell out the aims and objectives of a course of study.

Aims of Teaching Physical Sciences

Physical sciences can claim an honourable place in school curriculum if it can produce desirable changes in students.

The specific objectives of teaching physics must be based on some criteria in any society.

Thurber and Collette have proposed the following criteria for selection of aims:

(i) *Usefulness:* The knowledge gained should be useful to the students in their lives.

(ii) *Timeliness:* The knowledge given should be concerned with materials/objects with which student is familiar.

(iii) *Fitness:* The knowledge must fit into a sequence that leads him to broad objectives.

(iv) *Appropriate:* The learning should be appropriate for maturity and background of the students.

(v) *Practicability:* It means that experiences required for the development of learning should be possible.

Aims of Physical Science curriculum should be as follows:

(i) To make students interested in Physical science.

(ii) To familiarize the students with the important role played by physics in their daily life.

(iii) To develop in students a scientific culture.

(iv) To provide a training to students in methods of science.

(v) To emphasize upon students the role of physics on social behaviour.

(vi) To prepare students for those vocations which require a sound knowledge of Physical Science.

(vii) To increase students understanding to such a level that he can understand various concepts and theories which unify branches of Physical Science.

Objectives of Teaching Physical Sciences

By educational objectives, we mean explicit formulation of the ways in which students are expected to be changed by educative process. Objectives are not only the goals towards which the curriculum is shaped and towards which instruction is guided but they are also the goals that provide the detailed specification for the construction and use of evaluative techniques.

Probably the most common educational objective is the acquisition of knowledge. By knowledge, we mean that the student can give evidence that he remembers, either by recalling or by recognizing, some idea or phenomenon, which he has had experience in the educational process. Knowledge may also involve more complex processes of relating and judging.

Another important objective is development of intellectual abilities and skills. This has been labeled as 'critical thinking' by some, 'problem solving ' by others.

Arts or skills + knowledge = ability

'Arts and skills' refer to modes of operation and generalized technique for dealing with problem. The arts and skills emphasize the mental processes of organizing and re-organizing material to achieve a particular purpose. Intellectual abilities refer to situations in which the individual is expected to bring specific technical information to bear on a new problem.

Objectives are the specific and precise behavioural outcomes of teaching a particular topic or lesson of physical science. Objectives 'actually control other factors of physics teaching to a great extent, therefore more emphasis be laid on writing the objectives in behavioural terms for each unit of class room instructions in Physical science.

Programmed Instruction

(i) Historical Background of Programmed Instruction: The Greek philosopher Socrates is considered to be the first programmer. He was reported to have developed a programme in geometry, as recorded by his illustrious student Plato who makes a mention of it in his dialogue 'Man' (Chauhan, 1978: 40-41). The tutorial system adopted by British universities was the second stage in the development of programmed instruction. In the tutorial method of teacher there is constant exchange of ideas between pupil and tutor. There is discussion one of them asks and the other either answers or questions further. The findings of Thorndike (1874-1949) have a direct bearing on programming. His famous 'Law of Effect' pointing that, learning followed by satisfying state of affairs will last long; learning accompanied by dissatisfaction becomes weakened. Actions which are successful are more likely to be repeated than those which bring displeasure.

The teaching machine developed by the Pressy (1929) of Ohio State University, presents the student a question with four choices, only one of which is correct choice the machine presents the next item. Immediate feed back is provided for students' incorrect choice. Student's responding ends with the selection of right choice. Learning through this type of machine was significant also less time was taken to read the material (Dececco, 1968).

In thirties and forties Lumsdaine and Glased made sporadic attempts to mechanize teaching. Skinner (1954) developed a new learning theory known as 'Operant Conditioning', based on number of researches done on rats and pigeons. Applying principles of new technique of teaching and learning known as programmed instruction. Programmed Instruction has been so developed as to be regarded as a potential technique of managing learning in advanced countries. Hilgard (1975: 628-30) while referring to the developments in programmed instruction and teaching machine writes for more complex instructional devices have been developed beyond those of Pressy and Skinner. 'The programming is no more a single type of equipment.'

The term programmed instruction has been coined from principles of operant learning, developed in psychological laboratories on the basis of experimental studies conducted on animals by Skinner of Harvard University. These have been applied with considerable success to the development of self-instructional programmed books and teaching machines. Skinner and his associates had first started 'programmed learning' in 1943 by conditioning a pigeon to roll a small bowling of shaping behaviour in a laboratory experiment. It brought the strategy of programmed instructions. Skinner attended the opening day at his daughter's schools. He found that most of the class-room teaching is ineffective. He wanted to improve the classroom instruction and teaching.

He attempted to apply his operant conditioning theory of learning to teaching and preparing instruction. He published a paper entitled 'Science of Learning and Art of Teaching.' It provided the momentum to the concept of programming. He claimed that desirable change can be brought out by giving a continuous feed-back or reinforcement for desired responses. The operant conditioning is more significant for human learning. Skinner (1954) attempted to apply the principles of learning to education and to the use of teaching machines. There after, Pressey designed a teaching machine for testing purpose. While Skinner has not emphasized assignments and questions for assessing the student performance, Skinner tried 'Linear Programming'. Crowder (1964) a psychologist in U.S.A. developed a new strategy known as 'Branching Programming' or 'Intrinsic Programming'. He laid emphasis on task analysis rather than learning condition. In this technique, content is presented and multiple choice questions are asked to diagnose and to ascertain whether response is right or wrong.

(ii) Progress of Programmed Instruction in India: Early sixties mark the dawn of programmed learning in Indian History. The Department of Educational Psychology and Foundations of Education at National Council of Educational Research and Training (NCERT) in the year 1965 started spreading the information about programmed instruction to educational institutions of various kinds. Research in this field both at individual and at institutional level started gaining momentum. In M.S. University of Baroda, for the first time in 1966, in a course on 'Educational Technology and Programmed Instruction' at M.Ed. level was introduced. Indian Association of Programmed Learning was formed in the year 1967, especially with a view to undertake, promote and coordinate research in the field of Educational Technology. It also organizes in-service training and extension work to diffuse the information about programmed instruction. The NCERT, State Institutes of Education, Centre of Advanced Study in Education and few other universities have done a remarkable work in this area. Some of the areas they are exploring are:

(*i*) Programmed learning vis-à-vis traditional learning.

(*ii*) Administering programmes under supervised and non-supervised situations.

(*iii*) Effectiveness of response modes in programmed learning.

(*iv*) Developing different forms of programmed learning materials.

(*v*) Using programmed learning materials for remedial teaching in rural schools.

(*vi*) Effectiveness of programmed learning materials in terms of achievement of pupil and personality variables.

(*vii*) Relationship between anxiety, persistence and the performance on a programme. Progress of research in programmed instruction in India of the last decade and a half has been comprehensively dealt in Buch (1974-1979).

Programmed Learning

A variety of personalized instructional techniques and technologies were developed in the 1950's viz., programmed learning, teaching machines, cybernetics, personalized an effective strategy in the teaching learning process. It is a highly individualized strategy which has been found to be quite useful for classroom institution as well as self-learning or auto-instruction. Programmed Learning! Instruction emerged out of experimental research on operant conditioning which was formulated by Skinner (1968) and law of effect which was proposed by Thornlike (1712).

(i) Historical Background of Programmed Learning: Programmed learning has a long past. Socrates, the great philosopher teacher, is said to be one of the earliest programmers. He developed a programme in geometry which was recorded by his disciple Plato, in the 'Dialogue'. It is said Socrates guided his followers to knowledge through questions from 'fact to fact' and from 'insight to insight'

Programmed instruction owes its origin to the psychology of learning. Some direct relevance to programming is found in Thorndike's law of effect—a learner likes to repeat his performance or takes more interest in future learning if the present learning gives him pleasure or satisfaction. This concept of reinforcement by reward, or satisfaction is an important feature of programmed instruction. Sydney pressed, the inventor of a teaching machine, initiated programmed instruction, in an advanced form. In this device a question was followed by a number of answers. The machine would provide the next item only after the correct response key was pressed.

In the 1950s a number of devices were developed. Skinner and Games G. Holland devised an auto-institution method in 1954. Skinner used apparent conditioning to develop his linear model of programmed instruction. Norman developed another type of programmed learning i.e. branching in 1955.

In 1965, Stolurow developed his idea of "Computer Assisted Instruction" which revolutionized the idea of programmed learning.

The following table delineates some of the important contributions made for the growth development of Programmed Learning Introduction.

Growth and Development of Programmed Learning

Researcher	Year	Contribution
Socrates	430BC	Conversational programmes in geometry, Proceeding by Q/A – "fact & 'insight to insight'
Thorndike	1712D	Law of effect – reward encourage-ment/ reinforcement, Mechanical Devices for testing and scoring by multiple choice items.
Pressy	1945AD	Open and conditioning, principle of reinforcement.
Skinner	1950AD	Variation of branched progra-mmes with alternative subse-quence routes.
Robbery Marker	1960AD	Learner Controlled Instruction
Role	1962 AD	Task Analysis or Content Analysis.
Gallant	1962AD	"Mathematics"
Rothkoft	1965AD	Mathemagenics
Stolurow	1965 AD	Computer Assisted Instruction
Espich & Williams	1966 AD	Designing by flow chart schematics

(ii) Meaning of Programmed Learning/Instruction: Generally speaking the instructions provided by a teaching machine or programmed textbook is referred to as programmed instruction or programmed learning. Programmed learning involves instruction with carefully specified goals and skillfully arranged learning experiences which are self-instructional and self-corrective. Thus programmed instruction is a new path towards automation and individual learning/instruction.

Smith and More (1962) "Programmed institution is the process of arranging the material to be learned into a series of sequential steps, usually it moves the student from a familiar background into a complex and new set of concepts, principles and understanding".

Leith (1966) "A programme is a sequence of small steps of institutional material (called frames), most of which requires a response to be made by completing a blank space in a sentence. To ensure that required responses are given, a system of cuing is applied, and each response is verified by the provision of immediate knowledge of results. Such a sequence is intended to be worked at the learners 'own pace as individualized self-instruction".

"Programmed instruction is a planned sequence of instruction, leading to proficiency in terms of stimulus response relationship that have proven to be effective. (Espich and Williams)

"It is a method of designing a reproducible sequence of instructional events to produce a measurable and consistent effect on behaviour of each and every acceptable student." (Susan Markle)

"Programmed learning is the first application of laboratory technique utilized in the study of the learning process to the practical problems of education." (Skinner, 1954)

"Programmed learning as popularly understood is a method of giving individualized instruction, in which the student is active and proceeds at his own pace and is provided with immediate knowledge of results. The teacher is not physically present." (Gulati and Gulati, 1976)

The programmer, while developing programmed material has to follow the laws of behaviour and validate his strategy in terms of student learning".

Although Skinner's initial programmed instruction format has undergone many transformations, most adaptations retain three essential features: (1) an ordered sequence of items, either questions or statements to which the student is asked to respond; (2) the student's response, which may be in the form f filling in a blank, recalling the answer to a question, selecting from among a series of answers, or solving a problem; and (3) provision for immediate response confirmation, sometimes within the programme frame itself but usually in a different location, as on the next page in a programmed textbook or in a separate window in the teaching machine. (Joyce, Weil and Calhoun, 2000)

Programmed Instruction is a method of presenting new subject matters to students in a graded sequence of controlled steps. Students work through the programmed material by themselves at their own speed and after each step test their comprehension by answering an examination question or filling in a diagram. They are then immediately shown the correct answer or given additional information. Computers and other types of teaching machines are often used to present the material, although books may also be used. (The Columbia Encyclopedia, Sixth Edition. 2001-05, retrieved 2007)

Programmed Instruction consists of a network of statements and tests, which direct the student to new statements depending on his pattern of errors. It is based on a particular tool which is called teaching machine.

Based on the above definitions the meaning of programmed instruction can be described as a technique of giving or receiving individualized instruction from a variety of sources where in the instructional material is logically sequenced and broken into suitable small steps called frames.

(iii) Characteristics of Programmed Learning

(*i*) The content is broken into small easy steps and each step is presented in several sentences, each called a 'Frame'.

(*ii*) The frames are arranged sequentially.

(*iii*) Most of the frames require that the learner makes some kind of response - an answer to a question, an activity to demonstrate the understanding of the material - i.e. frequent response is elicited from the student.

(*iv*) The student is provided with immediate confirmation of the right answer i.e., the learner is provided immediate reinforcement. In case he is correct, his response is reinforced and if he is wrong, he may correct himself by receiving the correct answer.

(*v*) Units are arranged in a careful sequence such that it shapes the behaviour of a learner.

(*vi*) It is the interaction between the learner and learning material which is emphasized in programmed learning. Here, the learner is active and is motivated to learn and respond.

(*vii*) Programmed learning provides self-pacing and thus learning may occur at an individual rate rather than general, depending upon nature of the learner, learning material and learning situation.

(*viii*) It calls for the overt responses of the learner which can be readily observed, measured and effectively controlled.

(*ix*) It has provision for continuous evaluation which helps in improving the students' performance and quality of programmed learning material.

(*x*) The content and sequence of the frames are subject to actual tryout with the pupils and are revised on the data gathered based on the response of the learner.

(*xi*) Goals to be achieved are also evaluated and stated specifically.

(*xii*) In programmed learning, suitability and appropriateness of the material depends on the learner. If the learner makes mistakes, the programmed material should be rejected.

(iv) Principles of Programmed Learning: A good programmed learning material incorporates good principles of learning. The basic idea of programmed learning is that most efficient, pleasant and permanent learning must take place. The following are the principles on which programmed learning is based.

(*a*) *Principle of Small Steps:* A programme is made up of a large number of small, easy to take steps. A student can proceed from knowing very little about a topic to mastery of the subject by going through a programme.

(*b*) *Principle of Active Responding:* This principle rests on the assumption that a learner learns better by being active. Programming provides opportunity for learner to respond frequently. It not only presents material to the learner but also induces sustained activity.

(c) *Principle of Immediate Confirmation:* The psychological phenomenon of reinforcement is the basis of this principle. Necessity of providing immediate confirmation is important from two points of view - i) the learner will not wildly guess: ii) when the learner is not sure of the response he/she needs to be confirmed of the correctness of the response or provided with the right response.

(d) *Principle of Self-pacing:* Programmed learning is a technique of individualized learning. It is based on another basic assumption that learning can take place better if an individual is allowed to learn at his own pace. The pupil is not forced to move with other members of the class. Some students naturally learn more rapidly or more slowly than others. In a normal classroom so the students may be left behind as they are not able to keep pace with the teacher but here the learner is able to learn at his own pace. This principle controls individual difference in the process of learning.

(e) *Principle of Student Testing:* Continuous evaluation of the learning process helps in maximizing learning is another assumption on which programmed learning is based. The student leaves behind a record of his responses because he is required to write a response for each frame on a response sheet. This detailed record helps in revising the programme and also provides a feedback to the teacher about the students' progress.

(v) Basic Concepts in Programming

Concept	Interpretation
1. Frame	A single step of learning in programmed learning requires response from the learner after receiving information (stimuli) and finally provides a feed back.

...(Contd.)

Concept	Interpretation
2. Stimulus	A small bit of information followed by a question based on the information.
3. Response	The answer given by the learner.
4. Clue	A prompt or information contained in a frame to help the leaner to respond correctly.
5. Fading	A method of vanishing the presence of clues during the sequence of frames until the learner has mastered it.

(vi) Importance of programmed learning

1. It provides opportunities for the use of self instructional devices.
2. It leads to individualization of process of teaching learning.
3. It helps teacher to cater to individual difference.
4. The power of discrimination and making immediate and effective response is developed.
5. It helps in the development of integrative judgment and creative learning.
6. It helps teachers to devote more time for creative work.
7. It can be used at any time without any restrictions.
8. The programmes can be rewritten and revised.
9. The students proceed at their own pace. Hence are freed from the mental stress of competition.

Style of Programming

In programmed learning the presentation of the instructional material or subject matter to the learner in a form is termed as programming. Some of the programming styles are the following.

- Linear or Extrinsic Programming.
- Branching or Intrinsic Programming.
- Rule/Egrule System of Programming.
- Computer Assisted Instruction (CAI)
- Learner Controlled Instruction (LCI)

In programmed instruction the presentation of the instructional material in a suitable form is termed as programming. The various styles of programmed text designing are mentioned as follows:

1. **Linear or Extrinsic Programming:** The linear programming was propagated by Skinner. In this type of programming the instructional material is sequenced into small frames. The learner is required to respond at each step. In this programme each learner starts from the initial frame and ends at the terminal frame following the same sequence.
2. **Branching or Intrinsic Programming:** Branching programme was developed by Corroder. The content is sequenced into small frames and each frame is followed by a multiple choice question. If the learner selects the right answer he is reinforced regarding the correctness and then moves to the next frame. If the answer is wrong the learner is told and correct why he is wrong and led back to the main frame.
3. **Mathetics Programming:** This style of programming was formulated by Gilbert. Mathetics begins with an instructional plan and an analysis of what is to be taught which concentrates on learner activity. It is a programme where exercises are presented. It follows a backward chaining technique where in the mastery step (last step) is taught first, then the programmer supplies all the steps or prompts to lead to the mastery step.
4. **Rules system of Programming:** This was propagated by Homme and Glaser. It represents the deductive and inductive approach of teaching. Here a perfect rule or special example works as a stimulus for evoking the responses in terms of imperfect rule or perfect example. The verbal subject matter is divided into two classes. Rules to be learned and examples or illus traction suitable to the rule presented.
5. **Computer Assisted Instruction:** In computer Assisted instruction the computer interacts directly with the

learner. The computer is used to present lessons and give instruction to the learner. The learner then interacts by giving appropriate answers to the programmed questions. The computer is used in different modes like tutorial mode. Drill and practice made Discovery mode and simulation mode.

6. **Learner Controlled Instruction:** This was propagated by Mager. It is a method in which all the aspects of teaching learning are controlled by the learner. In traditional teaching it is the teacher who directs the process and in linear programming the programmer fixes the path of learning. The learner controlled instruction was devised as an alternative for the rigid learning path. Here the learner himself chooses his own path of learning develops his own sequence of learning develops his own sequence of learning and uses his own resources and creates favourable environment of learning.

The first three styles – linear, branching and mathetics - represent the actual basic formats. The Ruleg/Egrule system propagated by Glaser et. al., represents the inductive-deductive approaches of teaching. CAI and LCI are the ways and means of providing instructions.

(i) Linear or Extrinsic Programming: Skinner and his associates are the originators of the linear type of programme. This type of programming is directly related with his theory of apparent conditioning and is based on the assumption that human behaviour can be shaped or conditioned gradually, step by step with suitable reinforcement for each desired response. Here questions are asked directly and the learner is required to think and write down his answer - thus the answers are referred to as constructed responses'

In this type of programme, every learner starts from the initial frame and ends at the terminal frame following the same sequence. Every student must go through each and every frame in a straight line fashion - hence it called a linear programme. But each student has the liberty to complete the programme at his own pace and ability.

Format of Linear Programme

Frame-1	1. Information
	2. Questions
	3. Response
	4. Clue (Optional)
Frame-2	1. Correct answer to question in Formal (Feedback Reinforcement)
	2. Stimuli
	3. Question
	4. Response
	5. Clue (Optional)
Frame-3	1. Correct answer to question in Frame 2
	2. Information
	3. Question
	4. Response
	5. Clue optional

Fig. 1.2 : Format of Linear Programming

Subject matter is broken down into very small steps and each step is presented in proper sequence. The active responses of the learner are immediately reinforced in the succeeding frame. In some frames cues or prompts are provided to aid getting the correct response and to diminish errors.

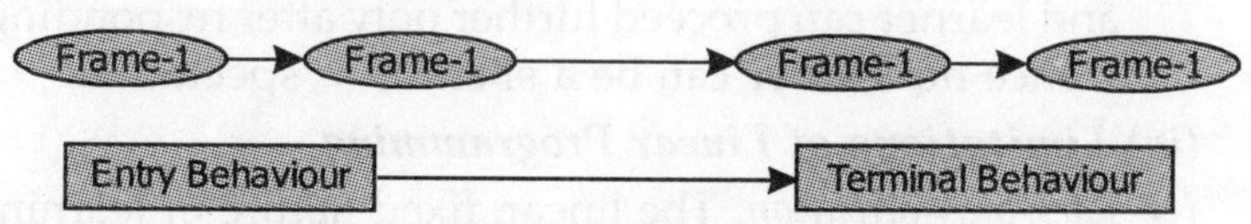

Path of Learning in Linear Programming

(ii) Principles of Linear Programming

- Principle of small steps.
- Principle of immediate confirmation.
- Principle of active responding.
- Principle of self-pacing.
- Principle of student testing.

(iii) Features of Linear Programming

(i) *Linear:* Every learner follows the same path. The learner starts from the initial frame and goes to terminal frame in the series of short following the same sequence.

(ii) *Small Steps:* Programme is composed of small steps which contain a single idea, example or rule.

(iii) *Controlled Response:* The responses and order are decided by the programmer and in each step only one response is required.

(iv) *Response is Emphasized:* Here importance is given to the response and the learner is forced to respond in each frame.

(v) *Provision for cues & prompts:* Provision for cues/prompts to minimize errors are made especially in the beginning frames.

(vi) *Feedback is quick:* The learner is able to compare his response with the programmers answer immediately. Hence it acts as a motivating factor.

(vii) *Self-pace:* Each learner works at his/her own speed and is discouraged from cheating.

(viii) *Active Response:* The responses are to be given after a critical observation and comprehension of the frame and learner can proceed further only after responding. Hence no learner can be a silent spectator.

(iv) Limitations of Linear Programming

(i) *Lack of Motivation:* The linear, fixed nature of learning tends to make it dull, uninspiring and uninteresting.

(ii) *Time Consumption:* Since the steps are small and many it consumes a lot of time to cover the subject matter.

(iii) *Freedom of Choice is curtailed:* Since the responses are controlled and learner has to answer in a few words, the creativity of the learner is not brought out.

(iv) *Guessing:* The blank type of responses and cues generally help the learner to guess the answer.

(v) *Costly:* The large number of steps makes the preparation and presentation costly as it requires lots of paper.

(vi) *Applicability:* It can be used in few areas where responses are measurable such as mathematics and science.

WRITING PROGRAMME

Stage 1

In the preceding chapters, we have described the preparation stage of writing a programme in which we have dealt with six steps involved in the stage. We have drawn two lines, basal and terminal. We know the entering behaviour of the learner and also we have specified the terminal behaviour which we wish to instill in the final repertoire of the learner. We have also analyzed the content at different levels of sophistication. In the present chapter our main purpose is to break the subject-matter into stimulus-response chains. We use two operations in writing frames which help us to raise the probability of correct responses. These operations are priming and prompting.

(i) Frame: In writing a programme (sequence of frames) two operations are very important which help the learner to respond correctly and to proceed successfully through the programme. Before we describe these operations in detail, let us understand a frame and its components

A frame may be defined as "a segment of information which is presented to the learner at a time". "The following examples will clarify the concept of the frame"

Example

Canis familiars is a technical term for the animal called—Dog. If we analyze the components of the above frame we find the following:

Design of a Frame

(i) *Stimulus:* There is stimulus which the learner needs and is motivated to respond.

(ii) *Response:* After reading the frame the learner responds this response is the second component of a frame.

(iii) *Reinforcement:* The learner compares his response with the response of the programmer and thus gets reinforcement.

Characteristics of a Good Frame

1. **Language:** The language of the frame should be neither too easy nor too difficult but should be consistent with the language development of the learner for whom the programme has been developed. It should be unambiguous, well-written and lively.
2. **Motivation:** The frame should provide motivation to the learner. It should be challenging and stimulating and should pose a problem to be solved by the learner.
3. **Unambiguity:** The frame should be free from any ambiguity. It should convey the same meaning to all the learners. What is said should be correct.
4. **Success:** The frame should be so constructed that there is maximum probability of success on the part of the learner.

Types of frames

1. **Introductory frames:** These are used to introduce n connects; Prompts and hints are judiciously used in these frames.
2. **Teaching frames:** New information is presented to the learner. These frames also contain prompts to ensure maximum probability of success.
3. **Practice frame:** After a concept has been taught to the learner, an adequate opportunity for practice to reinforce the desired behaviour is given through practice frames.
4. **Testing frames:** These frames are used to test the knowledge of the learner whether he has learned the concept taught. No prompt is used in this stage.

(ii) *Mechanism of Priming:* The mechanism of priming has been taken from literature into the language of programmed instruction. Priming the water pump is an old metaphor. When the water pump goes dry, we first pour in some water and then draw more water out of the pump. This metaphor is used in programmed instruction in the sense that when a programmer feels that learners would not be able to respond correctly, then he pours the information into the minds of the learners to enable them to respond correctly to the frames. Priming can be given in the following ways:

1. **Copying Frame:** Priming can be introduced in a frame through the process of copying the response which is provided in the frame. This type of priming is generally used when new technical vocabulary is taught.

   Example: The legal term for a genuine agreement between two minds consensus. If a lawyer says that there is this means that there is genuine agreement between the two parties.

2. **Echoic Response Priming:** This type of priming is used in teaching pronunciation to children. The stimulus is a sound pattern and the response is reproducing what is heard.

3. **Demonstration priming:** This type of priming is provided by demonstration and instructions to the learner.

(iii) Prompts: A prompt is a device that increases the probability out of a set of alternatives; a particular response will come to be omitted. It is a pure discriminative stimulus which helps to respond correctly. We can define a prompt as "an additional stimulus in the frame which raises the probability of correct responding".

Let us explain it with an example

Example

To reward an organism with food is to re—it with food.

Reinforce

Hence the introduction of re—helps the learner to respond correctly.

Functions of Prompts play an important role in a programme. The following functions of prompts have been identified by research workers in the field of programmed instruction:

The first function of prompts is the reduction of errors and error-rate. The use of prompts in a programme enables the learner to make, with minimum of error, the correct response. Prompts serve to make the occurrence of a response more probable and make possible the design of an internal sequence in which each learning step makes more likely one correct response in the next step. Thus they keep the error-rate of the programme low and save the time of the learner. Though the basic rationale of prompting is not the reduction of errors, prompts are devices which can help the process of modifying and improving stimulus control. The learner with the help of prompts determines the correct response.

The second function of prompts is to enrich the student's learning by helping him to discover new response. Beginners while making use of prompts in a programme should keep in mind that prompts should be used only at the introductory and teaching stages. They should be gradually withdrawn with the development of the programme so that the learner learns to perform and discover new knowledge without artificial prodding and with only the information and stimuli he will have available when he is to demonstrate subject mastery.

Prompts should be cautiously used. They should be based on the student's repertoire at a particular point in the learning process so that existing behaviour can be used to prompt out new behaviour.

Classification of Prompts

Prompts have been classified in different ways by programmers. Skinner classified all types of prompts into two broad categories whereas Patricia Calender has given six types of prompts. We will describe the classification by these two authors.

(A) Skinner's Classification of Prompts

1. **Formal Prompt:** A formal prompt gives an indication of the form the response will take. The following three examples explain the formal prompt.

   Example 1: Radiation carries h——— in every direction from the source

   Response: Heat

2. **Thematic Prompt:** A thematic prompt, as the name implies, depends on the general properties of the prompting stimulus rather than on its exact form. It is better known as a hint. It differs from the formal prompt in the directness with which it is employed. The formal prompt is a direct reminder whereas the thematic prompts may be concealed in other verbal behaviour. The following examples will explain;

   Example 1: When the hot wire glows brightly, we say that it gives off or sends out heat and......

   Response: Light

   Example 2: Canis familiars is a technical term for the animal called....

   Response: Dog

   Example 3: The Decalogue is another name for the............ commandments

   Response: Ten

Types of Formal Prompts

1. Partial Response Prompt: Sometimes a programmer provides a part of the desired response in the frame which is known as partial formal prompt. We experience in our daily life situations when the first word of a forgotten poem is enough to cue an entire line or stanza. In the same way, a frame which gives the first letter or letters of the correct response eliminates many possible alternatives of answer and at the same time keeps the frame simple.

(a) Partial Response Prompt: If at first you don't succeed You will conquer your tear.

2. Rhyming Formal Prompt: Rhyming prompt is just like the partial prompt in the sense that it gives at least the formal structure of the response.

(b) Rhyming Formal Prompt: Rubber does not conduct electricity; wood also has forbidden gaps or both are———

Response: Non Conductor

3. Literal Prompt: Often we find that a single response may occur in the presence of several stimuli. For instance, both the figure '5' and the word 'five' evoke the same spoken response as do both the symbol 'as' and the word 'dollar'. Whenever the student has been taught to respond correctly to one of several stimuli which call for the same response, his previous learning may be used to extend the response to the unlearned stimuli. A child in first grade learns to read English numerals long before he learns to read the number words. In the following frame the number '8' is gradually removed leaving only the word eight.

λ
λ Wavelength λ
λ
λ Wavelength λ
λ
Wavelength λ
Wavelength

Literal means the direct interchangeability of stimuli. The emphasis in this type of prompting is to get the behaviour to occur in the presence of a new stimulus which will come to guide behaviour in future Literal prompting like drill word tends to be somewhat barren and uninteresting. It can be used in teaching pronunciation.

4. Frame Structure Prompt: Sometimes the physical arrangement of a frame can be used to prompt the learner's response. The location of the blank and number of blanks can serve to prompt the type of response desired and minimize the occurrence of alternative response.

In the Kelvin scale, zero is approximately equal to 27C. The abbreviation "C" stands for ______________

This category of prompt gives direction to the learner as regards the response. Another category of structural prompt is the number of letters or blank places. Sometimes minor typography and format can play an important role in prompting the student's response. The following frame to respond correctly.

Types of Thematic Prompts

1. Thematic Prompts: Thematic prompts are quite different from formal prompts. They are matters of narrative, meaning, relevance and connotation. This category of prompts, if used skillfully, guides attention to the text and content of the subject-matter. The effectiveness of thematic prompt depends upon association between various aspects of the student's knowledge and skills. Such prompts help the students to interrelate the elements of their behaviour in order to extend their meanings and associations to new knowledge. Wise use of thematic prompting can produce rich and interesting learning sequences. The following are the important categories of thematic prompts.

Example: When the hot wire glows brightly, we say that it gives off or send out_____ & heat

Response: Light

Types of Thematic Prompts

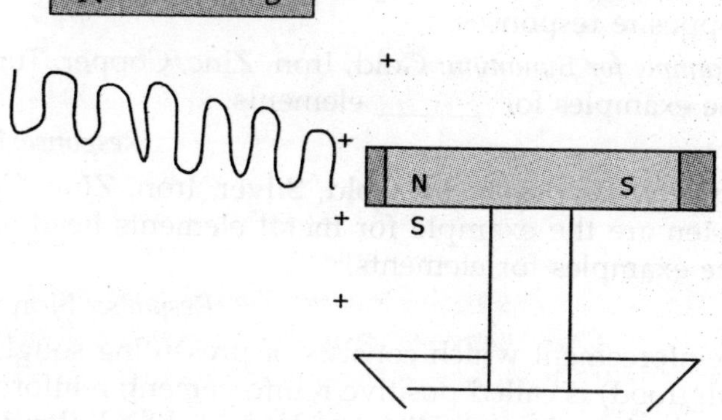

Which one of these indicates magnetic poles?

Fig. 1.3 : Response

2. Context-setting as Prompt: When a teacher indicates the topic of his conversation, a host of relevant response assume high strength while other behaviours which are pertinent other conversations are reduced in immediate strength. In the same way a frame can be labelled to suggest its context and consequently to limit the range of possible answers. This category prompt may be especially useful procedure when a programme covers several topics which must be interrelated.

The following' example has been taken from a programme on physiology:

Example: A glass prism will produce a good ____from a parallel beam of light

Response: Spectrum

3. Grammatical Structure as Prompt: Grammar can be used as prompt. When one says the pronoun 'we' it means he determines the form of the subsequent verb to be used. Similarly this' and 'these' 'that' and 'those' are followed by appropriate singular and plural form verbs.

Example: A candle flame is hot. It is an ______ source of light.

Response: Incandescent

4. Synonyms and Antonyms: Synonyms and antonyms can be used to limit the response range by prompting like and opposite responses.

Example for Synonym: Gold, Iron, Zinc, Copper, Tungsten are the examples for _______ elements.

Response: Metals

Example for Antonyms: Gold, Silver, Iron, Zinc, Copper, Tungsten are the example for metal elements head, carbon are the examples for elements.

Response: Non metals

Reinforcement which consists of presenting sought after stimuli (food) is called positive reinforcement; reinforcement which consists of terminating unpleasant stimuli (loud noise) is called ———reinforcement.

Response: Negative

5. Prompting with Thematic Redundancy: It is a well-known fact that we use more words to express a notion than a truly efficient use of language would call for. Such thematic redundancy can be very useful as a prompt in verbal programming.

6. Analogy as Prompt: Analogy may be used as prompt to respond correctly. The procedure of using analogy is to present a complete analogy in the text of a frame followed an incomplete analogy to which the student responds. The following three frames explain the use of analogy.

Example: Thus a centimeter works some what like pause. Just as 100 pause in one rupee 100 centimeters is__________

Response: 1 metre

7. Rules as Prompts: Response tendencies may be set up in frame by stating a general subject-matter rule. First, a general rule is stated in the frame followed by an incomplete example of rule which the student must complete. One rule may be used to prompt another similar rule. Rule frame exemplifies a deductive method of instruction. Often these frames give the student a feeling of accomplishment because he can make deductions from the rule or predict the results of using the rule in particular cases.

Example $E=mc^2$ c= velocity of light

E=520 Cal

M=20Kg

C= ?

8. Examples as Prompts: Examples as prompts are quite different rules. Here the examples are presented first and the student is asked to complete the rule. An example used as a prompt may be called an inductive frame as it leads from instance to general rules of examples.

A car moving to 10 Km with the per minute find the velocity of the moving car

$$\text{Velocity} = \frac{\text{Distance}}{\text{Time}} = \text{m/s}$$

(B) Patricia Callender's Classification of Prompts

Callender has classified prompts into the categories given below. She has not given any new category of prompting. All her categories have been dealt in the classification given above.

1. **Formal Prompt:** This type of prompt gives an indication of the form of response to the learner.

   Example: The capital of India is D...
2. **Copy Prompt:** In this type of prompt the learner copies the information given in the frame.
3. **Thematic Prompt:** As the name suggests, this type of prompting device gives hints towards the theme of the response. Thematic prompts are often associated with a pivotal word such as like, just as, etc.

   Example: The equator runs through the Amazon basin, so like the Congo basin this region has a (High/Low) temperature and a . ...rainfall. High
4. **Semantic Prompt:** In such types of prompts the responses are based on similarity of word roots with similar meaning used earlier in the frame on preceding frame.

   Example : A conifer derives its name from.....shaped fruit which these trees bear.

   Cone
5. **Visual Prompt:** The prompt may be provided by some visual aids as maps, charts, pictures, diagrams or figures.

   Example: The three sides of an equilateral triangle are equal. Tick the equilateral triangle in the following triangles.
6. **Temporal Sequence Prompt:** Such types of prompts are based on the sequence of the frames. The information required to make correct response is contained in the preceding frames. Thus we have briefly described two classification of prompts which can be added in the frames to enable the learner to respond correctly. The programmer should make use of different types of prompts in his programme to create novelty and interest in the learner.

Editing and Review of the Programme

After completing the first draft of the programme, the programmer should make a thorough edit and review of the draft. There are few programmers who are capable of writing programmes, perfect in all respects, in the first attempt which require no revision. Almost all programmers and, particularly, beginners, need a thorough editing of the first draft.

Main objectives of editing of the programme are:

1. To eliminate the ambiguities and other inadequacies before any student sees the programme.
2. To improve the logical sequence of the frames.
3. To sharpen and smoothen the programme.
4. To improve the technical accuracy aspect of the programme.
5. To examine the appropriate use of maps, charts and illustrations in the programme.

Types of Editing

There are three types of editing through which the first draft of the programme is processed. The three types of editing are technical accuracy, programming technique and composition edit. All the three types of editing cannot be done simultaneously so we have to perform editing in hierarchical order in such a way that no time is wasted in duplication. Experts in the field have suggested that first technical accuracy edit should be performed because it is very important in all the three types of edits. If the programme has some technical inaccuracy then the students will learn wrong things and no amount of composition or programming edits will correct the situation.

The second type of edit in hierarchy is programming technique edit. After editing the programme for technical accuracy, the programmer should edit the draft for programming technique edit. The programmer, finally, edits the programme for composition edit to give it a concrete shape.

Editing of a programme is a purely personal work of the programmer before it is put to test in front of a student. It is practically impossible to eliminate all the weaknesses of a programme through editing but a thorough edit will eliminate most of the inadequacies of the programme.

In the following section of this chapter we will describe the three types of editing in hierarchical order

1. Technical accuracy edit.
2. Programming technique edit.
3. Composition edit.

1. Technical Accuracy Edit: Technical accuracy edit, as the name suggests, is highly technical in the sense that it pertains to the technical accuracy of the material presented in the programme. The subject experts check the programme to determine whether or not the material presented is technically accurate.

The beginners, even if they are subject experts, should get their programme checked by some experts in the field. Too often, a programmer fails to find out his own errors. Probably while programming he may omit certain items. In doing so he may cause the student to develop an inaccurate concept. This omission may not be readily visible to the programmer but it will usually be quite apparent to another expert. Vocabulary should also be carefully scrutinized. The beginners should see that the vocabulary of the programme is neither too difficult nor too easy for the learners and that it is technically sound.

2. Programming Technique Edit: There are two types of programming technique edit. One is to edit the programme as a whole and the other is to edit the frames of the programme.

There are several aspects of programming technique edit which apply to the programme as a whole. The continuity of the programme is one of them. The programme must flow from item to item. There should be interrelationship between the different parts of the programme.

The programmer should also ask himself some questions about the development of ideas within his programme

(*i*) Are the ideas logically and methodically developed, with an adequate amount of supporting material?

(*ii*) Have examples and illustrations been used aptly to develop ideas?

(*iii*) Are the students familiar with the examples and illustrations given in the programme?

(*iv*) Can the students follow the line of reasoning through the programme as the material is developed?

(*v*) Does the programme work progress steadily towards a conclusion?

The programmer should sincerely answer the above questions and should modify his programme in the light of his answers.

The programmer should also give proper consideration to the size of the frame in the programme during programming technique edit. It has been suggested by experts to the beginners that they should neither keep too large nor too small step in the programme. Though the question of step size is under constant debate and the optimum step size is under constant debate and the optimum step for a particular student population can only be guessed at, the programmer must try to tailor his step to fit his group.

There are two types of frame sizes which need proper consideration, the inter-frame and the intra-frame. Inter-frame step size is the size of the step from one frame to the next; how big a jump is being taken from teaching point to teaching point? The intra-frame step size is the size of the concept presented within a single frame. How difficult is for him to apply the knowledge presented as he responds to the frame?

The last important factor which needs thorough consideration is to see whether or not the rules of construction technique were followed through out the programme in the course of writing or rewriting. It is possible that a frame or two may have benefit out inadvertently. The programmer should check the various types of frames and their proper placement in the programme. Practice frames that have been placed ahead of their respective frames, terminal frame, out of sequence, or a frame sequence incomplete, etc. should be checked.

The final aspect of the programming technique edit of the programme is the quality and aptness of the illustrations used. The placement of illustrations in relation to printed material may also be a factor to be thoroughly checked.

Programme Technique Edit -The Frames the purpose of the individual frame edit is to catch obvious faults before they affect the performance of the programme. The beginner should thoroughly edit each and every frame of the programme. A frame evaluation that considers several forms individually, with no regard to the material that preceded each frame or is to follow it, may not be valid. Inadequacies are suspected that exist only when that frame is taken out of context. Earlier frames may have precluded the inadequacies. However, much benefit can be gained from examining each frame and deliberately looking for inadequacies.

The programmer should use illustrations whenever applicable in a frame to clarify his points. But the frames in which an illustration is used must be so designed that the student is forced to make use of the illustration in one manner or another before forming his responses. He must ensure that the student will make use of the pictures, diagrams and charts used in the frames. Before using a picture or illustration in a frame, the programmer must be convinced that the illustration is meaningful and will help the student to make correct response. If the programmer is not convinced of the illustration, he must remove it.

The programmer should also check the art work of the programme. The picture and diagram should convey the idea which the programmer wants to convey. He should show an illustration to several people and ask them what they think it depicts. An illustration that conveys something other than what the programmer intends can do more harm than a thousand words.

The next step in a frame edit is to take a close look at the response required of the student.

The response which a student makes should be relevant. For maximum programme efficiency and effectiveness, each response the student makes should be a part of the terminal behaviour towards which he is being led.

In addition to the relevancy of the response, careful consideration would be made of the response that is used.

The following specific suggestions are given to improve the frames:

1. Frames should be written clearly in good English, Hindi or any regional language in which the programme is written. Whatever you want to convey through a frame, it should be correct and unambiguous.
2. Frames should be organized in some kind of logical order which may lead the learner to the specified goal in successive approximations of increasing difficulty.
3. The response required of the student in the frame should be rend it should lead the student towards the goal.
4. Frames should be considered as units of information, not as thirty words or less.
5. Study all the frames one by one and eliminate irrelevant material if there is any.
6. Make use of thematic prompts liberally. Prompt only when absolutely necessary.
7. Be very cautious in the use of prompts. You must examine your programme to see the introduction of prompts at the appropriate situations. The programme should neither be over prompted nor under-prompted. A reasonable number of prompts should be used to elicit the correct response. Prompts should be faded gradually in the programme to enable the learner to respond correctly without any prompt at the testing stage.

8. Provides a representative sample of examples covering a variety of conditions that the student should be able to cope with.
9. Examine thoroughly the content of the frames. Only relevant material should be retained.

3. Composition Edit: Editing a programme for composition is the same as editing any other written material for composition?. The programme is checked for grammatical mistakes, language of the frames, spelling, the ability to communicate, aptness and punctuation, etc. Also examined are such mechanical aspects of the material as the length of the blanks, uniformity of numbering system, placement of illustrations and adherence to some basic rules. The entire programme will present a more favourable appearance to the student if it is compositionally correct. Errors will probably influence some students to think poorly of the programme and to question the ability of the programmer.

A second factor that requires emphasis is the importance of maintaining a consistency through the programme the standpoint of what the student is expected to do. If necessary, the student should be instructed within each frame as to what his action should be the method of answering should be uniform in one type of frame. If one discrimination frame tells him to put an 'X' in the space to the left of each correct response, then all discrimination frames in the programme should ask him to do this. Needless to say, it is confusing for a student to make a check in one frame, to make an 'X' in the second and circle the correct answer in a third.

Some basic construction rides or given below as guidelines

1. Single blanks should not be continued on the next line.
2. Frames should be continued entirely on one page.
3. Blanks should be placed at or near the end of the frame.
4. A programmer may develop his own style guide to suit his own particular type to programmes, but he must be consistent throughout the programme that he develops.

Testing and the Evaluation of the Programme

Stage 3

Testing and evaluation of the programme is the last stage in the developmental process of a self-instructional programmed material. So far we have described the writing of the programme from the point of view of the programmer who, according to his own imagination, writes the frames and develops a logical sequence of the frames. His sequence of frames may or may not suit the needs of the student. At this stage, the programmer tests his material on students to evaluate its efficiency and effectiveness. If the programmer does not bring behavioural changes specified by the programmer, then it is modified in the light of the comments of the students

Everyone knows that programming is pragmatic in nature, which work is retained and which fails is rejected or modified in the light of suggestions given by the students. Therefore any attempt to improve and smoothen the programme may prove valuable when preparing self- instructional-programmed material either in a book form or for a teaching machine.

After editing the first draft of the programme, the programmer tests the programme to validate it in three phases on an individual, small group and on a large group field-testing in actual classroom situation. He also evaluates the programme in terms of its error rate, density and sequence progression.

Testing of the programme, in three different phases, is the most important step in writing a programme. It plays a crucial role in improving the content, sequence or organization of the frames for successful and effective programmed material. The programmer continues to revise the programme until he is convinced that the students are learning satisfactorily from it. Try outs of the programme reveal the inadequacies of the programme and the weak spots which need revision.

The programmer frequently finds that the final product after the try-outs is quite different from the original draft of the programme. Before giving it a final shape a programme is tested in three different phases, which are described below;

1. Individual Tryout: In individual try-out one-to-one, testing only one representative student for whom the programme is written is tested at a time. There is face-to— face interaction between the student and the programmer. Individual try-out gives an opportunity to the programmer to study the reactions of the learner immediately after the completion of the frame. The programmer can locate the stumbling blocks in his programme with the help of the student. Frames are usually written on cards (6′x4′). Only one card is presented to the students at a time. Before try-out, the programmer should establish proper rapport with the student to put him in the proper frame of mind. It should be made clear to him that he is going to help rewrite the programme and he is not being tested. The following instructions may be given to the students:

(*i*) It is a draft programme; you are to help in developing a successful programme for classroom teaching.

(*ii*) Tell frankly and freely any difficulty and inadequacy regarding the language, information and concepts, etc., of the frames.

(*iii*) Write down the responses of the frames on a separate sheet of paper (to be provided by the programmer).

(*iv*) The response of the frames is given on the back of the card but do not see it before writing your own response.

After administering a frame, discussion may be held with the student and his comments on the difficulties of individual frames may be noted. This try-out on an individual gives an opportunity to the programmer to evaluate the validity of his adjective devices. The programmer - should make copious notes of the comments and difficulties of the students in order to eliminate all inadequacies of the frames.

2. Small Group Tryout: After making necessary modifications and weeding out inadequacies in the frames on the basis of individual tryout, the programme is tried out on a small group of 5 to 10 average students for whom the programme is written. Here the programmer determines whether the programme succeeds in bringing desirable gains in learning.

The programmer, before testing the programme, should establish proper rapport with the students and should make it clear to them that they are taking a draft to the programme. They should help in the improvement of the programme. They should be clearly told that it is not a test of their abilities but a programme under revision, which is being tested. The programmer should bear in mind the following instructions before administering the programme.

(*i*) He should write the programme in definite format. Several types of formats can be used for presenting the programmed material such as four frames or three frames on a page. The responses of the frames may be written on the left hand side of the same frames or the alternate frames. Response may also be written at the foot of the same frame.

(*ii*) Definite instructions should be framed for proper guidance of the students.

(*iii*) The programmer may provide few frames to demonstrate the method of responding to acquaint the students of this new technique of teaching -learning.

(*iv*) The programmer should administer a pretest to determine the extent of knowledge of the students in the subject.

After following the above instructions, the programmer should distribute the programmed booklets among the students. He should ask the students to go through the material. The starting time should be noted down. Once the students start working on the programme, no help should be provided to them. They should be asked to locate the bottlenecks in the programme.

The time at which an individual student finishes the programme should be recorded. At the end of the programme, the programmer should discuss the difficulties with the students.

At completion of the programme, a post test is administered to all the students to find out the gains of training and to determine the success of the programme.

After finishing the administration of the post test, the programmer discusses the difficult areas as marked by the students.

The programmer statistically analyses the data collected on the programme in terms of error-rate, sequence progression and density. He modifies his programme in the light of statistical analysis. If the standards set are not met and if the programme reaches the standards set, then it is for field testing.

There is great difference between individual and small group try-outs, some of the important differences are given in the following table:

Individual tryout	Small group tryout
1. Only one individual is tested	1. 5 to 10 representatives students are tested
2. There is face-to-face interaction between the programmer and the student.	2. There is no face-to-face interaction, between the programmer and the student.
3. Programme is written on cards.	3. Programme is written in a definite format in the form of booklet.
4. Verbal instructions are given.	4. Instructions are written in programmed booklet.
5. Pre-tests and post-tests are not administered	Pre-test and post tests are administered
6. Data are not statistically analyzed	Data are statistically analyzed

3. Field Testing: The last step in the improvement of a programme is reached through the process of field testing when the programme is tested in actual class-room situation. It is administered to the population for whom it is meant to examine its utility. The programme, complete in all respects, is administered to a representative group of 50 or more students of an entire class. The ultimate object of field testing is to pinpoint the specific areas which need improvement in the programme. At this stage of testing, the programme is administered by the teacher or the instructor and not by the programmer. Pretests and posttests are given before and after the completion of the programme.

In addition to tryouts, the programme is analysed in terms of error rate, programme density and sequence of progression to improve the quality and the logical sequence of frames. These three types of analyses of the programme are attempted after small group and field testing operations.

(i) Error rate: The first measure of evaluating a programmed self-instructional material is to calculate its error rate.

The error rate of a programme is calculated on the basis of responses given by the learner obtainable on each frame of the programme. If, on a particular frame, the learner is not able to respond correctly, it is considered an error. Such analysis is made for each frame and from all the learners who are tested on a programmed instructional material. The formula to calculate error rate is like this the error made by individuals on all the frames is counted and the total numbers of errors is divided by total number of frames multiplied by the number of individuals taking the programme.

Let us explain the formula of calculation error rate with the help of hypothetical case. Suppose five students take a programme unit of ten frames and they commit five errors as shown in the chart given below.

The error may be plotted as shown below:

Individual	Frame 1	Frame 2	Frame 3	Frame 4	Frame 5	Frame 6	Frame 7	Frame 8	Frame 9	Frame 10	Total Errors
A			×								1
B			×				×				2
C									×		1
D					×						1
E											GT=5

(X indicates error)

$$\text{Error Rate} = \frac{\text{Total numbers of errors}}{\text{Total numbers of frames}} \times \frac{100}{\text{No. of Students}}$$

Programme Rate = It gives some relation of the responses required of the student and concept introduced in a programme.

Thus we can plot the error rate of a programme unit or programme as a whole.

Skinner (1948) recommends that in the use of self instructional devices, the training should be arranged so as to ensure the least occurrence of errors. He recommends 5 per cent to 10 per cent errors, for his linear style programme; on the other hand, Pressey (1945) is less concerned with error rate and he even states that errors can be useful. Crowder (1960) does not bother about high error rate. He believes that committing errors is basic to learning but errors should be detected and corrected immediately. He recommends 20 percent errors for his branching style of programming.

There is no evidence supporting either point of view. Two published studies indicate that a large error rate within the programme tends to produce a high error rate on the final criterion test.

The beginners should not think that a low error-rate is a positive proof to the effect that programme is working out effectively. Low error-rate may be due to easy programme or excessive prompting etc. The beginners should be very cautious in interpreting the findings obtainable from error analysis.

Determinants of Errors: There are certain sources of errors in a programme. The first is the illogical sequence of frames. If the frames of a programme have not been properly organized in increasing difficulty order from simple to complex and known to unknown, then the error- rate may be high. The well organised and better written programmes should presumably decrease the likelihood of errors.

The second source is the language of the programme. If the language is not consistent with the language ability of the learners then there is every possibility that learners will commit more errors. If the items have been worded ambiguously, the error-rate may increase.

The third source of errors is the general ability of the learners who, independent of their training, will contribute to the error rate. It is a general assumption that the ability of the students depend on their motivation, innate limitations, and the background of preparation they bring to the course in the first phase. The fourth source may be that the programmer may have assumed too much on the part of the student and at that point the continuity of the programme is broken. If it is broken, it means that too large a step has been taken.

The last source of errors may be inadequate use of prompts at the introductory stage of the programme.

(ii) Programme Density: The second measure to evaluate a programme is to calculate its density. The term density has been borrowed in programmed instruction from Physical science. It is used in the same way as in physics to see whether the programme is dense or sparse.

It has always been possible to measure the difficulty of a programme through conventional item analysis. Difficulty level can be related to step size. The analysis is, however, dependent upon the performance of the students. One cannot measure the difficulty level of an item without recourse to measurement of the behaviour that the item calls forth. This behaviour is subject to contamination by variables not under control of the programmer. Ideally an independent measure should be used. We have used the type/token ratio as the measure of the density of a programme (Green 1961). The analysis is done as follows. A tally is made of the number of different responses required of the student in a section of a programme. The number is divided by the total number of responses required.

$$\text{Density} = \frac{\text{Number of different responses}}{\text{Total Numbers of responses}}$$

$$\text{Conceptwise density} = \frac{\text{Concept type}}{\text{Total number of frames}}$$

$$= \frac{\text{Number of concepts}}{\text{Total number of frames}}$$

$$\text{Cumulative Density} = \frac{\text{Number of different responses}}{\text{Total Number of responses}}$$

Independent Density

According to Green (1961), this is the density of a single type composing a part of a programme. It is to independent density that error-rate is significantly related.

The second is cumulative density. Cumulative density takes into account the prior appearance of specific terms on preceding frames: Plotting the cumulative density over frames comprising sub-sections of programme gives the picture of the structure of the programme that is useful for experimental purposes. With an independent specification of the density of the programme, one can arbitrarily manipulate the programme to control the rate at which concepts are introduced.

Independent and cumulative density provides ways to specify precisely the composition of a programme in this regard. One can now equate programmes constructed by different techniques in terms of the rate at which they introduce material.

A programme would have a density of 1.00 if every response required by the programme were different. The programme would have minimal density if every response that is required of the student consisted of the same word. The tallies are of programmed answers. There is an artifact in this ratio, in that the value of the density ratio decreases as the size of the sample increases. Comparison, therefore, of two sections of a programme must be made on samples of equal size. We have found that the density of a type as we have defined it here is significantly related to the error-rate that students achieve with respect to that type. The denser the type, the higher the error rate.

We can calculate density in two ways, viz., (*a*) Independent density and (*b*) Cumulative density

The density function is an indirect measure of the rate at which material is introduced. Material occurs in the body of frames that is not directly represented by the density measure. However, examination of programmes to which this measure has been applied reveals that a greater density in the answers parallels greater repetition of that material written in the frames themselves. It should provide an indication of the degree to which material is weighed or repeated, even though the indication is indirect.

As suggested, the use to which the density function might be put in research is the assessment of the tolerance of a given population of students to the density of programmed instruction. A particular group will have higher tolerance, and programmes can be designed in advance for these populations. Parallel programmes can be constructed covering the same material with lesser density. We do not propose that the specification of programme density is a substitute for expensive evaluation, but time might be saved in the arduous task of programme writing, if the programmer knew beforehand that his programme was approximately within a range that was appropriate for his students.

An additional advantage of independent density is the insight it gives into the behaviour of the programmer. As mentioned above one of the most difficult tasks against which the neophyte programmer must guard himself is the tendency to write examination items rather than programmes.

Inspection of the independent density of programme samples produced by various programmers shows this tendency in that the programmers' initial work shows a higher independent density than does this later work of the same programmer. As programming skills are acquired, independent densities decrease. A decrease in cumulative reflects the exhaustion of the specialized vocabulary of the subject matter; a decrease in independent density reflects the acquisition of programming skills by the programmer.

Percentage Gain

$$\text{Individual \% gain} = \frac{\text{Post-test score—Pre-test scores}}{\text{Maximum possible scores—Pre-test score}} \times 100$$

$$\text{Mean \% gain} = \frac{\text{Mean Post-test score—Mean Pre-test scores}}{\text{Maximum possible scores—Mean Pre-test score}} \times 100$$

(iii) Sequence Progression: Sequence progression of frames is an important indicator of the authenticity of the programme. There are two methods to study the sequence of progression. One is to prepare a flow diagram and the second, more objective procedure is to arrange the scores of students in a rank order, taking the criterion test, and to study the sequence progression with reference to high and low rankers. The sequence of frames can be better understood from the following chart.

Sequence Progression Chart

Frame	1	2	3	4	5	6	7	8	9	10	11	12	13	14	15
15								×							
14									×	×					
13								×		×	×				
12						×		×		×	×				
11						×		×		×	×				
10			×			×			×	×	×			×	
9				×		×	×		×	×	×				
8						×	×		×	×	×	×		×	

(Evaluation of the Programme in terms of Criterion Test × indicates error)

If you examine the above chart you will find chunks of frames where proper sequencing is not in order. The programmer can fill the gaps and can improve the frames which may reduce the error-rate of the programme as a whole.

Process of Master Validation

The following steps are observed in master validation of self-instructional programmed material.

1. Administration of Pre-test: A pre-test is administered to see whether the students possess requisite knowledge to work on the programme. Those students who do not have the initial skills are not allowed to work on the programme.

2. Working on the Programme: Having selected the students with requisite knowledge, the programmer distributes the copy of the programme among them and makes it clear to them that the programme is being tested and not them. Their co-operation is sought to improve the programme. They are asked to note down the frames which present difficulty of any type. The time taken by each student is recorded.

3. Administration of Post-test: The post-test is administered at the completion of the programme to find out the exact gains obtained from the programme. Generally the pre-test and post-test are the same.

4. Analysis: The programmer makes the analysis of the errors of the students on frames. If a large number of students fail to respond correctly to the same frames, these frames are edited or revised.

5. Comparison of Criterion Behaviour with Terminal Behaviour: The programmer compares the criterion behaviour, the behaviour which he intends to achieve and the actual behaviour achieved by the learner after completing the programme.

6. Administration of Attitude Inventory: The attitude inventory is administered after the programme has been completed by the learners to find out the reactions of the learners. It reveals liking and disliking of the students from the programme. It serves a practical use in improving the lay-out, illustrations and examples in the programme. The programmer should ask specific questions in the inventory to elicit relevant information from the students on the programme.

STATEMENT OF THE PROBLEM

A Study of Effectiveness of Programmed Instruction as an Instructional Strategy in Physical Science

NEED OF THE STUDY

Since the recommendations of the secondary Education Commission report of 1952-53 we are teaching general science on compulsory basis throughout the school stages (from primary to secondary level) because of its multifarious and many sided values to human being. National Policy of Education (1986) remarkably suggests that —"science should be visualized as the vehicle to train the child to think, reason, analyse and articulate logically." Attainment or achievement in science is based on mastery of fundamental skills. The new curriculum in science at secondary school level demands for rapid learning and clear understanding of new curriculum (bi-semester system of education—newly introduced programme in the field of education).

The researcher had 15 years of teaching experience and observed the achievement of the students in science at secondary school level. It is his experience that the achievement of some students may be cent percent in science. The same case is observed in the SSLC examination of our state.

SCOPE OF THE STUDY

The present study was limited to IX standard students of Secondary Schools. The study was confined to the teaching of Physical Science of IX standard students of Bidar district, Karnataka state. The study was further confined to English medium schools only. The present study was also limited to cover the factors such as attitude towards Physical Science, achievement motivation, attitude towards programmed instruction.

OBJECTIVES OF THE STUDY

The present study was taken up with the following objectives:

1. To study the difference between pre and post test scores of academic achievement in physical science of secondary school students in experimental and conventional groups.
2. To study the difference between experimental and conventional groups with respect to pre-test, post-

test and their gain scores of academic achievement in physical science of secondary school students.

3. To study the difference between experimental and conventional groups with respect to pre-test, post-test and their gain scores of academic achievement in physical science of secondary school boys.
4. To study the difference between experimental and conventional groups with respect to pre-test, post-test and their gain scores of academic achievement in physical science of secondary school girls.
5. To study the difference between experimental and conventional groups with respect to attitude towards programmed instruction, achievement motivation scores of secondary school students.
6. To study the difference between experimental and conventional groups with respect to attitude towards programmed instruction, achievement motivation scores of secondary school boys.
7. To study the difference between experimental and conventional groups with respect to attitude towards programmed instruction, achievement motivation scores of secondary school girls.
8. To study the difference between secondary school boys and girls with respect to pre-test scores of academic achievement in physical science as a whole.
9. To study the difference between urban and rural secondary school students with respect to pre-test scores of academic achievement in physical science as a whole.
10. To study the difference between urban and rural secondary school students with respect to attitude towards programmed instruction, achievement motivation scores (both experiment and conventional).
11. To study the difference between different types of management (government, aided and unaided) with respect to pre-test and post-test academic achievement

in physical science scores of secondary school students as a whole.

12. To study the difference between different types of managements (government, aided and unaided) with respect to attitude towards programmed instruction, achievement motivation of secondary school students as a whole.
13. To study the difference between different groups of achievement motivation (high and low) with respect to pre-test scores, post-test achievement scores, attitude towards programmed instruction, achievement motivation scores of secondary school students as a whole.

Review of Related Research

Review of related literature, provides a comprehensive understanding about what has already been known about a topic. It forms the basis for subscribing rationale for having chosen the problem for the study. Review of related literature allows the researcher to acquaint himself with the current knowledge in the field or area in which he is going to conduct his research. It enables the researcher to define the limits of his study. It also helps the researcher to delimit and define his problem. The knowledge of the related literature brings the researcher up-to-date on the work, which others have done and thus state the objectives clearly and concisely.

By reviewing the related literature, the researcher can avoid unfruitful and useless problem areas. The researcher can select those areas in which positive findings are very likely to result and his endeavours are likely to add to the knowledge in a meaningful way. Through the review of related literature, the researcher can avoid unintentional duplication of well established facts. It is no use to replicate a study when the stability and validity of its results have been clearly established.

The review of related literature gives the researcher an understanding of the research methodology, which refers to the way, the study is to be conducted. It helps the researcher to know about the tools and instruments, which proved to be useful and promising in the previous studies. It also provides an insight into the statistical methods, through which the validity of the results is to be established.

The important specific reason for reviewing the related literature is to know about the recommendations of the previous researchers, listed in their studies for further research.

Good, Barr and Scates (1941) analyzed the purpose of review of related literature as given herewith: To show whether the available evidence material solves the problem adequately without further investigation, To provide ideas, theories, explanations or hypotheses valuable in formulating the present study, To suggest the research methods to the problems, To locate comparative data useful in interpretation of the results, To contribute to the general scholarship of the investigator, It helps the research worker to find what is already known, what others have attempted to find out, what methods of attack have been promising (or) disappointing and what problems remain to be solved, It furnishes him with indispensable suggestions about comparative data good procedures, likely method and tried techniques, It makes him alert to research possibilities that have been over looked and research approaches that have proved to be sterile, and It prevents pointless repetition of research.

From the above discussion, it is clear that for any worthwhile investigation, a review of literature in the field is of great help to the investigator. The studies tell us how much work has been already done in a certain field and provide necessary knowledge and insight into the methods used to collect, analyze, interpret data and the findings. It also suggests solutions and recommendations. Having realized the importance of related studies the investigator tried his best to study and record the related literature.

Programmed Instruction and Achievement

Ambiger (2009) investigated that the self instructional material (SIM) can be developed by using authentic and empirical sources of information on any subject. The development of the self instructional material requires lot of patience. In-depth and exhaustive literature survey is the simplest possible way of presentation and writing from the perspective of the learners. The Self-check potential, comparative is worth and the style of the SIM is very good. The SIM developed is excellent in terms of self sufficiency and ordinary in terms of the graphic presentation.

Basu (1973) found a significant difference among the different strategy means of multimedia programme on the overall achievement. The strategy of multi media programmed instruction enables learners to reach the level of mastery learner.

Berglund (1969) observed a negative relationship between the time spent on the programme and the percentage of confirmation provided.

Chauhan (1973) reported that the density of programme calculated by taking into account the number of frames and number of responses expected was found to be 1.117. The sequence progression for each unit was fairly normal and the opinion expressed by the student teachers was found to be favourable towards the programme.

Croom, Annie Pearl (1992) found the perception and opinions of the individualized learning packet and the teacher-directed methods as successful approaches for the teaching and learning of selected badminton skills.

Das (1966) stated that there is no significant gain in teacher's professional awareness when the university and college teachers were taught through self learning material. When taught through self learning materials the teacher's perception became significantly more favourable towards professional demands placed on them by his/her profession.

Das (1986) reported the effect of self learning materials was arrived by comparing the pre-test and post-test scores of professional awareness scores of teachers taught by self-learning materials.

Gupta (1973) observed the programme density for the frames on definition ranged from 0.4 to 0.5 and the error rate for the frames on structures ranged from 0.4 to 0.8. The average density and error rates for the complete programme taking the parts on definitions and structures together were 0.06 and 2.0 respectively.

Gupta (1979) stated that the Analytic Synthetic method was significantly more effective in terms of overall geometry achievement than the Narration Explanation method in class 9th but both the methods were equally effective in class 8th.

Hulteen, et. al. (1969) found that the students who read the programmed text book by means of a text book was significantly greater than those who read by means of a projector.

Kapadia (1972) found no significant relationship between self sufficiency and achievement on linear and branched type of programs.

Kulik and Kulik (1991) investigated the effectiveness of software incorporating self paced instruction and found that software improved learning outcomes (speed of learning and achievement) by consistent 20%.

Kumar (1977) observed that programmed learning material had a direct bearing on the minds of learners who understood things more clearly with programmes.

Kumari (1983) observed that there was a significant difference between the post-test scores of the experimental group and those of the control group.

Kuruvilla (1977) stated that Eighty percent of the students who had learnt-through different types of programmes had scored eighty percent or above. The branching form was significantly more effective than other forms when students' performance and time were taken as criteria. There was positive and significant relationship between performance of students of post-test and reading comprehension on each form separately.

Malvinder (1979) observed that providing feedback according to different schemes appears to be a poor determinate of performance. The best performance was observed at knowledge level and second best at comprehension and least at application level.

Mavi (1981) found that Ninety five percent of the learners were able to respond correctly to 95 per cent of the frames. The Cumulative density calculated by taking into account the number of fames and the number of responses expected did not exceed 0.50. Sequence progression for information through the frames was fairly normal. On unit tests, the success reached by learners ranged from 85 to 91 percent. The opinion expressed by the students was found to be favourable towards the programme.

Mohanty (1984) observed that school college cooperation was found poor in almost all institutions where the student teaching programs were going on.

Noble (1969) reported that the performance from programmed instruction is related more to organizational, social and administrative factors than to individual differences.

Patel (1975) stated that high and low 1.8 groups of students performed better with programmed learning material (PLM) than with the conventional teaching.

Shah (1981) found that the total time for computing the programmed material on the selected units in Mathematics for class V was twenty four hours and forty minutes. The reactions of the students and the teachers were favourable.

Trivedi (1980) observed that for class VI, the programmed learning material was more effective than the conventional method of teaching whereas for class V and VII, both the methods were equally effective in terms of pupils' achievement.

Programmed Instruction and Attitude

Govinda (1976) stated that a programmed text was as effective as structured lectures. Eighty percent of the students had favourable attitude towards programmed learning. Students with more favourable attitude achieved higher scores. There was no significant relationship between attitude of students towards programmed learning and their intelligence.

Kuruvilla (1977) observed that Most of the students had positive attitude towards programmed learning.

Programmed Instruction and Gender

Bhaskara (1992) found that verbal creativity instructional material significantly improved the creative thinking abilities of middle and low creative potential boys and girls.

Kumar (1977) found that girls and boys had the same ability to understand the things whether they learnt by programmed material by teacher in traditional way. Learning was not affected by their sex.

Shahapur (2009) reported that the male students shown more interest in learning through programmed learning methods than conventional methods of teaching.

Trivedi (1980) observed that in the case of class VI, girls learn better than boys through the use of programmed materials, whereas in the case of classes V and VII, there was no significant difference between the mean scores of boys and girls learning through the programmed materials

Programmed Instruction and Intelligence

Bhaskara (1992) found that verbal creativity instructional material significantly improved the creative thinking abilities of middle and low creative potential students.

Kapadia (1972) reported that intelligence was positively related to achievement of linear and branched instruction.

Programmed Instruction and Learning

Berglund (1969) stated that there is no evidence of differential effect among the various conditions on the subjects' ratings of the degree of difficulty of the programme.

Crandall, et.al. (2002) reported that students who learned from such hypertext-enriched instructional material were better able to apply concepts to new accounting cases than those who learned from instructional material that contained identical content but lacked the concept-case application hyperlinks.

Jamieson (1969) observed that the youngest and oldest groups learn significantly better by the guided discovery method. The subjects tended to prefer the experimental methods of learning rather than the methods of learning to which they were accustomed.

Patel (1975) found that the average time taken by the group learning programmed learning material (PLM) was less than that of the group taught by the traditional method.

Shitole (1976) observed the superiority of programmed learning method over the traditional one, irrespective of the category and sex of the student. Programmed learning method required less time than the traditional one.

Umino (1999) found that learners using self instructional broadcast materials are not necessarily as passive as might be expected.

Programmed Instruction and Locality

Bhaskara (1992) found that verbal creativity instructional material significantly improved the creative thinking abilities of middle and low creative potential students from rural and urban areas.

Kumar (1977) observed that the students of rural areas did better than the students of urban area whether they had learnt by programmes or they were taught by the teacher.

Programmed Instruction and Management

Mohanty (1984) observed that the functioning of government institutions was better than that of private institution.

Rausaria, et. al. (2001) investigated the use of self-instructional materials (SIMs) in distance learning at Indira Gandhi National Open University (IGNOU) and State Open Universities (SOUs) in India on the need for Correspondence Course Institutes in conventional Indian universities to transform printed course materials into SIMs.

Programmed Instruction and Motivation

Desai (1981) observed that pupils took active interest in reading and learning physics through programmed material.

Kuruvilla (1977) reported that there was positive and significant relationship between performance of students on post-test- and academic motivation on linear overt, branching and response prompt forms, but-skip programme had a positively significant relationship.

Wedman (1992) found that the students who used multi-media self-instructional materials in self-study are more likely to be motivated in a self-study course than students who used the text only. Students who had prior experience with self-study are more likely to be motivated in a self-study course than students who have no prior experience.

Programmed Instruction and Personality

Kapadia (1972) stated that anxiety was negatively related to achievement on the linear program. There is no significant relationship between introversion, extroversion and achievement of linear and branched type of programs.

Kumar (1978) investigated the interaction between extraversion and instructions through linear programme and conventional methods of instructions.

Malvinder (1979) reported that the mean performance of high average and low anxiety groups are not significantly different from each other at knowledge, comprehension and application levels. The two order interaction of anxiety and feedback and the three order interaction of anxiety, feedback and categories were not found significant.

Programmed Instruction and Socio Economic Status

Bhaskara (1992) found that verbal creativity instructional material significantly improved the creative thinking abilities of middle and low creative potential students of high and middle socio economic status.

Programmed Instruction and Teaching

Bajpai (1970) investigated that the inductive programs were significantly superior as compared to lecture or traditional method of teaching.

Gupta (1979) found that the Analytic Synthetic and Narration Explanation methods of teaching were equally effective in terms of knowledge, comprehension (understanding), application and skill objectives in class 8th and application objectives in class 9th but the Analytic Synthetic method was definitely more effective than the Narration Explanation method.

Kaur (2004) reported that the self-instructional material may go a long way in improving the general teaching competence of student-teachers in general and developing teaching skills in particular.

Khan (1972) stated that programmed instruction technique was more effective than the usual classroom procedures of teaching.

Kumari (1983) found that the programmed learning material was effective compared to the traditional method of teaching, in achievement in principles of education in sub-tests 1, 2, and 3. Programmed learning material was found to be effective for both the higher level and the lower level objectives when compared with class teaching method.

Mohanty (1984) observed that the manner in which the criticism lessons were held was not proper. Superiors do not observe lessons completely. They rarely discuss their observation in lesson – plan journals with the trainees.

Patel (1975) found that the programmed learning material (PLM) proved to be more effective than conventional method. Students from different strata of the social performed better with programmed learning material than with conventional teaching.

Pikas (1969) reported that traditional teaching is superior to programmed learning in practical application.

Rahim (1969) found that programmed instruction technique was more effective than the usual classroom procedures of teaching.

Shahapur (2009) stated that the programmed instruction is more effective than conventional methods of teaching.

Suthar (1981) observed that the programmed learning material was superior to the traditional way of teaching, irrespective of different variables.

Programmed Instruction and Attitude-Motivation

Govinda (1976) observed no significant relationship between attitude of students towards programmed learning and their academic motivation.

Programmed Instruction and Intelligence-Achievement

Govinda (1976) stated that Intelligence and achievement motivation had no definite effect on achievement of programmed text.

Gupta (1979) observed that the Analytic Synthetic method was significantly superior in terms of overall geometry achievement in case of high and low intelligence.

Programmed Instruction and Intelligence-Attitude

Govinda (1976) reported no significant relationship between attitude of students towards programmed learning and their intelligence.

Thus, the review of the related literature helped to develop a clear insight into the problem and in selecting the present problem, namely, A Study of Effectiveness of Programmed Instruction as an Instructional Strategy in Physical Science.

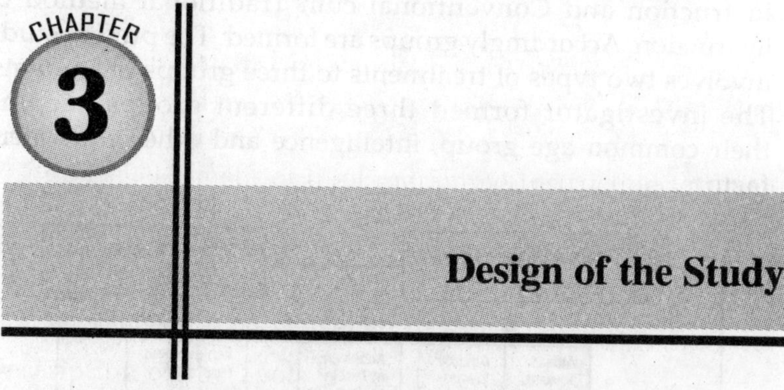

Chapter 3

Design of the Study

The main objective of the present study was to study the effectiveness of programmed instruction as an instructional strategy in physical science. In the Chapter-II provided the appropriate Literature on the present study. It gives more information about the rationale of the problem, objectives of the study, tools and methods used to collect the required data and major findings of the previous studies on the lines of the same study, it through light upon how to tackle the problem in scientific and technical manner. This is also essential for designing the present study. For this purpose the details of the sample selected, the tools and techniques used are discussed in this chapter. The objectives and hypothesis formulated helped the researcher to frame the methodology of the study and to proceed to reach the achievable target.

RESEARCH DESIGN OF THE STUDY

The procedure followed and the conduct of Experiment is shown below; by a pictorial representation.

The present study is an experimental design involving control and experimental groups. Effects on different treatments determined by pre-test and post-test. The design of the study is as follows:

1. Formation of groups: The main objective of the study is to know the achievement and retention of students in Physical Science of IX standard classes taught through Programmed

Instruction and Conventional cum Traditional method of instruction. Accordingly groups are formed. The present study involves two types of treatments to three groups of students. The investigator formed three different groups keeping their common age group, intelligence and other equivalent factors.

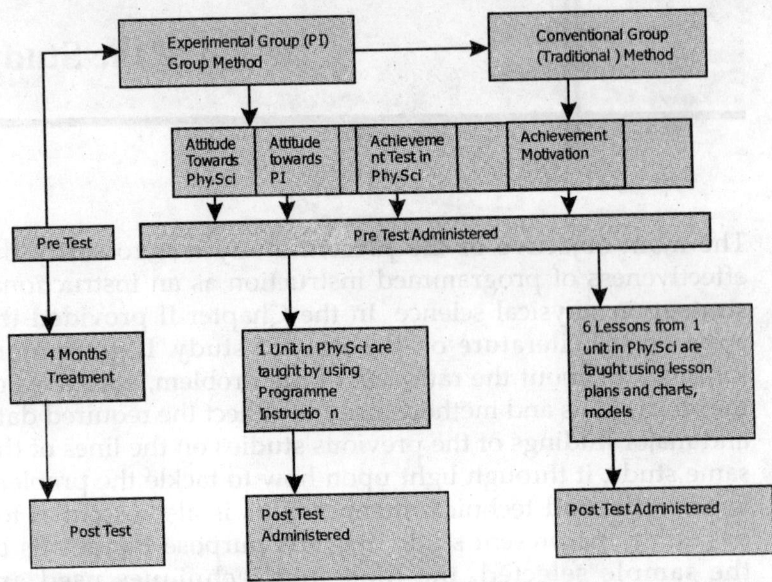

Group-1: Control group: The investigator gave group intelligence test to all the students and IQ of the each student was calculated and then he selected 50 Boys and 50 Girls having similar intelligence.

Control Group, 50 Boys + 50 Girls = 100

Group-2: Experimental Group: The investigator administered group intelligence test to all the students and calculated the IQ of each student and then he selected *50* Boys and 50 Girls having similar intelligence.

Experimental Group = 50 Boys + 50 Girls = 100.

The selection of the schools and students list is given below.

Table 3.1: Showing Formation of Groups

Type of School	Type of Group	Boys	Girls	Total
Aided	ExperimentalControl	99	99	18
Private	Experimental Control	88	88	16
Government	Experimental Control	88	88	16
	Total	**50**	**50**	**100**

Mechanism of Groups Formed for the Study

(a) Control group: In this group the teacher taught the unit in his/her usual method using some kinds of teaching materials and learning materials. The factors controlled are methods of teaching, use of teaching aids, students participation, their level of IQ, age, experience, attitude and duration of time are important.

(b) Experimental group: In this type of treatment, the teacher allowed all the students to the computer lab and gives information about computer and its accessories and its method of operating. With the help of the ready made compact disk on various aspects related to Physical science displayed in different intervals of time when students are free to arrive. After having some kind of practical orientation with the computer and likings of the students, they will be asked to view and respond to the series of contents presented through CDs and encouraged, their knowledge and achievement and retention power were evaluated through some set of instructions.

OPERATIONAL DEFINITIONS OF KEY TERMS

Some common technical terms frequently appear in the report during the course of investigation and they have been used with specific meaning and purpose. They are defined as follows:

- ***Achievement:*** Achievement is the end product of all educational endeavors, the main concern of all educational efforts is to see that the learner achieves. Performance of the students in different school subjects including Physical science in schools or colleges in a standardized series of educational tests is termed as achievement. The term is used to describe the performance of the students in various subjects of school curriculum.

- ***Achievement Test:*** Test designed to measure the effects of teaching or training in a particular area of the subject is defined as achievement test.
- ***Attitude:*** Attitude may be positive or negative depending upon the nature of thinking power of a person. It is the dispositional readiness to respond to the situation, person, object or to activity in a consistent manner which has been learned and has become one's typical mode of response.
- ***Attitude towards Physical Science:*** The present study widely uses the term to study the specific mode of behaviour and response of the students with respect to their feelings, thinking and opinion about Physical Science.
- ***Conventional Method:*** It is a Teacher-Centered and Traditional Method of teaching with a due weightage given to Chalk and Talk. It is based on Herbartian Stages of teaching using lesson plans, charts and maps. Lecture and Demonstration methods will be followed, simultaneously or in separate steps.
- ***Experimental Group:*** A Representative sample of particular group to whom the researcher applies various tools and techniques to arrive at desired goals and objectives.
- ***Intelligence:*** It is the mental state of an individual. It differs from individual to individual. Some may be superior, some may be average and some may be dull. To a particular stimulus the individual expects a particular response. It includes alertness with respect to actual situation, cognitive faculties like observation, memory, imagination, conception, reasoning, thinking and computation.

- ***Lesson Plan:*** It is an outline of the lesson to be presented by the teacher in a planned way. It is composed of contents, objectives to be achieved and methods to be followed.
- ***Pre-test:*** A test to be given to the students before taking a training or teaching. It is just to know the background, knowledge and experience of them in a little period of time and test.
- ***Post test:*** It is administered at the end of the training or teaching given, all the necessary information and training His/Her performance, strengths or weakness will be evaluated.
- ***Achievement Motivation:*** Achievement motivation is a persons' motive and influences on his/her work affects the level of performance of work. Individuals with high achievement motivation to find successful performance intrinsically satisfying.
- ***Academic Achievement:*** The knowledge attained or the skills developed in the school subjects usually determined by test.
- ***Retention:*** Retention is a part of the process of memory. We are aware that, learning experiences or information about events, things and the people we encounter are retained or stored or recorded. How much is retained and how long retained material lasts depends on learning, motivation forgetting etc.,
- ***Repetition:*** Repetition or practice, meaningful learning, whole or part learning, motivation, passage of time and feedback, influences retention.

VARIABLES OF THE STUDY

A variable, as the name implies, is something which varies. This is the simplest and broadest way of defining a variable. However, a behaviour scientist attempts to define a variable more precisely and specifically. From his point of view, variables may be defined as those attributes of objects, events, things and beings which can be measured. In other words, variables are the characters or conditions that are manipulated, controlled or observed by the experimenter. Intelligence, anxiety, aptitude, adjustment, satisfaction income, education, authoritarianism, achievements, etc., are the examples of variables commonly employed in psychology, sociology and education.

A variable is held constant in order to assess or clarify the relationship between two other variables. Control variable should not be confused with controlled variable, which is an alternative term for independent variable.

Variables are necessary requisites for any worthwhile research for the purpose of comparison. For the present study, the following variables are considered.

The variables considered in the study were

(A) Control Variables: The control variable is something that is constant and unchanged in an experiment. It is the variable that remains unchanged or held constant to prevent its effects on the outcome and therefore may verify the behavior of and the relationship between independent and dependent variables. Control variables are important in scientific experiments to test the validity of the results.

1. Intelligence
2. Treatment of Method of Teaching

(B) Dependent Variables: The dependent variable is a functional relation whose value is dependent upon, or influenced by, an independent variable. it is one factor whose value changes when the independent variable is changed. It is the variable whose value is measured to determine the extent of the effect of another variable to it, as in an experiment.

1. Achievement and Retention in Physical Science

(C) Independent Variables: The independent variable is a functional relation whose value is independent, or is not affected by other variables. This variable is manipulated in an experiment. The factor that affects the value of variables is dependent to it.

1. Conventional Method

2. Programmed Instruction
5. Attitude towards Physical Science
6. Attitude towards Programmed Instruction
7. Achievement Motivation

The above stated variables were selected by taking into account the relative effectiveness of programmed instruction and conventional instruction in terms of achievement and retention in Physical Science. Also the selection of the above problem is based on review of related literature, researcher's experience, observation and opinion from experts.

HYPOTHESES OF THE STUDY

Hypothesis is a guess, a supposition or a tentative inference as to the existence of some fact, condition or relationship relative to some phenomenon which serves to explain such facts as already are known to exist in a given area of research and to guide the search for the new truth.

A hypothesis may be defined as 'a proposition or a set of propositions set forth as an explanation for the occurrence of some specified group or phenomena either asserted merely as a provisional conjecture to guide some investigation or accepted as highly probable in the light of established facts'.

The following hypotheses were formulated in the present study.

1. Hypothesis: There is no significant difference between pre and post test of academic achievement in physical science of secondary school students in experimental and conventional groups.

1A. Sub-Hypothesis: There is no significant difference between pre and post test of academic achievement in physical science of secondary school boys in experimental and conventional groups.

1B. Sub-Hypothesis: There is no significant difference between pre and post test of academic achievement in physical science of secondary school girls in experimental group and conventional group.

2. Hypothesis: There is no significant difference between experimental and conventional groups with respect to pre-test, post-test and their gain of academic achievement in physical science of secondary school students.

3. Hypothesis: There is no significant difference between experimental and conventional groups with respect to pre-test, post-test and their gain of academic achievement in physical science of secondary school boys.

4. Hypothesis: There is no significant difference between experimental and conventional groups with respect to pre-test, post-test and their gain of academic achievement in physical science of secondary school girls.

5. Hypothesis: There is no significant difference between experimental and conventional groups with respect to attitude towards physical science, attitude towards programmed instruction, achievement motivation of secondary schools students.

6. Hypothesis: There is no significant difference between experimental and conventional groups with respect to attitude towards physical science, attitude towards programmed instruction, achievement motivation of secondary school boys.

7. Hypothesis: There is no significant difference between experimental and conventional groups with respect to attitude towards physical science, attitude towards programmed instruction, achievement motivation of secondary schools girls.

8. Hypothesis: There is no significant difference between boys and girls of secondary schools with respect to pre-test of academic achievement in physical science as a whole..

8A. Sub-Hypothesis: There is no significant difference between boys and girls of secondary schools with respect to pre-test of academic achievement in physical science in experimental group.

8B. Sub-Hypothesis: There is no significant difference between boys and girls of secondary schools with respect to pre-test of academic achievement in physical science in conventional group.

9. Hypothesis: There is no significant difference between boys and girls of secondary schools with respect to attitude towards physical science, attitude towards programmed instruction, achievement motivation (both experimental and conventional).

9A. Sub-Hypothesis: There is no significant difference between boys and girls of secondary schools with respect to attitude towards physical science, attitude towards programmed instruction, achievement motivation in experimental group.

9B. Sub-Hypothesis: There is no significant difference between boys and girls of secondary schools with respect to attitude towards physical science, attitude towards programmed instruction, achievement motivation in conventional group.

10. Hypothesis: There is no significant difference between urban and rural secondary school students with respect to pre-test of academic achievement in physical science as a whole.

10A. Sub-Hypothesis: There is no significant difference between urban and rural secondary school students with respect to pre-test of academic achievement in physical science in experimental group.

10B. Sub-Hypothesis: There is no significant difference between urban and rural secondary school students with respect to pre-test of academic achievement in physical science in conventional group.

11. Hypothesis: There is no significant difference between urban and rural secondary school students with respect to attitude towards physical science, attitude towards programmed instruction, achievement motivation (both experimental and conventional).

11A. Sub-Hypothesis: There is no significant difference between urban and rural secondary school students with respect to attitude towards physical science, attitude towards programmed instruction, achievement motivation in experimental group.

11B. Sub-Hypothesis: There is no significant difference between urban and rural secondary school students with respect to attitude towards physical science, attitude towards programmed instruction, achievement motivation in conventional group.

12. Hypothesis: There is no significant difference between different types of management (government, aided and unaided) with respect to pre-test and post-test academic achievement in physical science of secondary schools as a whole.

12A. Sub-Hypothesis: There is no significant difference between different types of management (government, aided and unaided) with respect to pre -est and post-test academic achievement in physical science of secondary schools in experimental group

12B. Sub-Hypothesis: There is no significant difference between different types of management (government, aided and unaided) with respect to pre-test and post-test academic achievement in physical science of secondary schools in conventional group.

13. Hypothesis: There is no significant difference between different types of managements (government, aided and unaided) with respect to attitude towards physical science, attitude towards programmed instruction, achievement motivation of secondary schools as a whole.

13A. Sub-Hypothesis: There is no significant difference between different types of managements (government, aided and unaided) with respect to attitude towards physical science, attitude towards programmed instruction, achievement motivation of secondary schools in experimental group.

13B. Sub-Hypothesis: There is no significant difference between different types of managements (government, aided and unaided) with respect to attitude towards physical science, attitude towards programmed instruction, achievement motivation of secondary schools in conventional group.

14. Hypothesis: There is no significant difference between different groups of achievement motivation (high and low) with respect to pre-test, post-test achievement, attitude towards physical science, attitude towards programmed instruction, achievement motivation of secondary schools as a whole.

14A. Sub-Hypothesis: There is no significant difference between different groups of achievement motivation (high and low) with respect to pre-test, post-test achievement, attitude towards physical science, attitude towards programmed instruction, achievement motivation of secondary schools in experimental group.

14B. Sub-Hypothesis: There is no significant difference between different groups of achievement motivation (high and low) with respect to pre-test, post-test achievement, attitude towards physical science, attitude towards programmed instruction, achievement motivation of secondary schools in conventional group.

15. Hypothesis: There is no significant relationship between attitude towards physical science, attitude towards programmed instruction, achievement motivation and achievement in physical science of secondary school students as a whole.

16. Hypothesis: There is no significant relationship between attitude towards physical science, attitude towards programmed instruction, achievement motivation and achievement in physical science of secondary school students in conventional group.

17. Hypothesis: There is no significant relationship between attitude towards physical science, attitude towards programmed instruction, achievement motivation and achievement in physical science of secondary school boys in conventional group.

18. Hypothesis: There is no significant relationship between attitude towards physical science, attitude towards programmed instruction, achievement motivation and achievement in physical science of secondary school girls in conventional group.

19. Hypothesis: There is no significant relationship between attitude towards physical science, attitude towards programmed instruction, achievement motivation and achievement in physical science of secondary school students in experimental group.

20. Hypothesis: There is no significant relationship between attitude towards physical science, attitude towards programmed instruction, achievement motivation and achievement in physical science of secondary school boys in experimental group.

21. Hypothesis: There is no significant relationship between attitude towards physical science, attitude towards programmed instruction, achievement motivation and achievement in physical science of secondary school girls in experimental group.

22. Hypothesis: There is no significant relationship between attitude towards physical science, attitude towards programmed instruction, achievement motivation and achievement in physical science of secondary school boys.

23. Hypothesis: There is no significant relationship between attitude towards physical science, attitude towards programmed instruction, achievement motivation and achievement in physical science of secondary school girls.

24. Hypothesis: There is no significant relationship between attitude towards physical science, attitude towards programmed instruction, achievement motivation and achievement in physical science of students of urban secondary schools.

25. Hypothesis: There is no significant relationship between attitude towards physical science, attitude towards programmed instruction, achievement motivation and achievement in physical science of students of rural secondary schools.

26. Hypothesis: Attitude towards physical science, attitude towards programmed instruction, achievement motivations are would not be significant predictors of academic achievement in physical science of secondary school students as a whole.

27. Hypothesis: Attitude towards physical science, attitude towards programmed instruction, achievement motivations are would not be significant predictors of academic achievement in physical science of secondary school students in conventional group.

28. Hypothesis: Attitude towards physical science, attitude towards programmed instruction, achievement motivations are would not be significant predictors of academic achievement in physical science of secondary school students in experimental group.

29. Hypothesis: Attitude towards physical science, attitude towards programmed instruction, achievement motivations are would not be significant predictors of academic achievement in physical science of secondary school boys in conventional group.

30. Hypothesis: Attitude towards physical science, attitude towards programmed instruction, achievement motivations are would not be significant predictors of academic achievement in physical science of secondary school girls in conventional group.

31. Hypothesis: Attitude towards physical science, attitude towards programmed instruction, achievement motivations are would not be significant predictors of academic achievement in physical science of secondary school boys in experimental group.

32. Hypothesis: Attitude towards physical science, attitude towards programmed instruction, achievement motivations are would not be significant predictors of academic achievement in physical science of secondary school girls in experimental group.

33. Hypothesis: There is no significant direct and indirect effect of attitude towards physical science, attitude towards programmed instruction, achievement motivation test on achievement in physical science of secondary school students as a whole.

34. Hypothesis: There is no significant direct and indirect effect of attitude towards physical science, attitude towards programmed instruction, achievement motivation test on achievement in physical science of secondary school students in conventional group.

35. Hypothesis: There is no significant direct and indirect effect of attitude towards physical science, attitude towards programmed instruction, achievement motivation test on achievement in physical science of secondary school students in experimental group.

36. Hypothesis: There is no significant direct and indirect effect of attitude towards physical science, attitude towards programmed instruction, achievement motivation test on achievement in physical science of secondary school boys in conventional group.

37. Hypothesis: There is no significant direct and indirect effect of attitude towards physical science, attitude towards programmed instruction, achievement motivation test on achievement in physical science of secondary school girls in conventional group.

38. Hypothesis: There is no significant direct and indirect effect of attitude towards physical science, attitude towards programmed instruction, achievement motivation test on achievement in physical science of secondary school boys in experimental group.

39. Hypothesis: There is no significant direct and indirect effect of attitude towards physical science, attitude towards programmed instruction, achievement motivation test on achievement in physical science of secondary school girls in experimental group.

SAMPLE OF THE STUDY

Bort (1967) says, "In any educational study, it is desirable to select a sample in such a way that the research worker is assured that certain sub group in a population or represented in the sample in proportion to their number in the population itself. Such samples are usually referred to as representative sample".

The present study focused on a sample of 100 in two groups, namely, Conventional or Traditional instruction group and Programmed instruction Group containing both boys and girls of different Socio-Economic and Educational Background.

The sample is a true representative of the student population. While choosing the samples the following points are kept in mind:

1. Common Syllabus cum Units from Physical Science is selected in applicable to IX standard of Karnataka State.
2. IX Class where in both Boys and Girls are studying in the same class (Co-educational class) having similar intelligence.
3. Teachers are selected from the same school to co-operate in the completion of the research work.
4. Such IX classes where in which English and Kannada are the medium of instruction but here adopted English as the medium of instruction to collect the required information.

Keeping the above factors in mind the investigator consulted with the management, principal and headmaster of these schools and appraised the necessity of visiting and collecting the information from the seven schools.

S.No.	Name of the School	No. of Pupils
1.	Garu Nanak Public School, Private	15
2.	St.-Joseph Public School, Private	15
3.	Millennium Public School, Private	15
4.	Unique Public School, Aided	15
5.	Gayana Sudha School, Aided	15
6.	National School, Aided	15
7.	Government School (Municipal School)	10
	Total	**100**

TOOLS OF THE STUDY

A research tool plays a major role in any worthwhile research as it is the sole factor in determining the sound data and in arriving at perfect conclusions about the problem on hand, which ultimately, helps in providing suitable remedial measures to solve the problem concerned.

The selection and use of the tools can be done in two ways. The first one is to construct a tool independently by the investigator for his own study. Here, there are many problems in doing so. Preparation and standardization of a perfect tool itself is a major task and one can safely say that it is a doctoral study. On construction of their own tools, Anand and Padma (1987) felt that "A note of caution has to be struck when a researcher develops a tool for his study by merely pooling some items and does not subject it to the sophisticated techniques of tool construction. The result would be then, obviously, a poor quality research". With this, one can say that preparation and standardization of tools is a major task, and one should take care of aspects like selection of area and sample, pooling up of statements related to the area, consulting the experts and application of sophisticated statistical techniques. (Bhaskara Rao, 1997).

The other way of selection and use of tools is right selection of tools from already standardized ones available in the field of study. Here again locating the tools and identifying their usefulness to the study on hand is a tedious job. Even then, this technique is very useful when a research work is studied in depth, when the research work involves a good number of variables and when there is scarcity of time and other resources. Some people believe that some of the instruments available do not measure up to their standards. In some instances, consideration should be given to the logistics of the situation. Lacking time and financial resources for the construction of a test, many researchers can not expect to produce a better instrument. In these cases, the most logical procedure that one can follow is to choose the best instrument available for this purpose. (Bhaskara Rao, 1997)

The tools used for the collection of the data were:

1. Construction of Achievement Test in Physical Science for IXth Standard Students.

2. Achievement Motivation Test (ACMT).
3. Preparation of Lesson Plans for Conventional Instructions.
4. Development of the Programme Instruction Package (PI).
5. Programmed Instruction Attitude Scale (PIAS).
6. Attitude Scale to Measure Attitude towards Physical Science.

Description of the Tools

1. Construction of Achievement Test in Physical Science for IX Standard Students: The researcher has followed the steps as laid down by Taxler and North (1957) and the construction of the achievement test. They have suggested the following steps:

- A survey of the aims and objectives and the subject for which the test is made, was done through textbooks and courses of Study (syllabus).
- A decision was taken concerning the weight ages to the different objectives.
- Preparation of the test items based on the various objectives.
- The setting up of a trial form of the test including at least 50 per cent more items than were used in the final form.
- Submission of the trial form to specialists for criticism.
- Administration of the trial form to a group of pupils who were at the level for which the test was planned.
- A statistical analysis of the items of difficulty and discrimination was carried out.
- The comments of the specialists (experts) on the trial form items were taken into consideration. Selection of the best items for the final form of the test was done on the basis of the item analysis.
- The establishment of norms for various ages, grades or years of study.

- The formulating of precise directions for administering and scoring so that it would be possible for all persons giving the test and scoring it to obtain comparable results.

The collection and reporting of complete statistical data on the reliability and validity of the test.

- The following were the stages and steps involved in the process of construction of Achievement Test :

Stage -I

Step-1 Preparation of Blue Print, and

Step-2 Pooling and Writing of Item

Stage –II

Step-3 Item –Analysis in term of

(*i*) Difficulty Index, and

(*ii*) Item-Validity

Stage-III

Step -4 Finalization of items based on Item Analysis

Stage-IV

Step-5 Evaluation of the test in terms of

(*i*) Reliability, and

(*ii*) Validity

The above stated stages and steps are described in detail in the following pages.

Stage-I: Preparation of Blueprint

A three dimensional blueprint showing coverage of content, instructional objectives and types of items was prepared by referring the IX standard text book of physical science, and in consultation with the guiding teacher and personal experience. This blue-print is given in the Table No. 3.2.

(*a*) Defining the objectives of the Test: The first step involved in the construction of the test is to prepare a specialization table. This includes the development of a table which depicts consideration of objectives of different units of the course. The basic procedure is to set up a two dimensional

Table 3.2 : Blueprint for the Achievement Test in Physical Science (Pre-Test)

(A) Physical science

Sl.No.	Objectives / Forms of Qns → Content ↓ Areas	K(OT)	U(OT)	A(OT)	Total
1.	Motion	$(4)_4$	$(2)_2$	—	$(6)_6$
2.	Velocity	—	$(7)_7$	—	$(7)_7$
3.	First Law of Motion	$(2)_2$	—	$(1)_1$	$(3)_3$
4.	Newton's Law of Motion	$(3)_3$	$(4)_4$	—	$(7)_7$
5.	Newton's First Law	—	$(11)_{11}$	—	$(11)_{11}$
6.	Newton's Second Law	$(6)_6$	$(2)_2$	—	$(8)_8$
7.	Newton's Third Law	$(14)_{14}$	$(1)_1$	—	$(15)_{15}$
8.	S.I. Unit of Force	$(2)_2$	$(1)_1$	—	$(3)_3$
9.	Mass of body	$(7)_7$	$(2)_2$	—	$(9)_9$
10.	Mass	$(5)_5$	—	—	$(5)_5$
11.	Momentum	$(3)_3$	$(7)_7$	—	$(10)_{10}$
12.	Impulse	$(2)_2$	$(3)_3$	—	$(5)_5$
13.	Friction	$(4)_4$	$(7)_7$	—	$(11)_{11}$
14.	Application of Friction	$(6)_6$	$(2)_2$	—	$(8)_8$
	Sub Total	$(58)_{58}$	$(49)_{49}$	$(1)_1$	$(108)_{108}$

Note: The number inside the bracket indicate the total marks and the numbers outside the bracket indicate the number of items.K refers to knowledge, U refers to understanding, A refers to Application objectives. When it is calculated for 100 items and for 100 marks the objectives have the following weight ages. Knowledge = 39.5, Understanding = 55.5, Application = 5, Total = 100 items, 100 Marks.

chart one axis is represented the subject matter or content and on the other, the types of behaviour that the test intends to measure the utilization of two dimensional chart helps to ensure adequate coverage of the area in the test with reference to both specific content and the types of behavior expected out of teaching learning process.

Initially, 40... multiple choice/Fill in the blanks items were constructed. Both open and closed end questionnaire were developed and administered. The items were then presented to a group of experts consisting of research workers and experienced Teachers, Specialists, Educators, Counsellors and Administrators. See Appendix-A for the pre- test in Physical science.

The suggestions given by experts are made use of in refining the items. Based on the discussions with the experts, the researcher selected 100 items for tryout. See Appendix-A for the post test (Experimental Achievement Test) in Physical science.

(*b*) Expected Previous Knowledge: The students of IX standard have already studied some of the contents of Physical science syllabus in the VIII standard. They are the continued units of IX standard syllabus.

(*c*) Selection of Objectives: Construction of achievement test is also based on the identification of objectives. Every content in the unit of Physical science is based on the achievement of one or more objectives. It is based on the classification made by Bloom (1956). He classified all the available educational objectives in cognitive, affective and psycho-motor domains. These objectives are in the form of knowledge, understanding, application, appreciation, interest, attitude, curiosity, skill etc. The specifications of some objectives are listed in the following table.

Table 3.3 : Showing Specification to Educational Objectives

Sl.No.	Objectives	Specifications (The pupil will be able to respond in the following way)
1	Knowledge	Recall, Recognize
2	Understanding	Citing examples, illustrate, defines, detects errors, observe the relationships, explains, compares, contrasts, classifies
3	Application	Analyses, verifies results, interprets, gives reason, establishes relationship, selects and uses appropriate instruments, formulae, rules, theorems etc.
4	Appreciation	Appreciates the contribution of great physical science, continues their works, shows curiosity, interest, attitude in physical science works, etc.
5	Skill	Selects appropriate instruments, rules, formulae, theorems, etc.,

Step-2: Pooling and Writing of Items

Keeping in view the requirements of the blue print, 100 items were pooled and written for final test. These items were collected from text books of Physical science prescribed for IX standard. See Appendix for pre and post test in Physical science along with the directions and scoring key.

STAGE–II

Step-3: Item Analysis

(*i*) Difficulty index: After administering the test to 100 pupils and on scoring them, the responses were subjected to item analysis and the present test constructed.

After completing the scoring of all test answer papers, the answer papers were arranged in the order of from highest to the lowest. The top 27 per cent of total group formed the high group and the bottom 27 per cent formed the low group.

The individual responses to each item for each group (i.e. 27 per cent higher group and 27 per cent lower group) were tallied and the total number of correct responses for each item in each group was found out, the difficulty level of each item was determined using the formula,

$$\text{Difficulty Index D} = \frac{pH + pL}{N_t} \times 100$$

Where p_H: the number in High group getting the item right.

p_L: the number of low group getting the item right.

N_t: the total number of students in both the groups.

The index of discrimination of each item was calculated by using the formula:

$$\text{Index of discrimination} = \frac{pH + pL}{N}$$

N = the total number of either in high group or low group

This index is valuable index for evaluating the quality of text item. It has been regarded as an indicator of validity. So, the selection of items for the final test depends upon the index of discrimination.

The criterion in using this index as suggested by Ebel (1966) is made use in the present study.

Index of D	Item evaluation
0.4 and above	very good items.
0.3 to 0.39	Reasonably good, but possible to be Subjected to improvement.
0.2 to 0.29	Marginal items usually needing Improvement
0.10 to 0.19	Poor items to be rejected or improved by revision.

The index of D of an item is determined by the extent to which the given item discriminates among examinees who differ sharply in the function measured by the test.

After item analysis the researcher has selected items for the final test.

The Table No 3.4 indicating item difficulty indices is given below:

Table 3.4 : Difficulty indices of 100 items of Physical Science Achievement Test (N=100)

Item No.	Type of item	Percentage of Higher groupValue (HGV)% P_H	Percentage of Lower groupValue (LGV)%P_L	Difficulty index $DI=(P_H+P_L)/2$
1	2	3	4	5
1	0	76.00	47.00	61.50
2	0	78.00	49.00	63.50
3	0	98.05	42.55	63.50
4	0	96.20	46.25	71.22
5	0	94.35	14.80	54.57
6	0	96.20	51.80	74.00
7	0	94.35	44.50	69.43
8	0	61.43	15.15	38.29
9	0	98.05	61.05	79.55
10	0	98.05	64.75	81.40

1	2	3	4	5
11	0	96.20	55.50	75.85
12	0	74.00	14.80	44.40
13	0	94.35	24.05	59.20
14	0	99.90	61.05	80.47
15	0	74.00	14.80	44.40
16	0	98.05	57.35	77.70
17	0	68.10	44.65	56.37
18	0	85.10	44.40	64.75
19	0	57.35	7.40	32.37
20	0	68.35	21.51	44.93
21	0	96.20	35.15	65.67
22	0	64.53	22.50	43.53
23	0	92.50	27.75	60.12
24	0	94.35	38.85	66.60
25	0	99.90	22.20	61.05
26	0	79.55	5.55	42.55
27	0	57.35	7.40	32.37
28	0	68.10	44.65	56.37
29	0	53.81	18.14	35.98
30	0	79.55	5.55	42.55
31	0	81.35	35.13	58.24
32	0	85.10	44.40	64.75
33	0	61.05	25.90	43.47
34	0	50.70	22.20	36.45
35	0	37.00	24.05	30.52
36	0	73.12	22.41	47.76
37	0	79.63	33.11	56.07
38	0	61.05	24.31	42.27
39	0	53.65	20.50	37.07
40	0	85.41	33.13	59.27
41	0	42.55	15.50	29.02
42	0	74.31	25.14	49.73
43	0	81.25	40.25	60.75

1	2	3	4	5
44	0	81.33	41.33	61.33
45	0	71.12	23.13	47.12
46	0	61.43	21.51	41.47
47	0	74.16	24.53	49.35
48	0	83.25	37.00	60.12
49	0	79.55	20.35	49.95
50	0	37.00	24.05	30.52
51	0	57.35	8.91	33.13
52	0	81.40	48.10	64.75
53	0	39.50	19.41	29.46
54	0	85.10	33.30	59.20
55	0	49.25	30.51	39.88
56	0	79.55	29.60	54.57
57	0	83.25	37.00	60.12
58	0	83.25	22.20	52.72
59	0	58.70	23.21	40.95
60	0	85.10	35.15	60.12
61	0	62.90	12.95	37.92
62	0	79.55	29.60	54.57
63	0	42.55	12.95	27.57
64	0	62.55	12.95	37.92
65	0	85.10	35.15	60.12
66	0	83.25	37.00	60.12
67	0	79.55	40.70	60.12
68	0	61.05	25.90	43.47
69	0	74.00	25.90	49.95
70	0	79.55	29.60	54.57
71	0	41.61	15.68	28.65
72	0	45.00	29.60	42.30
73	0	59.35	19.45	39.40
74	0	53.65	18.50	36.07
75	0	57.75	35.15	46.45
76	0	81.40	48.10	64.75

1	2	3	4	5
77	0	61.05	25.90	43.47
78	0	85.70	33.30	59.50
79	0	75.85	36.15	56.00
80	0	75.85	27.75	51.80
81	0	74.00	27.75	50.87
82	0	64.75	31.45	48.10
83	0	59.60	24.05	41.82
84	0	63.51	35.51	49.51
85	0	83.25	33.30	58.27
86	0	50.70	22.20	36.45
87	0	77.70	31.45	54.57
88	0	59.81	40.31	50.06
89	0	61.45	23.20	42.33
90	0	63.90	26.90	45.40
91	0	83.25	43.30	63.27
92	0	75.00	44.65	59.83
93	0	51.70	23.20	37.45
94	0	74.00	43.65	58.82
95	0	75.85	35.15	55.50
96	0	63.51	30.51	47.01
97	0	79.63	33.41	56.52
98	0	71.01	35.73	53.37
99	0	62.90	25.90	44.40
100	0	61.45	22.20	41.82

Where 'O' = Objective type item

***(ii)* Item Validity:** Then, in order to determine item validities of objective type questions by serial, co-efficient techniques were done using the corresponding ABACUS.

STAGE–III

Step-4: Finalization of Items Based on Item Analysis

100 test items were constituted for the post test. It may be added here that too easy and too difficulty items and items giving rise to co-efficient of correlation less than 0.25 were deleted.

Table 3.5 : Validities of Items of Physical Science Achievement Test (N=100)

Item No.	Type of item	Percentage of Pupils passed in the higher % pH	Percentage Pupils passed in the lower group value (LGV)	R_b/rP_b	Value
1	2	3	4	5	6
1	0	76.00	47.00	rP_b	0.61
2	0	78.00	49.00	rP_b	0.39
3	0	98.00	42.55	rP_b	0.67
4	0	96.00	46.25	rP_b	0.63
5	0	94.35	14.80	rP_b	0.77
6	0	96.35	51.80	rP_b	0.61
7	0	94.35	44.50	rP_b	0.61
8	0	61.43	15.15	rP_b	0.58
9	0	98.05	61.05	rP_b	0.61
10	0	98.05	64.75	rP_b	0.70
11	0	96.20	55.50	rP_b	0.58
12	0	74.00	14.80	rP_b	0.63
13	0	94.35	24.05	rP_b	0.62
14	0	99.90	61.05	rP_b	0.63
15	0	74.00	14.80	rP_b	0.63
16	0	98.05	61.05	rP_b	0.61
17	0	68.10	57.35	rP_b	0.26
18	0	85.10	44.65	rP_b	0.49
19	0	57.35	07.40	rP_b	0.61
20	0	68.35	21.51	rP_b	0.74
21	0	96.20	44.40	rP_b	0.67
22	0	64.53	35.15	rP_b	0.43
23	0	92.50	22.53	rP_b	0.68

1	2	3	4	5	6
24	0	94.35	38.85	rP_b	0.63
25	0	99.90	22.20	rP_b	0.77
26	0	79.90	05.55	rP_b	0.74
27	0	57.35	07.40	rP_b	0.61
28	0	68.10	44.65	rP_b	0.26
29	0	53.81	18.14	rP_b	0.42
30	0	79.55	05.50	rP_b	0.74
31	0	81.35	35.13	rP_b	0.52
32	0	85.10	44.40	rP_b	-0.43
33	0	61.05	25.90	rP_b	-0.38
34	0	50.70	22.05	rP_b	-0.13
35	0	37.00	24.05	rP_b	-0.13
36	0	73.12	21.41	rP_b	0.54
37	0	79.63	33.11	rP_b	-0.48
38	0	61.05	24.31	rP_b	0.43
39	0	53.65	20.50	rP_b	0.48
40	0	85.41	33.13	rP_b	0.60
41	0	42.55	15.50	rP_b	0.39
42	0	74.31	25.14	rP_b	0.54
43	0	81.25	40.25	rP_b	0.48
44	0	81.33	41.33	rP_b	0.51
45	0	71.12	23.13	rP_b	0.53
46	0	61.43	21.51	rP_b	0.45
47	0	76.16	24.53	rP_b	0.54
48	0	83.25	37.00	rP_b	0.52
49	0	79.55	20.35	rP_b	0.63
50	0	37.00	24.05	rP_b	0.13
51	0	57.25	08.92	rP_b	0.58
52	0	81.40	48.10	rP_b	0.41
53	0	39.50	19.41	rP_b	0.38
54	0	85.10	33.30	rP_b	0.63

1	2	3	4	5	6
55	0	49.25	30.51	rP_b	0.29
56	0	79.55	29.60	rP_b	0.54
57	0	83.25	37.00	rP_b	0.52
58	0	83.25	22.20	rP_b	0.64
59	0	58.70	23.21	rP_b	0.42
60	0	85.10	35.15	rP_b	0.56
61	0	62.90	12.95	rP_b	0.59
62	0	79.55	29.60	rP_b	0.54
63	0	42.55	12.95	rP_b	0.42
64	0	62.90	12.95	rP_b	0.62
65	0	85.10	35.15	rP_b	0.55
66	0	83.25	37.00	rP_b	0.52
67	0	79.55	40.70	rP_b	0.44
68	0	61.05	25.90	rP_b	-0.40
69	0	74.00	25.90	rP_b	0.54
70	0	79.55	29.60	rP_b	0.40
71	0	41.61	15.68	rP_b	0.39
72	0	55.00	29.60	rP_b	0.26
73	0	59.35	19.45	rP_b	0.50
74	0	53.65	18.50	rP_b	0.32
75	0	57.75	35.15	rP_b	0.25
76	0	81.40	48.10	rP_b	0.23
77	0	61.05	25.90	rP_b	0.32
78	0	85.70	33.30	rP_b	0.58
79	0	75.85	35.15	rP_b	0.29
80	0	75.85	27.75	rP_b	0.54
81	0	74.00	27.75	rP_b	0.52
82	0	64.75	31.45	rP_b	0.41
83	0	59.60	24.05	rP_b	0.42
84	0	63.51	35.51	rP_b	0.29
85	0	83.25	33.30	rP_b	0.54

1	2	3	4	5	6
86	0	50.70	22.20	rP_b	0.30
87	0	77.70	31.45	rP_b	0.53
88	0	59.81	40.31	rP_b	0.30
89	0	61.45	23.20	rP_b	0.45
90	0	63.90	26.90	rP_b	0.49
91	0	83.25	43.30	rP_b	0.38
92	0	75.00	44.65	rP_b	0.38
93	0	51.70	23.20	rP_b	0.32
94	0	74.00	43.65	rP_b	0.43
95	0	75.85	35.15	rP_b	0.51
96	0	63.51	30.51	rP_b	0.40
97	0	79.63	33.41	rP_b	0.53
98	0	71.01	25.90	rP_b	0.50
99	0	62.90	25.90	rP_b	0.50
100	0	61.45	22.20	rP_b	0.44

Where 'O' = Objective type item

rP_b = Point Bi serial Co-efficient for objective type items

STAGE-IV

Step-5: Evaluation of the Physical Science Achievement Test

(*i*) Reliability of the Test: Reliability is an important characteristic of any measuring tool. Reliability refers to the accuracy of the measurement obtained in a test.

It is determined by test and Retest method.

The Researcher established the reliability of the test using test and Retest methods having gap of more than 15 days between the first and the final administration of the test. The stability coefficient of the test was found to be 0.6435 (N= 100) and the consistency reliability 0.9889 for the computation of stability coefficient.

(*ii*) Validity of the Test: Concurrent validity of the test is computed which is found significant, concurrent validity of the test is 0.639 for its computation. Validity refers to the degree to which the test actually measures what it purports to measure. Fundamentally, all procedures for determining test validity are concerned with the relationships between performances on the test and other independently. The intrinsic validity of the test ranges from 0.799 to 0.970.

Observable Facts about the Behaviour Characteristics under Consideration of Content Validity

Anastasia (1968) says, Content validity involves essentially the systematic examination of the test content to determine whether it covers a representative sample of the behaviour domain to be measured. Validation procedure is commonly used in evaluating achievement tests. This type of test, it will be recalled and designed to measure how well the individual has mastered a specific skill or course of study. It might thus appear that a mere inspection of the content of the test should suffice to establish its validity for such a purpose.

Establishing Content Validity

Content Validity is built into achievement test by choosing appropriate items. The researcher thoroughly went through the Physical science syllabus prescribed by the Directorate of Text Books, Government of Karnataka for IX Standard Class.

The content validity of the test was examined in terms of coverage of content, instructional objectives and type of items.

From the above table it is evident that, the test has content validity. It covers all the topics adequately. According to some experienced teachers and experts the test has content validity.

The other items followed in the construction of Achievement Test are given below:

(1) Sample for Tryout: A sample of 100 pupils of IX Standard from aided, private and government school were selected. The names of the schools were already mentioned.

(2) Administration of the Test: The correct procedure of administration of the test plays an important role in the test development. Pupils were told about the

Table 3.6 : Classification of 100 Items of the Post-test in Terms of Content, Instructional Objectives and Type of Items

Sl.No.	Forms of Questions & Objectives → ↓ Content Areas	K(OT)	U(OT)	A(OT)	Total
1.	Motion	$(9)_9$	$(11)_{10}$	—	$(20)_{20}$
2.	Velocity	$(14)_{14}$	$(3)_3$	—	$(17)_{17}$
3.	Mass	$(2)_2$	$(3)_3$	—	$(5)_5$
4.	Quantum	$(3)_3$	$(1)_1$	—	$(4)_4$
5.	Newton's First law of Motion	—	$(9)_9$	$(2)_2$	$(11)_{11}$
6.	Newton's Second law of Motion	—	$(4)_4$	$(1)_1$	$(5)_5$
7.	Newton's Third law of Motion	$(2)_2$	—	—	$(2)_2$
8.	Momentum	$(9)_9$	$(3)_3$	—	$(12)_{12}$
9.	Impulse	$(2)_2$	$(2)_2$	—	$(4)_4$
10.	Friction	$(10)_{10}$	$(7)_7$	—	$(17)_{17}$
	Total	$(51)_{51}$	$(46)_{46}$	$(3)_3$	$(100)_{100}$

Note: The numbers inside the bracket indicate the total marks and the numbers outside the bracket indicate the number of items.

purpose of the test. They were acquainted with the procedure to be followed in answering the questions and the way of recording their responses in the answer sheet. Examples were included and the direction written on the Black Board. They were asked to tick the correct answer of each item, in case of multiple choice questions write correct answers to fill in the blank questions. Time was noted before starting the test and also at the time when each student completed it.

(3) **Scoring of the Test:** The scoring of the test was done by hand with the help of a pre-determined key. Each right response was given one mark and the items in which the student had written more than one choice answer was considered as wrong. The number of

correct responses determined the individuals' raw score on the test. These raw of the students and their responses were used in selecting the items for the final administration.

(4) **Allotment of time for the Test:** The time allowance for the test should be generous. This is more important in the tryout stage, during the tryout of the test 65 minutes were given i.e. one minute was given for answering one test item.

The test was administered in English medium.

(5) **Assembling the Test:** The test items and the final form were arranged in the increasing order of difficulty within the sub-group of Physical Science. In this way, easy questions were placed in the beginning and weaker pupils might not feel too discouraged to answer. Difficult and time consuming questions were placed near the end of each sub group so that the pupils spending an excessive amount of time did not do it to the exclusion of other questions.

(6) **Final Administration of the Test:** A period of 90 minutes is normally required for the administration of the test. A preliminary activity like distribution of materials, reading directions and explaining solved examples requires another 10-15 minutes.

(7) **Directions for Scoring:** The raw score on Achievement Test for each student was obtained by counting the number of correct answers. No credit was given to wrong answers.

(8) **Selection of Materials of Instruction:** The emphasis was given to the contents of the Text Books prescribed by the Department of Education and also the time duration in its presentation; contents were selected based on the learning conditions and levels of performance of the students. Equal weightage was given in terms of Age, IQ and abilities of the students in the teaching of Physical Science at the secondary school level. Hence, 200 test items were constructed

in the Pre test (test) period and 100 test items were constructed at post test (Re-test) period.

(9) Summary of the Achievement Test: The achievement test in Physical Science measures the extent to which important objectives to be attained by the students in IX Standard. While consulting the subject experts of the locality, they have expressed to give weightages not only for the achievement in knowledge or information gathered by the students, but also to achieve the other important objectives like understanding, application, skill and appreciation. List of objectives identified are already enclosed in the Table Nos. 3.2, 3.3 and 3.6.

Further, statistical analysis was done to determine the

1. Weightage to difficulty level
2. Weightage to content areas, and
3. Weightage to different objectives along with Blue print for test administration.

2. Achievement Motivation Test (ACMT)

It was conducted as per the guidelines given in the scale designed by Bhargava (1994). Here in this scale, there are 50 different questions based on different kinds of self motivational factors. There is no question of a right or wrong answer. Only to select alternative and also to measure n-Ach (Need achievement), each question was based on three preferences like A, B, C and link with incomplete sentences under consideration. The direction and scoring key of the scale is given in the Appendix.

3. Preparation of Lesson Plants for Conventional Instructions

The investigator has prepared lesson plans on law of motion Unit of physical Science form IX standard text book.

4. Development of the Programme Instruction Package (PI)

For the development of PI package 1 unit was selected from the IX standard Physical science text book prescribed by DSERT, Bangalore. These units were also used in Conventional instruction lesson planning and teaching. Overview of the chapters, specification objectives and content analysis are listed below. Regarding content validity and reliability of both Conventional Instruction and PI are the same.

The following chapters are selected for preparing Programmed Instruction Packages from the syllabus of IX Standard Physical Science prepared by Directorate of Text Books, Bangalore. These chapters are basically important for students.

Chapter: **Law of Motion**

This chapter is basically importance for students: Law of Motion

5. Programmed Instruction Attitude Scale (PIAS)

This scale is developed by Haseen Taj,. It consists of 54 statements (40 statements are positive and 14 are negative) to represent attitudes on the use of programmed instruction in classroom teaching. Every student is asked to Indicate what he/she believes, rather than what he/she thinks by ticking (√) at the appropriate choice from SA (Strongly Agree), A (Agree), DA (Disagree) and SD (Strongly Disagree). These Statements indicate that there is no right or wrong answers. It is only an opinion regarding the use of Programmed Instructional.

6. Attitude Scale to Measure Attitude Towards Physical Science

Attitude towards Physical Science was measured by using an attitude scale constructed and standardized by Sunny (1987) in the P.G. Department of Education, University of Calicutt, Kerala. The scale is a five point Likert type attitude scale. The attitude scale consists of 41 statements of which half of them measures a positive affect and the remaining negative affect towards Physical Science. The scale has been developed to measure 7 constructs of attitude towards Physical Science namely (1) Value of Physical Science in society (2) Awareness of oneself in dealing with Physical Science (3) Anxiety towards Physical Science (4) Motivation in Physical Science (5)

Perception of Physical Science teacher (6) Enjoyment in Physical Science (7) Universalism of Physical Science.

For the positive statements (Favourable statements) 5,4,3,2,1 were respectively given to a marking SA, U, D and SD for negative statements (unfavourable statements) 1,2,3,4,5 respectively were given for marking SA, U, D and SD.

Reliability and validity are the two essential characteristics of a measuring instrument. Reliability of the scale was found using split half method and the consistency reliability of the test was found to be 0.78. The stability coefficient of the Attitude towards Physical Science scale is 0.77. The indices of reliability and validity show that, the scale is a reasonably reliable and valid tool to measure the attitude of the students towards Physical Science. Please see Appendix-G for the scale along with direction.

The intrinsic validity of the Attitude towards Physical Science scale ranges from 0.877 to 0.883 which is significant.

This scale is used and administered to experimental and control groups of English medium students to assess their attitude towards Physical science.

Chapter 4

Data Analysis

The data, however valid, reliable and adequate may be, it does not serve any useful purpose unless it is carefully processed, systematically classified and tabulated, scientifically analyzed, intelligently interpreted and rationally concluded.

After the data had been collected, it was processed and tabulated using Microsoft Excel - 2000 Software. The data collected on dependent variable i.e. pre and post test of academic achievement of students in physical science and independent variables i.e. Attitude towards physical science, Attitude towards programmed instruction, Achievement motivation in both conventional and experimental groups of secondary school students. Then the data were analyzed with reference to the objectives and hypotheses and then analyzed by using descriptive statistics, differential analysis with paired and unpaired t-test, one way Analysis of variance Scheffes multiple post-hoc procedure, Pearson's correlation coefficient, Regression analysis and Path analysis, by using SPSS 11.0 statistical software and the results obtained there by have been interpreted.

It is also the intention of the investigator to find the out whether differences in the independent variables namely gender (boys, girls), location (urban, rural), types of management (Government, aided, unaided) of secondary school students with respect to their academic achievement in Physical science and consequently others.

For the purpose of convenience, the different sections of chapter IV of the study have been organized under the following sections:

1. Descriptive statistics
2. Differential statistics
3. Co-relational analysis between dependent variables, i.e., academic achievement in physical science and independent variables of secondary school students
4. Regression analysis of a dependent variable on the independent variables to qualitative Effect of independent variables on a dependent variable i.e. academic achievement in physical science
5. Path analysis of independent variables on the dependent variables (i.e., direct and indirect effects of independent variables on achievement in physical science)

1. Descriptive Statistics: In this section, the mean and standard values of pre-test and post-test, academic achievement in Physical science, Attitude towards physical science, Attitude towards programmed instruction, Achievement motivation in both conventional and Experimental groups are calculated and presented in the following table.

Table 4.1 : The Mean and SD Values of Different Variables in Experimental Group by Gender of the Student (N =100)

Variable	Summary	Experimental group		
		Boys (N=50)	Girls (N=50)	Total (N=100)
Pre-test of academic achievement in physical science	Mean	40.36	32.54	36.45
	SD.	7.81	9.55	9.52
Post-test of academic achievement in physical science	Mean	60.96	53.16	57.06
	SD	6.99	14.21	11.81
Attitude towards Physical science	Mean	107.50	104.02	105.76
	SD	15.43	20.01	17.86
Attitude towards programmed instruction	Mean	93.46	91.94	92.70
	SD	12.61	14.81	13.71
Achievement motivation	Mean	43.58	46.64	45.11
	SD	18.10	17.50	17.78

The mean and SD values of pre-test and post-test, academic achievement in physical science, attitude towards physical science, attitude towards programmed instruction, achievement motivation in experimental group by gender of the students are presented in the above table. The mean of pre-test academic achievement in physical science of students of secondary schools in experimental group is 36.45±9.52 and post-test academic achievement in physical science of students of secondary schools in experimental group is 57.06±11.81. The mean and SD academic achievement in physical science, physical science, attitude towards physical science, attitude towards programmed instruction, achievement motivation in Experimental group is presented in the above table and the following Figure.

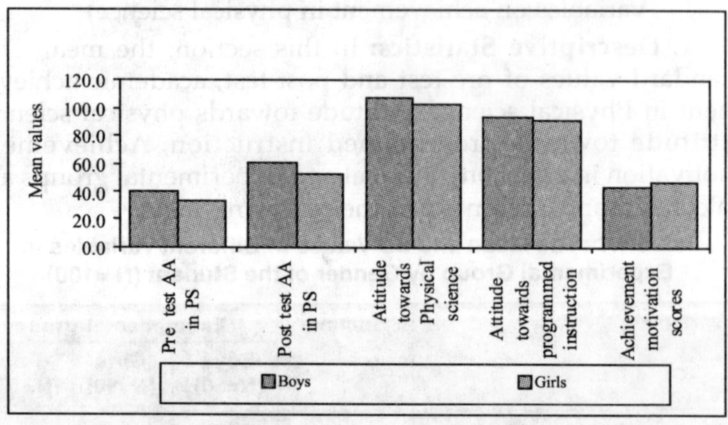

Fig. 4.1 : Comparison of mean values of different variable among boys and girls in Experimental Group

The mean and SD values of pre test and post test academic achievement in physical science, attitude towards physical science, attitude towards programmed instruction, achievement motivation in Conventional group by gender of the student are presented in the above table. The mean pre test academic achievement in physical science of students of secondary schools in conventional group is 36.21±11.52 and post test academic achievement in physical science of students

Table 4.2 : The Mean and SD Values of Different Variables in Conventional Group by Gender of the Student (N=100).

Variable	Summary	Conventional group		
		Boys (N=50)	Girls (N=50)	Total (N=100)
Pre-test of academic achievement in physical science	Mean	34.82	37.60	36.21
	SD	11.23	11.74	11.52
Post-test of academic achievement in physical science	Mean	49.48	46.08	47.78
	SD.	11.43	16.55	14.25
Attitude towards Physical science	Mean	101.36	98.56	99.96
	SD	21.72	23.78	22.70
Attitude towards programmed instruction	Mean	88.96	87.80	88.38
	SD	15.09	14.22	14.60
Achievement motivation	Mean	39.48	38.38	38.93
	SD	12.43	12.57	12.45

of secondary schools in conventional group is 47.78±14.25. The mean and SD academic achievement in physical science, physical science, attitude towards physical science, attitude towards programmed instruction, achievement motivation in Conventional group is presented in the above table and the following Figure.

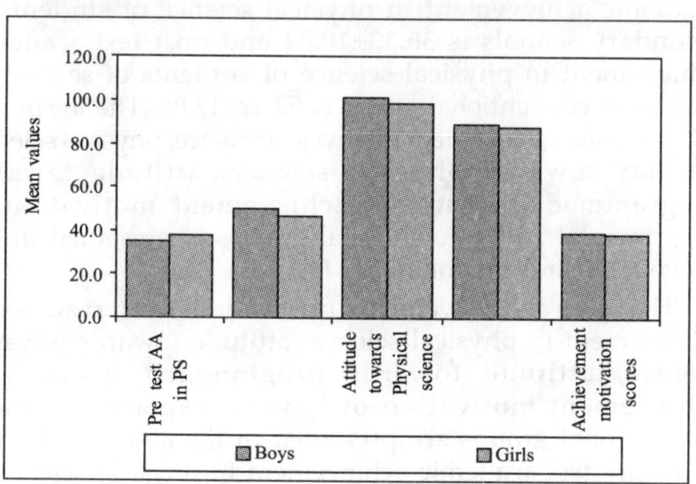

Fig. 4.2 : Comparison of mean values of different variables among boys and girls in conventional group

Table 4.3 : Mean and SD Values of Different Variables in Experimental (PI) and Conventional Groups (n=100)

Variable	Summary	Experimental Group (N=50)	Conventional Group (N=50)	Total (N=100)
Pre-test of academic achievement in physical science	Mean	36.45	36.21	36.33
	SD	9.52	11.52	10.54
Post-test of academic achievement in physical science	Mean	57.06	47.78	52.42
	SD	11.81	14.25	13.86
Attitude towards Physical science	Mean	105.76	99.96	102.86
	SD	17.86	22.70	20.58
Attitude towards programmed instruction	Mean	92.70	88.38	90.54
	SD	13.71	14.60	14.29
Achievement motivation	Mean	45.11	38.93	42.02
	SD	17.78	12.45	15.62

The mean and SD values of pre test and post test academic achievement in physical science, attitude towards physical science, attitude towards programmed instruction, achievement motivation in experimental and conventional groups are presented in the above table. The mean pre test academic achievement in physical science of students of secondary schools is 36.33±10.54 and post test academic achievement in physical science of students of secondary schools in conventional group is 52.42±13.86. The mean and SD academic achievement in physical science, physical science, attitude towards physical science, attitude towards programmed instruction, achievement motivation in experimental and conventional groups is presented in the above table and the following Figure.

The mean and SD values of pre test and post test academic achievement in physical science, attitude towards physical science, attitude towards programmed instruction, achievement motivation of boys in experimental and conventional groups are presented in the above table. The mean pre test academic achievement in physical science of students of secondary schools is 37.59±10.02 and post test academic achievement in physical science of students of

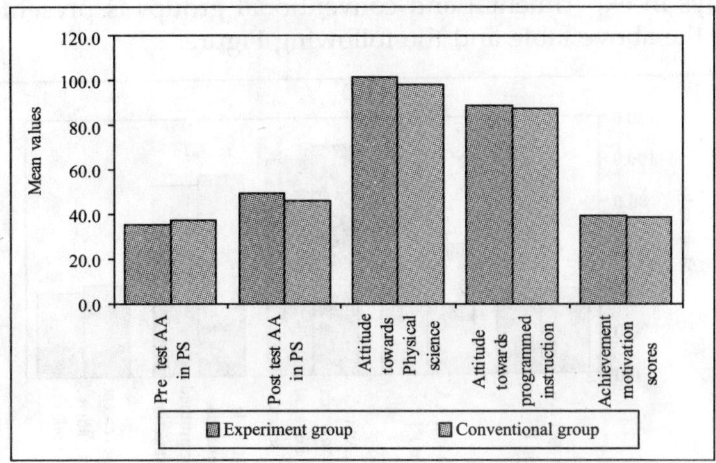

Fig. 4.3 : Comparison of mean values of different variables a in experimental and conventional group

Table 4.4: Mean and SD Values of Different Variables of Boys in Experimental and Conventional Groups (n=100)

Variable	Summary	Experimental Group (N=50)	Conventional Group (N=50)	Total (N=100)
Pre-test of academic achievement in physical science	Mean	40.36	34.82	37.59
	SD	7.81	11.23	10.02
Post-test of academic achievement in physical science	Mean	60.96	49.48	55.22
	SD	6.99	11.43	11.05
Attitude towards Physical science	Mean	107.50	101.36	104.43
	SD	15.43	21.72	19.00
Attitude towards programmed instruction	Mean	93.46	88.96	91.21
	SD	12.61	15.09	14.02
Achievement motivation	Mean	43.58	39.48	41.53
	SD	18.10	12.43	15.59

secondary schools in conventional group is 55.22±11.05. The mean and SD academic achievement in physical science, physical science, attitude towards physical science, attitude towards programmed instruction, achievement motivation of boys in experimental and conventional groups is presented in the above table and the following Figure.

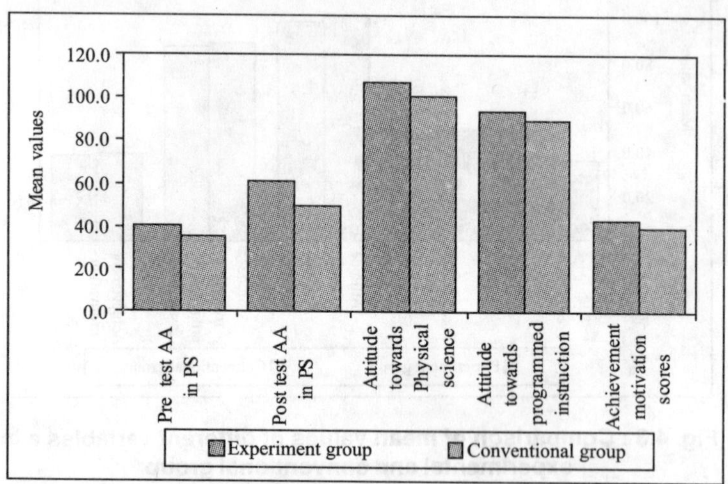

Fig. 4.4 : Comparison of mean values of different variables among boys in experimental and conventional groups

Table 4.5 : Mean and SD Values of Different Variables of Girls in Experimental and Conventional Group (N = 100)

Variable	Summary	Experimental Group (N=50)	Conventional Group (N=50)	Total (N=100) (N=100)
Pre test of academic achievement in physical science	Mean	32.54	37.60	35.07
	SD	9.55	11.74	10.95
Post test of academic achievement in physical science	Mean	53.16	46.08	49.62
	SD	14.21	16.55	15.75
Attitude towards Physical science	Mean	104.02	98.56	101.29
	SD	20.01	23.78	22.04
Attitude towards programmed instruction	Mean	91.94	87.80	89.87
	SD	14.81	14.22	14.59
Achievement motivation	Mean	46.64	38.38	42.51
	SD	17.50	12.57	15.72

The mean and SD values of pre test and post test academic achievement in physical science, attitude towards physical science, attitude towards programmed instruction, achievement motivation of girls in experimental and conventional groups are presented in the above table. The mean pre test academic achievement in physical science of students of secondary schools is 35.07±10.95 and post test academic achievement in physical science of students of secondary schools in conventional group is 49.62±15.75. The mean and SD academic achievement in physical science, physical science, attitude towards physical science, attitude towards programmed instruction, achievement motivation of girls in experimental and conventional groups is presented in the above table and the following Figure.

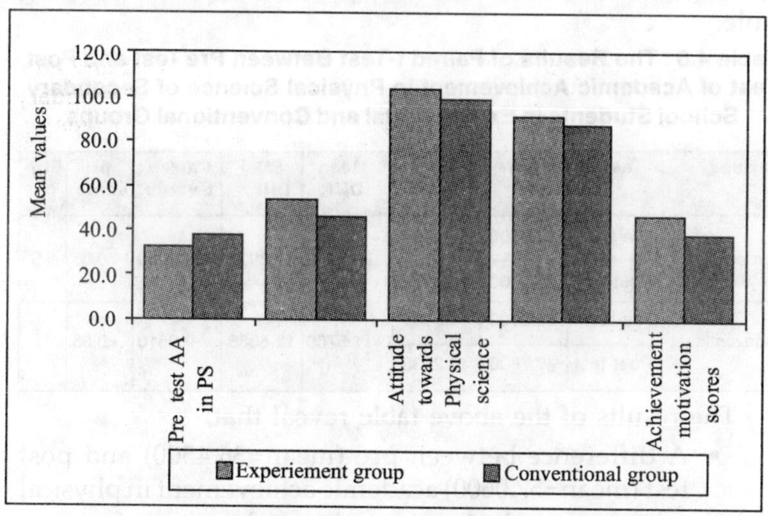

Fig. 4.5 : Comparison of mean values of different variables among girls in experimental and conventional groups

2. Differential Statistics: The differences between the pre test and post test of achievement in both Experimental and Conventional groups. Also significant differences between experimental and conventional groups, boys and girls, rural and urban school students; types of management were compared with respect to pre and post test of academic achievement of students in physical science and independent variables i.e. Attitude towards physical science, Attitude towards programmed instruction, Achievement motivation in both conventional and Experimental groups of secondary school students by using paired, unpaired and one way ANOVA t-test and the results were discussed in the preceding section.

Hypothesis: There is no significant difference between pre and post test of academic achievement in physical science of secondary school students in experimental and conventional groups.

To test this, the paired t-test was applied between pre test and post test and results are presented in the following table.

Table 4.6 : The Results of Paired t-Test Between Pre Test and Post Test of Academic Achievement in Physical Science of Secondary School Students in Experimental and Conventional Groups

Groups	Test	Mean	SD	Mean Diff.	SD Diff.	Paired t-value	p-value	Signi.
Experimental	Pre-test	36.4500	9.5234	-20.6100	11.3937	-18.0890	<0.05	S
	Post-test	57.0600	11.8132					
Conventional	Pre-test	36.2100	11.5166	-11.5700	12.5338	-9.2310	<0.05	S
	Post-test	47.7800	14.2535					

The results of the above table reveal that,

- A difference between pre (mean=36.4500) and post test (mean=57.0600) academic achievement in physical science of students in experimental group is found to be significant (t=-18.0890, <0.05, S) at 5 per cent level of significance. Hence the null hypothesis is rejected and alternative hypothesis is accepted. It means that, the post tests of academic achievement in physical science of students are high as compared to pre test of academic achievement in physical science of students in experimental group.
- A difference between pre (mean=36.2100) and post test (mean=47.7800) academic achievement in physical

science of students in conventional group is found to be significant (t=-18.0890, <0.05, S) at 5 per cent level of significance. Hence the null hypothesis is rejected and alternative hypothesis is accepted. It means that, the post tests of academic achievement in physical science of students are high as compared to pre test of academic achievement in physical science of students in conventional group.

Sub Hypothesis: There is no significant difference between pre test and post test of academic achievement in physical science of secondary school boys in experimental and conventional groups.

To test this, the paired t-test was applied between pre test and post test and results are presented in the following table.

Table 4.7 : The Results of Paired t-Test between Pre Test and Post Test of Academic Achievement in Physical Science of Secondary School Boys in Experimental and Conventional Groups

Groups	Test	Mean	SD	Mean Diff.	SD Diff.	Paired t-value	p-value	Signi.
Experimental	Pre test	40.3600	7.8057	-20.6000	8.4274	-17.2847	<0.05	S
	Post test	60.9600	6.9926					
Conventional	Pre test	34.8200	11.2299	-14.6600	8.7706	-11.8193	<0.05	S
	Post test	49.4800	11.4344					

The results of the above table reveal that,

- A difference between pre (mean=40.3600) and post test (mean=60.9600) academic achievement in physical science of boys in experimental group is found to be significant (t=-17.2847, <0.05, S) at 5 per cent level of significance. Hence the null hypothesis is rejected and alternative hypothesis is accepted. It means that, the post test of academic achievement in physical science of students is high as compared to pre test of academic achievement in physical science of boys in experimental group.

- A difference between pre (mean=34.8200) and post test (mean=49.4800) academic achievement in physical science of boys in conventional group is found to be significant (t=-11.8193, <0.05, S) at 5 per cent level of significance. Hence the null hypothesis is rejected and alternative hypothesis is accepted. It means that, the post tests of academic achievement in physical science of boys are high as compared to pre test of academic achievement in physical science of students in conventional group.

Sub Hypothesis: There is no significant difference between pre test and post test of academic achievement in physical science of secondary school girls in experimental group and conventional group.

To test this, the paired t-test was applied between pre test and post test and results are presented in the following table.

Table 4.8: Results of Paired t-Test Between Pre Test and Post Test of Academic Achievement in Physical Science of Secondary School Girls in Experimental and Conventional Groups

Groups	Test	Mean	SD	Mean Diff.	SD Diff.	Paired t-value	p-value	Signi.
Experimental	Pre-test	32.5400	9.5452	-20.6200	13.8297	-10.5429	<0.05	S
	Post test	53.1600	14.2132					
Conventional	Pre-test	37.6000	11.7439	-8.4800	14.8657	-4.0336	<0.05	S
	Post test	46.0800	16.5478					

The results of the above table reveal that,

- A difference between pre (mean=32.5400) and post test (mean=53.1600) academic achievement in physical science of girls in experimental group is found to be significant (t=-10.5429, <0.05, S) at 5 per cent level of significance. Hence the null hypothesis is rejected and alternative hypothesis is accepted. It means that, the post test of academic achievement in physical science of students is high as compared to pre test of academic achievement in physical science of girls in experimental group.

- A difference between pre (mean=37.6000) and post test (mean=46.0800) academic achievement in physical science of girls in conventional group is found to be significant (t=-4.0336, <0.05, S) at 5 per cent level of significance. Hence the null hypothesis is rejected and alternative hypothesis is accepted. It means that, the post tests of academic achievement in physical science of girls are high as compared to pre test of academic achievement in physical science of students in conventional group.

Hypothesis: There is no significant difference between experimental and conventional groups with respect to pre test, post test and their gain of academic achievement in physical science of secondary school students.

To test this, the student's unpaired t-test was applied and results are presented in the following table.

Table 4.9 : The Results of Unpaired t-test between Experimental and Conventional Groups with Respect to Pre Test, Post Test and their Gain of Academic Achievement in Physical Science of Secondary School Students

Variable	Groups	Mean	SD	Unpaired t-value	P-value	Signi.
Pre-test	Experimental	36.4500	9.5234	0.1606	>0.05	NS
	Conventional	36.2100	11.5166			
Post-test	Experimental	57.0600	11.8132	5.0128	<0.05	S
	Conventional	47.7800	14.2535			
Gain	Experimental	20.6100	11.3937	5.3370	<0.05	S
	Conventional	11.5700	12.5338			

From the results of the above table it is observed that,

- The experimental and conventional groups do not differ significantly with respect to pre test of academic achievement in physical science of secondary school students (t=0.1606, >0.05, NS) at 5 per cent level of significance. Hence, the null hypothesis is accepted and alternative hypothesis is rejected. It means that, the pre test of academic achievement in physical science of secondary school students are similar in experimental and conventional group.

- The Experimental and conventional groups differ significantly with respect to post test of academic achievement in physical science of secondary school students (t=5.0128, <0.05, S) at 5 per cent level of significance. Hence, the null hypothesis is rejected and alternative hypothesis is accepted. It means that, the post test of academic achievement in physical science of secondary school students are high in experimental group as compared to conventional group.
- The experimental and conventional groups differ significantly with respect to gain of pre and post test of academic achievement in physical science of secondary school students (t=5.3370, <0.05, S) at 5 per cent level of significance. Hence, the null hypothesis is rejected and alternative hypothesis is accepted. It means that, the gain of pre and post test of academic achievement in physical science of secondary school students are high in experimental group as compared to conventional group.

Hypothesis: There is no significant difference between experimental and conventional groups with respect to pre test, post test and their gain of academic achievement in physical science of secondary school boys.

To test this, the student's unpaired t-test was applied and results are presented in the following table.

From the results of the above table it is observed that,

- The experimental and conventional groups differ significantly with respect to pre test of academic achievement in physical science of secondary school

Table-4.10: The Results of Unpaired t-test between Experimental and Conventional Groups with Respect to Pre Test, Post Test and their Gain of Academic Achievement in Physical Science of Secondary School Boys

Variable	Groups	Mean	SD	Unpaired t-value	P-value	Signi.
Pre-test	Experimental	40.3600	7.8057	2.8644	<0.05	S
	Conventional	34.8200	11.2299			
Post-test	Experimental	60.9600	6.9926	6.0565	<0.05	S
	Conventional	49.4800	11.4344			
Gain	Experimental	20.6000	8.4274	3.4532	<0.05	S
	Conventional	14.6600	8.7706			

boys (t=2.8644, <0.05, S) at 5 per cent level of significance. Hence, the null hypothesis is rejected and alternative hypothesis is accepted. It means that, the pre tests of academic achievement in physical science of secondary school boys are high in experimental group as compared to conventional group.

- The experimental and conventional groups differ significantly with respect to post test of academic achievement in physical science of secondary school boys (t=6.0565, <0.05, S) at 5 per cent level of significance. Hence, the null hypothesis is rejected and alternative hypothesis is accepted. It means that, the post tests of academic achievement in physical science of secondary school boys are high in experimental group as compared to conventional group.
- The experimental and conventional groups differ significantly with respect to gain of pre and post test of academic achievement in physical science of secondary school boys (t=3.4532, <0.05, S) at 5% level of significance. Hence, the null hypothesis is rejected and alternative hypothesis is accepted. It means that, the gain of pre and post test of academic achievement

in physical science of secondary school boys are high in experimental group as compared to conventional group.

Hypothesis: There is no significant difference between experimental and conventional groups with respect to pre test, post test and their gain of academic achievement in physical science of secondary school girls.

To test this, the student's unpaired t-test was applied and results are presented in the following table.

Table 4.11 : The Results of Unpaired t-Test between Experimental and Conventional Groups with Respect to Pre Test, Post Test and their Gain of Academic Achievement in Physical Science of Secondary School Girls

Variable	Groups	Mean	SD	Unpaired t-value	P-value	Signi.
Pre-test	Experimental	37.6000	11.7439	2.3642	<0.05	S
	Conventional	32.5400	9.5452			
Pre-test	Experimental	53.1600	14.2132	2.2950	<0.05	S
	Conventional	46.0800	16.5478			
Gain	Experimental	15.5600	18.8789	0.5092	>0.05	NS
	Conventional	13.5400	20.7504			

From the results of the above table it is observed that,

- The experimental and conventional groups differ significantly with respect to pre test of academic achievement in physical science of secondary school girls (t=2.3642, <0.05, S) at 5 per cent level of significance. Hence, the null hypothesis is rejected and alternative hypothesis is accepted. It means that, the pre tests of academic achievement in physical science of secondary school girls are high in experimental group as compared to conventional group.
- The experimental and conventional groups differ significantly with respect to post test of academic achievement in physical science of secondary school

girls (t=2.2950, <0.05, S) at 5 per cent level of significance. Hence, the null hypothesis is rejected and alternative hypothesis is accepted. It means that, the post tests of academic achievement in physical science of secondary school girls are high in experimental group as compared to conventional group.

- The experimental and conventional groups do not differ significantly with respect to gain of pre and post test f academic achievement in physical science of secondary school girls (t=0.5092, >0.05, NS) at 5 per cent level of significance. Hence, the null hypothesis is accepted and alternative hypothesis is rejected. It means that, the gain of pre and post test of academic achievement in physical science of secondary school girls are similar in experimental group and conventional group.

Hypothesis: There is no significant difference between experimental and conventional groups with respect to attitude towards physical science, attitude towards programmed instruction, achievement motivation of secondary schools students.

To test this, the student's unpaired t-test was applied and results are presented in the following table.

From the results of the above table it is observed that,

- The experimental and conventional groups differ significantly with respect to attitude towards physical science of secondary school students (t=2.0078, <0.05, S) at 5 per cent level of significance. Hence, the null hypothesis is rejected and alternative hypothesis is accepted. It means that, the attitude towards physical science of secondary school students is high in experimental group as compared to conventional group.
- The experimental and conventional groups differ significantly with respect to attitude towards programmed instruction of secondary school students

Table 4.12 : The Results of Unpaired t-Test between Experimental and Conventional Groups with Respect to attitude Towards Physical Science, Attitude Towards Programmed Instruction, Achievement Motivation of Secondary Schools Students

Variable	Groups	Mean	SD	Unpaired t-value	P-value	Signi.
Attitude towards Physical science	Experimental	105.7600	17.8621	2.0078	<0.05	S
	Conventional	99.9600	22.7023			
Attitude towards progra-mmed instruction	Experimental	92.7000	13.7080	2.1572	<0.05	S
	Conventional	88.3800	14.5989			
Achieve-ment motivation	Experimental	45.1100	17.7803	2.8470	<0.05	S
	Conventional	38.9300	12.4521			

(t=2.1572, <0.05, S) at 5 per cent level of significance. Hence, the null hypothesis is rejected and alternative hypothesis is accepted. It means that, the attitude towards programmed instruction of secondary school students is high in experimental group as compared to conventional group.

- The experimental and conventional groups differ significantly with respect to achievement motivation of secondary school students (t=2.8470, <0.05, S) at 5 per cent level of significance. Hence, the null hypothesis is rejected and alternative hypothesis is accepted. It means that, the achievement motivation of secondary school students is high in experimental group as compared to conventional group.

Hypothesis: There is no significant difference between experimental and conventional groups with respect to attitude towards physical science, attitude towards programmed instruction, achievement motivation of secondary schools boys.

To test this, the student's unpaired t-test was applied and results are presented in the following table.

Table 4.13 : The Results of Unpaired t-Test between Experimental and Conventional Groups with Respect to attitude Towards Physical Science, Attitude Towards Programmed Instruction, Achievement Motivation of Secondary Schools Boys

Variable	Groups	Mean	SD	Unpaired t-value	P-value	Signl.
Attitude towards Physical science	Experimental	107.5000	15.4289	1.6295	>0.05	NS
	Conventional	101.3600	21.7225			
Attitude towards progra-mmed instruction	Experimental	93.4600	12.6123	1.6179	>0.05	NS
	Conventional	88.9600	15.0902			
Achieve-ment motivation	Experiment	43.5800	18.1030	1.3201	>0.05	NS
	Conventional	39.4800	12.4347			

From the results of the above table it is observed that,

- The experimental and conventional groups do not differ significantly with respect to attitude towards physical science of secondary school boys (t=1.6295, >0.05, NS) at 5 per cent level of significance. Hence, the null hypothesis is accepted and alternative hypothesis is rejected. It means that, the attitudes towards physical science of secondary school boys are similar in experimental group and conventional group.
- The experimental and conventional groups do not differ significantly with respect to attitude towards programmed instruction of secondary school boys (t=1.6179, >0.05, NS) at 5 per cent level of significance. Hence, the null hypothesis is accepted and alternative hypothesis is rejected. It means that, the attitude towards programmed instruction of secondary school boys is similar in experimental group and conventional group.
- The experimental and conventional groups do not differ significantly with respect to achievement

motivation of secondary school boys (t=1.3201, >0.05, NS) at 5 per cent level of significance. Hence, the null hypothesis is accepted and alternative hypothesis is rejected. It means that, the achievement motivation of secondary school boys is similar in experimental group and conventional group.

Hypothesis: There is no significant difference between experimental and conventional groups with respect to attitude towards physical science, attitude towards programmed instruction, achievement motivation of secondary schools girls

To test this, the student's unpaired t-test was applied and results are presented in the following table.

Table 4.14: The Results of Unpaired t-Test between Experimental and Conventional Groups with Respect to Attitude Towards Physical Science, Attitude Towards Programmed Instruction, Achievement Motivation of Secondary Schools Girls

Variable	Groups	Mean	SD	Unpaired t-value	P-value	Signi.
Attitude towards Physical science	Experimental	104.0200	20.0097	1.2423	>0.05	NS
	Conventional	98.5600	23.7789			
Attitude towards progra-mmed instruction	Experimental	91.9400	14.8123	1.4257	>0.05	NS
	Conventional	87.8000	14.2198			
Achieve-ment motivation	Experimental	46.6400	17.4996	2.7107	<0.05	S
	Conventional	38.3800	12.5712			

From the results of the above table it is observed that,

- The experimental and conventional groups do not differ significantly with respect to attitude towards physical science of secondary school girls (t=1.2423, >0.05, NS) at 5 per cent level of significance. Hence, the null hypothesis is accepted and alternative hypothesis is rejected. It means that, the attitudes towards physical science of secondary school girls are similar in experimental group and conventional group.

- The experimental and conventional groups do not differ significantly with respect to attitude towards programmed instruction of secondary school girls (t=1.4257, >0.05, NS) at 5 per cent level of significance. Hence, the null hypothesis is accepted and alternative hypothesis is rejected. It means that, the attitude towards programmed instruction of secondary school girls is similar in experimental group and conventional group.
- The experimental and conventional groups differ significantly with respect to achievement motivation of secondary school girls (t=2.7107, <0.05, S) at 5 per cent level of significance. Hence, the null hypothesis is rejected and alternative hypothesis is accepted. It means that, the achievement motivation of secondary school girls are high in experimental group as compared to conventional group.

Hypothesis: There is no significant difference between boys and girls of secondary schools with respect to pre test of academic achievement in physical science as a whole.

To test this, the student's unpaired t-test was applied and results are presented in the following table.

Table 4.15 : Results of t-test between Boys and Girls of Secondary Schools with Respect to Pre Test of Academic Achievement in Physical Science

Variable	Groups	Mean	SD	Unpaired t-value	P-value	Signl.
Pre test achievement	Boys	37.5900	10.0162	1.6984	>0.05	NS
	Girls	35.0700	10.9464			
Post test achievement	Boys	55.2200	11.0541	2.9098	<0.05	S
	Girls	49.6200	15.7536			
Achievement gain	Boys	17.6300	9.0628	1.4167	>0.05	NS
	Girls	14.5500	19.7624			

From the results of the above table it is observed that,

- Boy and girls of secondary schools do not differ significantly with respect to pre test academic achievements in physical science (t=1.6984, >0.05, NS) at 5 per cent level of significance. Hence, the null hypothesis is accepted and alternative hypothesis is rejected. It means that, the boys and girls of secondary schools have similar pre test academic achievements in physical science.
- The boys and girls of secondary schools differ significantly with respect to post test academic achievements in physical science (t=2.9098,<0.05, S) at 5 per cent level of significance. Hence, the null hypothesis is rejected and alternative hypothesis is accepted. It means that, the boys of secondary schools are high in post test academic achievements in physical science as compared to girls of secondary schools.
- The boys and girls of secondary schools do not differ significantly with respect to gain of pre test and post academic achievements in physical science (t=1.4167, >0.05, NS) at 5 per cent level of significance. Hence, the null hypothesis is accepted and alternative hypothesis is rejected. It means that, the boys and girls of secondary schools have similar gain of pre test and post academic achievements in physical science.

Sub Hypothesis: There is no significant difference between boys and girls of secondary schools with respect to pre test of academic achievement in physical science in experimental group.

To test this, the student's unpaired t-test was applied and results are presented in the following table.

From the results of the above table it is observed that,

- The boys and girls of secondary schools do not differ significantly with respect to pre test academic achievements in physical science in experiment group (t=1.3840, >0.05, NS) at 5 per cent level of significance.

Table 4.16: Results of t-Test between Boys and Girls of Secondary Schools with Respect to Pre Test of Academic Achievement in Physical Science in Experimental Group

Variable	Groups	Mean	SD	Unpaired t-value	P-value	Signl.
Pre test achieve-ment	Boys	40.3600	7.8057	1.3840	>0.05	NS
	Girls	37.6000	11.7439			
Post test achieve-ment	Boys	60.9600	6.9926	3.4819	<0.05	S
	Girls	53.1600	14.2132			
Achieve-ment gain	Boys	20.6000	8.4274	1.7238	>0.05	NS
	Girls	15.5600	18.8789			

Hence, the null hypothesis is accepted and alternative hypothesis is rejected. It means that, the boys and girls of secondary schools have similar pre test academic achievements in physical science in experimental group.

- The boys and girls of secondary schools differ significantly with respect to post test academic achievements in physical science in experiment group (t=3.4819,<0.05, S) at 5 per cent level of significance. Hence, the null hypothesis is rejected and alternative hypothesis is accepted. It means that, the boys of secondary schools have high in post test academic achievements in physical science as compared to girls of secondary schools in experimental group.
- The boys and girls of secondary schools do not differ significantly with respect to gain of pre test and post academic achievements in physical science in experimental group (t=1.7238, >0.05, NS) at 5 per cent level of significance. Hence, the null hypothesis is accepted and alternative hypothesis is rejected. It means that, the boys and girls of secondary schools have similar gain of pre test and post academic achievements in physical science in experimental group.

Sub Hypothesis: There is no significant difference between boys and girls of secondary schools with respect to pre test of academic achievement in physical science in conventional group.

To test this, the student's unpaired t-test was applied and results are presented in the following table.

Table 4.17: Results of t-Test between Boys and Girls of Secondary Schools with Respect to Pre Test of Academic Achievement in Physical Science in Conventional Group

Variable	Groups	Mean	SD	Unpaired t-value	P-value	Signi.
Pre test achievement	Boys	34.8200	11.2299	1.0939	>0.05	NS
	Girls	32.5400	9.5452			
Post test achievement	Boys	49.4800	11.4344	1.1953	>0.05	NS
	Girls	46.0800	16.5478			
Achievement gain	Boys	14.6600	8.7706	0.3515	>0.05	NS
	Girls	13.5400	20.7504			

From the results of the above table it is observed that,

- The boys and girls of secondary schools do not differ significantly with respect to pre test academic achievement in physical science in conventional group (t=1.0939, >0.05, NS) at 5 per cent level of significance. Hence, the null hypothesis is accepted and alternative hypothesis is rejected. It means that, the boys and girls of secondary schools have similar pre test academic achievements in physical science in conventional group.
- The boys and girls of secondary schools do not differ significantly with respect to post test academic achievement in physical science in conventional group (t=1.1953,>0.05, NS) at 5 per cent level of significance. Hence, the null hypothesis is accepted and alternative hypothesis is rejected. It means that, the boys and girls of secondary schools have similar post test

academic achievements in physical science in conventional group.

- The boys and girls of secondary schools do not differ significantly with respect to gain of pre test and post academic achievement in physical science in conventional group (t=0.3515, >0.05, NS) at 5 per cent level of significance. Hence, the null hypothesis is accepted and alternative hypothesis is rejected. It means that, the boys and girls of secondary schools have similar gain of pre test and post academic achievement in physical science in conventional group.

Hypothesis: There is no significant difference between boys and girls of secondary schools with respect to attitude towards physical science, attitude towards programmed instruction, achievement motivation (both experimental and conventional).

To test this, the student's unpaired t-test was applied and results are presented in the following table.

Table 4.18 : Results of t-Test between Boys and Girls of Secondary Schools with Respect to Attitude Towards Physical Science, Attitude Towards Programmed Instruction, Achievement Motivation

Variable	Groups	Mean	SD	Unpaired t-value	P-value	Signi.
Attitude towards Physical science	Boys	104.4300	18.9972	1.0793	>0.05	NS
	Girls	101.2900	22.0355			
Attitude towards programmed instruction	Boys	91.2100	14.0197	0.6621	>0.05	NS
	Girls	89.8700	14.5946			
Achievement motivation	Boys	41.5300	15.5878	-0.4427	>0.05	NS
	Girls	42.5100	15.7169			

From the results of the above table we seen that the followings:

- The boys and girls of secondary schools do not differ significantly with respect to attitude towards physical science (t=1.0793, >0.05, NS) at 5 per cent level of significance. Hence, the null hypothesis is accepted and alternative hypothesis is rejected. It means that, the boys and girls of secondary schools have similar attitude towards physical science.
- The boys and girls of secondary schools do not differ significantly with respect to attitude towards programmed instruction (t=0.6621, >0.05, NS) at 5 per cent level of significance. Hence, the null hypothesis is accepted and alternative hypothesis is rejected. It means that, the boys and girls of secondary schools have similar attitude towards programmed instruction.
- The boys and girls of secondary schools do not differ significantly with respect to achievement motivation (t=-0.4427, >0.05, NS) at 5 per cent level of significance. Hence, the null hypothesis is accepted and alternative hypothesis is rejected. It means that, the boys and girls of secondary schools have similar achievement motivation.

Sub Hypothesis: There is no significant difference between boys and girls of secondary schools with respect to attitude towards physical science, attitude towards programmed instruction, achievement motivation in experiment group.

To test this, the student's unpaired t-test was applied and results are presented in the following table.

From the results of the above table we seen that the followings:

- The boys and girls of secondary schools do not differ significantly with respect to attitude towards physical science in experimental group (t=0.9739, >0.05, NS)

Table 4.19 : Results of t-Test between Boys and Girls of Secondary Schools with Respect to Attitude Towards Physical Science, Attitude Towards Programmed Instruction, Achievement Motivation in Experimental Group

Variable	Groups	Mean	SD	Unpaired t-value	P-value	Signl.
Attitude towards Physical science	Boys	107.5000	15.4289	0.9739	>0.05	NS
	Girls	104.0200	20.0097			
Attitude towards progra-mmed instruc-tion	Boys	93.4600	12.6123	0.5525	>0.05	NS
	Girls	91.9400	14.8123			
Achieve-ment motiva-tion	Boys	43.5800	18.1030	-0.8594	>0.05	NS
	Girls	46.6400	17.4996			

at 5 per cent level of significance. Hence, the null hypothesis is accepted and alternative hypothesis is rejected. It means that, the boys and girls of secondary schools have similar attitude towards physical science in experimental group.

- The boys and girls of secondary schools do not differ significantly with respect to attitude towards programmed instruction in experimental group (t=0.5525, >0.05, NS) at 5 per cent level of significance. Hence, the null hypothesis is accepted and alternative hypothesis is rejected. It means that, the boys and girls of secondary schools have similar attitude towards programmed instruction in experimental group.
- The boys and girls of secondary schools do not differ significantly with respect to achievement motivation in experimental group (t=-0.8594, >0.05, NS) at 5 per cent level of significance. Hence, the null hypothesis is accepted and alternative hypothesis is rejected. It

means that, the boys and girls of secondary schools have similar achievement motivation in experimental group.

Sub Hypothesis: There is no significant difference between boys and girls of secondary schools with respect to attitude towards physical science, attitude towards programmed instruction, achievement motivation in conventional group.

To test this, the student's unpaired t-test was applied and results are presented in the following table.

Table 4.20: Results of t-Test between Boys and Girls of Secondary Schools with Respect to Attitude Towards Physical Science, Attitude Towards Programmed Instruction, Achievement Motivation in Conventional Group

Variable	Gender	Mean	SD	Unpaired t-value	P-value	Signi.
Attitude towards Physical science	Boys	101.3600	21.7225	0.6147	>0.05	NS
	Girls	98.5600	23.7789			
Attitude towards progra-mmed instruc-tion	Boys	88.9600	15.0902	0.3956	>0.05	NS
	Girls	87.8000	14.2198			
Achieve-ment motiva-tion	Boys	39.4800	12.4347	0.4399	>0.05	NS
	Girls	38.3800	12.5712			

From the results of the above table we seen that the followings:

- The boys and girls of secondary schools do not differ significantly with respect to attitude towards physical science in conventional group (t=0.6147, >0.05, NS) at 5 per cent level of significance. Hence, the null hypothesis is accepted and alternative hypothesis is rejected. It means that, the boys and girls of secondary schools have similar attitude towards physical science in conventional group.

- The boys and girls of secondary schools do not differ significantly with respect to attitude towards programmed instruction in conventional group (t=0.3956, >0.05, NS) at 5 per cent level of significance. Hence, the null hypothesis is accepted and alternative hypothesis is rejected. It means that, the boys and girls of secondary schools have similar attitude towards programmed instruction in conventional group.
- The boys and girls of secondary schools do not differ significantly with respect to achievement motivation in conventional group (t0.4399, >0.05, NS) at 5 per cent level of significance. Hence, the null hypothesis is accepted and alternative hypothesis is rejected. It means that, the boys and girls of secondary schools have similar achievement motivation in conventional group.

Hypothesis: There is no significant difference between urban and rural secondary school students with respect to pre test of academic achievement in physical science as a whole.

To test this, the student's unpaired t-test was applied and results are presented in the following table.

Table 4.21: Results of t-Test between Urban and Rural Secondary School Students with Respect to Pre Test of Academic Achievement in Physical Science

Variable	Location	Mean	SD	Unpaired t-value	P-value	Signi.
Pre test achievement	Urban	38.8700	10.8801	3.5028	>0.05	NS
	Rural	33.7900	9.5888			
Post test achievement	Urban	56.7600	10.7601	4.6519	<0.05	S
	Rural	48.0800	15.2439			
Achievement gain	Urban	17.8900	12.4177	1.6589	>0.05	NS
	Rural	14.2900	17.7970			

From the results of the above table it is observed that,

- The urban and rural secondary school students do not differ significantly with respect to pre test academic achievements in physical science (t=3.5028, <0.05, S) at 5 per cent level of significance. Hence, the null hypothesis is rejected and alternative hypothesis is accepted. It means that, the urban and rural secondary school students have similar pre test academic achievements in physical science.
- The urban and rural secondary school students differ significantly with respect to post test academic achievements in physical science (t=4.6519,<0.05, S) at 5 per cent level of significance. Hence, the null hypothesis is rejected and alternative hypothesis is accepted. It means that, the urban and rural secondary school students have different post test academic achievements in physical science.
- The urban and rural secondary school students do not differ significantly with respect to gain of pre test and post academic achievements in physical science (t=1.6589, >0.05, NS) at 5 per cent level of significance. Hence, the null hypothesis is accepted and alternative hypothesis is rejected. It means that, the urban and rural secondary school students have similar gain of pre test and post academic achievements in physical science.

Sub Hypothesis: There is no significant difference between urban and rural secondary school students with respect to pre test of academic achievement in physical science in experimental group.

To test this, the student's unpaired t-test was applied and results are presented in the following table.

From the results of the above table it is observed that,

- The urban and rural secondary school students differ significantly with respect to pre test academic achievements in physical science in experimental group

Table 4.22 : Results of t-Test between Urban and Rural Secondary School Students with Respect to Pre Test of Academic Achievement in Physical Science in Experimental Group

Variable	Location	Mean	SD	Unpaired t-value	P-value	Signi.
Pre-test achievement	Urban	42.5000	9.4074	3.7370	<0.05	S
	Rural	35.4600	9.4312			
Post-test achievement	Urban	60.9800	6.7988	3.5020	<0.05	S
	Rural	53.1400	14.2957			
Achievement gain	Urban	18.4800	10.3475	0.2697	>0.05	NS
	Rural	17.6800	18.2482			

(t=3.7370, <0.05, S) at 5 per cent level of significance. Hence, the null hypothesis is rejected and alternative hypothesis is accepted. It means that, the urban and rural secondary school students have different pre test academic achievements in physical science in experimental group.

- The urban and rural secondary school students differ significantly with respect to post test academic achievements in physical science in experiment group (t=3.5020,<0.05, S) at 5 per cent level of significance. Hence, the null hypothesis is rejected and alternative hypothesis is accepted. It means that, the urban and rural secondary school students have different post test academic achievements in physical science in experimental group.
- The urban and rural secondary school students do not differ significantly with respect to gain of pre test and post academic achievements in physical science in experimental group (t=0.2697, >0.05, NS) at 5 per cent level of significance. Hence, the null hypothesis is accepted and alternative hypothesis is rejected. It means that, the urban and rural secondary school students have similar gain of pre test and post

academic achievements in physical science in experimental group.

Sub Hypothesis: There is no significant difference between urban and rural secondary school students with respect to pre test of academic achievement in physical science in conventional group.

To test this, the student's unpaired t-test was applied and results are presented in the following table.

Table 4.23: Results of t-Test between Urban and rural Secondary School Students with Respect to Pre Test of Academic Achievement in Physical Science in Conventional Group

Variable	Location	Mean	SD	Unpaired t-value	P-value	Signi.
Pre-test achievement	Urban	35.2400	11.1256	1.5049	>0.05	NS
	Rural	32.1200	9.5461			
Post-test achievement	Urban	52.5400	12.3027	3.5272	<0.05	S
	Rural	43.0200	14.5903			
Achievement gain	Urban	17.3000	14.2746	2.0502	<0.05	S
	Rural	10.9000	16.8369			

From the results of the above table it is observed that,

- The urban and rural secondary school students do not differ significantly with respect to pre test academic achievements in physical science in conventional group (t=1.5049, >0.05, NS) at 5 per cent level of significance. Hence, the null hypothesis is accepted and alternative hypothesis is rejected. It means that, the urban and rural secondary school students have similar pre test academic achievements in physical science in conventional group.
- The urban and rural secondary school students differ significantly with respect to post test academic achievements in physical science in conventional group (t=3.5272,<0.05, S) at 5 per cent level of significance. Hence, the null hypothesis is rejected and alternative

hypothesis is accepted. It means that, the urban secondary school students have high in post test academic achievements in physical science than the post test academic achievements in physical science in conventional group.

- The urban and rural secondary school students differ significantly with respect to gain of pre test and post academic achievements in physical science in conventional group (t=2.0502, <0.05, S) at 5 per cent level of significance. Hence, the null hypothesis is rejected and alternative hypothesis is accepted. It means that, the urban and rural secondary school students have different gain of pre test and post academic achievements in physical science in conventional group.

Hypothesis: There is no significant difference between urban and rural secondary school students with respect to attitude towards physical science, attitude towards programmed instruction, achievement motivation (both experimental and conventional).

Table 4.24: Results of t-Test between Urban and Rural Secondary School Students with Respect to Attitude Towards Physical Science, Attitude Towards Programmed Instruction, Achievement Motivation

Variable	Location	Mean	SD	Unpaired t-value	P-value	Signl.
Attitude towards Physical science	Urban	106.7400	21.7570	2.7082	<0.05	S
	Rural	98.9800	18.6455			
Attitude towards progra-mmed instruc-tion	Urban	93.6300	16.5363	3.1247	<0.05	S
	Rural	87.4500	10.8501			
Achieve-ment motiva-tion	Urban	44.4900	17.5542	2.2591	<0.05	S
	Rural	39.5500	13.0387			

To test this, the student's unpaired t-test was applied and results are presented in the following table.

From the results of the above table we seen that the followings:

- The urban and rural secondary school students do not differ significantly with respect to attitude towards physical science (t=1.0793, >0.05, NS) at 5 per cent level of significance. Hence, the null hypothesis is rejected and alternative hypothesis is accepted. It means that, the urban and rural secondary school students have different attitude towards physical science.
- The urban and rural secondary school students do not differ significantly with respect to attitude towards programmed instruction (t=0.6621, >0.05, NS) at 5 per cent level of significance. Hence, the null hypothesis is rejected and alternative hypothesis is accepted. It means that, the urban and rural secondary school students have different attitude towards programmed instruction.
- The urban and rural secondary school students do not differ significantly with respect to achievement motivation (t=-0.4427, >0.05, NS) at 5 per cent level of significance. Hence, the null hypothesis is rejected and alternative hypothesis is accepted. It means that, the urban and rural secondary school students have different achievement motivation.

Sub Hypothesis: There is no significant difference between urban and rural secondary school students with respect to attitude towards physical science, attitude towards programmed instruction, achievement motivation in experiment group.

To test this, the student's unpaired t-test was applied and results are presented in the following table.

Table 4.25: Results of t-Test between Urban and rural Secondary School Students with Respect to Attitude Towards Physical Science, Attitude Towards Programmed Instruction, Achievement Motivation in Experimental Group

Variable	Location	Mean	SD	Unpaired t-value	P-value	Signi.
Attitude towards Physical science	Urban	109.7600	17.2480	2.2867	<0.05	S
	Rural	101.7600	17.7334			
Attitude towards progra-mmed instruc-tion	Urban	96.0200	14.6601	2.4844	<0.05	S
	Rural	89.3800	11.9265			
Achieve-ment motiva-tion	Urban	46.8000	20.2666	0.9500	>0.05	NS
	Rural	43.4200	14.9053			

From the results of the above table the followings observations are made.

- The urban and rural secondary school students differ significantly with respect to attitude towards physical science in experimental group (t=2.2867, <0.05, S) at 5 per cent level of significance. Hence, the null hypothesis is rejected and alternative hypothesis is accepted. It means that, the urban secondary school students have high attitude towards physical science in experimental group when compared to rural secondary school students.
- The urban and rural secondary school students differ significantly with respect to attitude towards programmed instruction in experimental group (t=2.4844, <0.05, S) at 5 per cent level of significance. Hence, the null hypothesis is rejected and alternative hypothesis is accepted. It means that, the urban secondary school students have high attitude towards

programmed instruction in experiment group when compared to rural secondary school students..

- The urban and rural secondary school students do not differ significantly with respect to achievement motivation in experimental group (t=0.9500, >0.05, NS) at 5 per cent level of significance. Hence, the null hypothesis is accepted and alternative hypothesis is rejected. It means that, the urban and rural secondary school students have similar achievement motivation in experimental group.

Sub Hypothesis: There is no significant difference between urban and rural secondary school students with respect to attitude towards physical science, attitude towards programmed instruction, achievement motivation in conventional group.

To test this, the student's unpaired t-test was applied and results are presented in the following table.

Table 4.26: Results of t-Test between Urban and Rural Secondary School Students with Respect to Attitude Towards Physical Science, Attitude Towards Programmed Instruction, Achievement Motivation in Conventional Group

Variable	Location	Mean	SD	Unpaired t-value	P-value	Signi.
Attitude towards Physical science	Urban	103.7200	25.3039	1.6712	>0.05	NS
	Rural	96.2000	19.2915			
Attitude towards programmed instruction	Urban	91.2400	18.0527	1.9881	<0.05	S
	Rural	85.5200	9.3814			
Achievement motivation	Urban	42.1800	14.1763	2.6910	<0.05	S
	Rural	35.6800	9.5264			

From the results of the above table the following conclusion were drawn:

- The urban and rural secondary school students do not differ significantly with respect to attitude towards physical science in conventional group (t=1.6712, >0.05, NS) at 5 per cent level of significance. Hence, the null hypothesis is accepted and alternative hypothesis is rejected. It means that, the urban and rural secondary school students have similar attitude towards physical science in conventional group.
- The urban and rural secondary school students differ significantly with respect to attitude towards programmed instruction in conventional group (t=1.9881, <0.05, S) at 5 per cent level of significance. Hence, the null hypothesis is rejected and alternative hypothesis is accepted. It means that, the urban secondary school students have high attitude towards programmed instruction in conventional group when compared to rural secondary school students.
- The urban and rural secondary school students do not differ significantly with respect to achievement motivation in conventional group (t=2.9610, >0.05, S) at 5 per cent level of significance. Hence, the null hypothesis is accepted and alternative hypothesis is accepted. It means that, the urban secondary school students have high on achievement motivation in conventional group as compared to rural secondary school students.

Hypothesis: There is no significant difference between different types of management (Government, aided and unaided) with respect to pre test and post test academic achievement in physical science of secondary schools as a whole.

To test this, the one-way analysis of variance -test was applied and results are presented in the following table.

From the above table, it is clearly seen that;

- The types of management (Government, aided and unaided) do not differ significantly with respect to pre test of academic achievement in physical science

Table 4.27 : Results of ANOVA Test between Different Types of Management (Government, Aided and Unaided) with Respect to Pre Test and Post Test Achievement in Physical Science of Secondary Schools as a Whole

Variable	SS Effect	df Effect	MS Effect	SS Error	df Error	MS value	F-value	p-value	Signi. value
Pre-test achievement	301	2	150	21810	196	111	1.3503	>0.05	NS
Post-test achievement	6572	2	3286	31477	196	161	20.4610	<0.05	S
Gain achievement	7639	2	3820	39408	196	201	18.9975	<0.05	S

(F=1.3503, >0.05, NS) at 5 per cent level of significance. Hence, the null hypothesis is accepted and alternative hypothesis is rejected. It means that, the types of management (Government, aided and unaided) students have similar pre test of academic achievement in physical science.

- The types of management (Government, aided and unaided) differ significantly with respect to post test of academic achievement in physical science (F=20.4610, <0.05, S) at 5 per cent level of significance. Hence, the null hypothesis is rejected and alternative hypothesis is accepted. It means that, the types of management (Government, aided and unaided) students have different post test of academic achievement in physical science.
- The types of management (Government, aided and unaided) differ significantly with respect to gain of pre and post test of academic achievement in physical science (F=18.9975, <0.05, S) at 5 per cent level of significance. Hence, the null hypothesis is rejected and alternative hypothesis is accepted. It means that, the types of management (Government, aided and unaided) students have different gain of pre and post test of academic achievement in physical science.

If F is significant to know pair wise comparison of types of management by applying the Schaffe's multiple comparison post hoc procedure and the results are presented in the following table.

Table 4.28: Pair Wise Comparison of Types of Management (Government, Aided and Unaided) with Respect to Pre Test and Post Test Achievement in Physical Science of Secondary Schools by Scheffe's Multiple Post Hoc Procedure

Variable	Managements	Government	Aided	Unaided
Pre test academic achievement	Mean	37.1740	37.1140	34.4670
	Government	—	—	—
	Aided	0.9994	—	—
	Unaided	0.3495	0.3634	—
Post test academic achievement	Mean	44.6960	58.0000	54.5670
	Government	—	—	—
	Aided	0.0000*	—	—
	Unaided	0.0001*	0.3077	—
Gain of pre and post test academic achievement	Mean	7.5217	20.8860	20.1000
	Government	—	—	—
	Aided	0.0000*	—	—
	Unaided	0.0000*	0.9516	—

*$p<0.05$

The results of the above table clearly indicated that,

- The students belonging to Government and aided, Government and unaided management secondary schools differ significantly with respect to post test of academic achievement in physical sciences at 5 per cent level of significance. It means that, the students belonging to aided secondary schools have high post test of academic achievement in physical sciences as compared to unaided and Government schools students.
- The students belong to Government and aided, Government and unaided management secondary

schools differ significantly with respect to gain of pre and post test of academic achievement in physical sciences at 5 per cent level of significance. It means that, the students belonging to aided secondary schools have high gain of pre and post test of academic achievement in physical sciences as compared to unaided and Government schools students.

Sub Hypothesis: There is no significant difference between different types of management (Government, aided and unaided) with respect to pre test and post test academic achievement in physical science of secondary schools in experimental group.

To test this, the one-way analysis of variance-test was applied and results are presented in the following table.

Table 4.29: Results of ANOVA Test between Different Types of Management (Government, Aided and Unaided) with Respect to Pre Test and Post Test Achievement in Physical Science of Secondary Schools in Experimental Group

Variable	SS Effect	df Effect	MS Effect	SS Error	df Error	MS value	F-value	p-value	Signi. value
Pre test achievement	212	2	106	9722	97	100	1.0595	>0.05	NS
Post test achievement	647	2	323	13169	97	136	2.3818	>0.05	NS
Gain achievement	1133	2	566	20447	97	211	2.6863	>0.05	NS

From the above table, it is clearly seen that;

- The types of management (Government, aided and unaided) do not differ significantly with respect to pre test of academic achievement in physical science in experimental group (F=1.0595, >0.05, NS) at 5 per cent level of significance. Hence, the null hypothesis is accepted and alternative hypothesis is rejected. It means that, the types of management (Government, aided and unaided) students have similar pre test of academic achievement in physical science in experimental group.

- The types of management (Government, aided and unaided) do not differ significantly with respect to post test of academic achievement in physical science in experiment group (F=2.3818, >0.05, S) at 5 per cent level of significance. Hence, the null hypothesis is accepted and alternative hypothesis is rejected. It means that, the types of management (Government, aided and unaided) students have similar post test of academic achievement in physical science in experimental group.
- The types of management (Government, aided and unaided) do not differ significantly with respect to gain of pre and post test of academic achievement in physical science in experimental group (F=2.6863, >0.05, S) at 5 per cent level of significance. Hence, the null hypothesis is accepted and alternative hypothesis is rejected. It means that, the types of management (Government, aided and unaided) students have similar gain of pre and post test of academic achievement in physical science in experimental group.

Sub Hypothesis: There is no significant difference between different types of management (Government, aided and unaided) with respect to pre test and post test academic achievement in physical science of secondary schools in conventional group.

Table 4.29: Results of ANOVA Test between Different Types of Management (Government, Aided and Unaided) with Respect to Pre Test and Post Test Achievement in Physical Science of Secondary Schools in Conventional Group

Variable	SS Effect	df Effect	MS Effect	SS Error	df Error	MS value	F-value	p-value	Signi. value
Pre-test achievement	100	2	50	10674	97	110	0.4538	>0.05	NS
Post-test achievement	7554	2	3777	12559	97	129	29.1712	<0.05	S
Gain achievement	7854	2	3927	17045	97	176	22.3490	<0.05	S

To test this, the one-way analysis of variance-test was applied and results are presented in the following table.

From the above table, it is clearly seen that;

- The types of management (Government, aided and unaided) do not differ significantly with respect to pre test of academic achievement in physical science in conventional group (F=0.4538, >0.05, NS) at 5 per cent level of significance. Hence, the null hypothesis is accepted and alternative hypothesis is rejected. It means that, the types of management (Government, aided and unaided) students have similar pre test of academic achievement in physical science in conventional group.
- The types of management (Government, aided and unaided) differ significantly with respect to post test of academic achievement in physical science in conventional group (F=29.1712, <0.05, S) at 5 per cent level of significance. Hence, the null hypothesis is rejected and alternative hypothesis is accepted. It means that, the types of management (Government, aided and unaided) students have different post test of academic achievement in physical science in conventional group.
- The types of management (Government, aided and unaided) differ significantly with respect to gain of pre and post test of academic achievement in physical science in conventional group (F=22.3490, <0.05, S) at 5 per cent level of significance. Hence, the null hypothesis is rejected and alternative hypothesis is accepted. It means that, the types of management (Government, aided and unaided) students have different gain of pre and post test of academic achievement in physical science in conventional group.

If F is significant to know pair wise comparison of types of management by applying the Scheffe's multiple comparison post hoc procedure and the results are presented in the following table.

Table 4.30 : Pair Wise Comparison of Types of Management (Government, Aided and Unaided) with Respect to Pre Test and Post Test Achievement in Physical Science of Secondary Schools by Scheffe's Multiple Post Hoc Procedure

Variable	Managements	Government	Aided	Unaided
Pre-test academic achievement	Mean	34.1710	34.4860	32.1670
	Government	—	—	—
	Aided	0.9922	—	—
	Unaided	0.7452	0.6749	—
Post-test academic achievement	Mean	36.3140	56.4570	51.0330
	Government	—	—	—
	Aided	0.0000*	—	—
	Unaided	0.0000*	0.1651	—
Gain of pre and post test academic achievement	Mean	2.1429	21.9710	18.8670
	Government	—	—	—
	Aided	0.0000*	—	—
	Unaided	0.0000*	0.6433	—

*p<0.05

The results of the above table clearly indicated that,

- The students belonging to Government and aided, Government and unaided management secondary schools differ significantly with respect to post test of academic achievement in physical sciences in conventional group at 5 per cent level of significance. It means that, the students belonging to aided secondary schools have high in post test of academic achievement in physical sciences as compared to unaided and Government schools students in conventional group.
- The students who belong to Government and aided, Government and unaided management secondary schools differ significantly with respect to gain of pre test and post test of academic achievement in physical sciences in conventional group at 5 per cent level of significance. It means that, the students belonging to

aided secondary schools have high gain of pre and post test of academic achievement in physical sciences as compared to unaided and Government schools students in conventional group.

Hypothesis: There is no significant difference between different types of management (Government, aided and unaided) with respect to attitude towards physical science, attitude towards programmed instruction, achievement motivation of secondary schools as a whole.

To test this, the one-way analysis of variance -test was applied and results are presented in the following table.

Table 4.31: Results of ANOVA Test between Different Types of Management (Government, Aided and Unaided) with Respect to Attitude Towards Physical Science, Attitude Towards Programmed Instruction, Achievement Motivation of Secondary Schools as a Whole

Variable	SS Effect	df Effect	MS Effect	SS Error	df Error	MS value	F-value	p-value	Signi. value
Attitude towards Physical science	11539	2	5770	72753	197	369	15.6233	<0.05	S
Attitude towards programmed instruction	5208	2	2604	35428	197	180	14.4802	<0.05	S
Achievement motivation	3419	2	1709	45139	197	229	7.4601	<0.05	S

From the above Table, it is clearly known that ;

- The types of management (Government, aided and unaided) differ significantly with respect to Attitude towards Physical science (F=15.6233, <0.05, S) at 5% level of significance. Hence, the null hypothesis is rejected and alternative hypothesis is accepted. It means that, the types of management (Government, aided and unaided) have different Attitude towards Physical science.

- The types of management (Government, aided and unaided) differ significantly with respect to Attitude towards programmed instruction (F=14.4802, <0.05, S) at 5 per cent level of significance. Hence, the null hypothesis is rejected and alternative hypothesis is accepted. It means that, the types of management (Government, aided and unaided) students have different Attitude towards programmed instruction.
- The types of management (Government, aided and unaided) differ significantly with respect to achievement motivation (F=7.4601, <0.05, S) at 5 per cent level of significance. Hence, the null hypothesis is rejected and alternative hypothesis is accepted. It means that, the types of management (Government, aided and unaided) students have different achievement motivation.

If F is significant to know pair wise comparison of types of management by applying the Scheffe's multiple comparison

Table 4.32: Pair Wise Comparison of Types of Management (Government, Aided and Unaided) with Respect to Attitude towards Physical Science, Attitude towards Programmed Instruction, and Achievement Motivation of Secondary Schools by Scheffe's Multiple Post Hoc Procedure

Variable	Managements	Government	Aided	Unaided
Attitude towards physical science	Mean	92.7570	110.2000	106.0800
	Government	—	—	—
	Aided	0.0000*	—	—
	Unaided	0.0006*	0.4778	—
Attitude towards programmed instruction	Mean	84.6000	96.7860	90.1830
	Government	—	—	—
	Aided	0.0000*	—	—
	Unaided	0.0432*	0.0215	—
Achievement motivation	Mean	37.3430	47.1860	41.4500
	Government	-		
	Aided	0.0008*	-	
	Unaided	0.3066	0.1010	-

*p<0.05

post hoc procedure and the results are presented in the following table.

The results of the above table clearly indicated that:

- The students who belong to Government and aided, Government and unaided management secondary schools differ significantly with respect to attitude towards physical science at 5 per cent level of significance. It means that, the students belonging to aided secondary schools have high attitude towards physical science as compared to unaided and Government schools students.
- The students who belong to Government and aided, Government and unaided management secondary schools differ significantly with respect to attitude towards programmed instruction at 5 per cent level of significance. It means that, the students belonging to aided secondary schools have high attitude towards programmed instruction as compared to unaided and Government schools students.
- The students belong to Government and aided management secondary schools differ significantly with respect to achievement motivation at 5 per cent level of significance. It means that, the students belonging to aided secondary schools have high achievement motivation as compared to unaided and Government schools students.

Sub Hypothesis: There is no significant difference between different types of management (Government, aided and unaided) with respect to attitude towards physical science, attitude towards programmed instruction, achievement motivation of secondary schools in experimental group.

To test this, the one-way analysis of variance-test was applied and results are presented in the following table.

Table 4.33 : Results of ANOVA Test between Different Types of Management (Government, Aided and Unaided) with Respect to Attitude towards Physical Science, Attitude towards Programmed Instruction, Achievement Motivation of Secondary Schools in Experimental Group

Variable	SS Effect	df Effect	MS Effect	SS Error	df Error	MS value	F-value	p-value	Signi. value
Attitude towards Physical science	279	2	140	31307	97	323	0.4329	>0.05	NS
Attitude towards programmed instruction	684	2	342	17919	97	185	1.8511	>0.05	NS
Achievement motivation	264	2	132	31034	97	320	0.4129	>0.05	NS

From the above Table, it is clearly known that:

- The types of management (Government, aided and unaided) do not differ significantly with respect to Attitude towards Physical science in experimental group (F=0.4329, >0.05, NS) at 5 per cent level of significance. Hence, the null hypothesis is accepted and alternative hypothesis is rejected. It means that, the types of management (Government, aided and unaided) have similar Attitude towards Physical science in experimental group.
- The types of management (Government, aided and unaided) do not differ significantly with respect to Attitude towards programmed instruction in experimental group (F=1.8511, >0.05, NS) at 5 per cent level of significance. Hence, the null hypothesis is accepted and alternative hypothesis is rejected. It means that, the types of management (Government, aided and unaided) students have similar Attitude towards programmed instruction in experimental group.

- The types of management (Government, aided and unaided) do not differ significantly with respect to achievement motivation in experimental group (F=0.4129, >0.05, NS) at 5 per cent level of significance. Hence, the null hypothesis is accepted and alternative hypothesis is rejected. It means that, the types of management (Government, aided and unaided) students have similar achievement motivation in experimental group.

Sub Hypothesis: There is no significant difference between different types of management (Government, aided and unaided) with respect to attitude towards physical science, attitude towards programmed instruction, achievement motivation of secondary schools in conventional group.

To test this, the one-way analysis of variance-test was applied and results are presented in the following table.

Table 4.34: Results of ANOVA Test between Different Types of Management (Government, Aided and Unaided) with Respect to Attitude towards Physical Science, Attitude towards Programmed Instruction, Achievement Motivation of Secondary Schools in Conventional Group

Variable	SS Effect	df Effect	MS Effect	SS Error	df Error	MS value	F-value	p-value	Signi. value
Attitude towards Physical science	20100	2	10050	30924	97	319	31.5240	<0.05	S
Attitude towards programmed instruction	7547	2	3774	13552	97	140	27.0100	<0.05	S
Achievement motivation	5665	2	2833	9685	97	100	28.3689	<0.05	S

From the above Table, it is clearly known that;

- The types of management (Government, aided and unaided) differ significantly with respect to Attitude towards Physical science in conventional group (F=31.5240, <0.05, S) at 5 per cent level of significance. Hence, the null hypothesis is rejected and alternative hypothesis is accepted. It means that, the types of management (Government, aided and unaided) have different Attitude towards Physical science in conventional group.

- The types of management (Government, aided and unaided) differ significantly with respect to Attitude towards programmed instruction in conventional group (F=27.0100, <0.05, S) at 5 per cent level of significance. Hence, the null hypothesis is rejected and alternative hypothesis is accepted. It means that, the types of management (Government, aided and unaided) students have different Attitude towards programmed instruction in conventional group.
- The types of management (Government, aided and unaided) differ significantly with respect to achievement motivation in conventional group (F=28.3689, <0.05, S) at 5 per cent level of significance. Hence, the null hypothesis is rejected and alternative hypothesis is accepted. It means that, the types of management (Government, aided and unaided) students have different achievement motivation in conventional group.

If F is significant to know pair wise comparison of types of management by applying the Schaffer's multiple comparison post hoc procedure and the results are presented in the following table.

From the results of the above table clearly indicated that,

- The students who belong to Government and aided Government and unaided management secondary schools differ significantly with respect to attitude towards physical science at 5 per cent level of significance. It means that, the students belonging to aided secondary schools have high attitude towards physical science as compared to unaided and Government schools students in conventional group.

Table 4.35: Pair Wise Comparison of Types of Management (Government, Aided and Unaided) with Respect to Attitude towards Physical Science, Attitude towards Programmed Instruction, and Achievement Motivation of Secondary Schools by Schaffer's Multiple Post Hoc Procedure

Variable	Managements	Government	Aided	Unaided
Attitude towards physical science	Mean	80.8000	112.3700	107.8300
	Government	—	—	—
	Aided	0.0000*	—	—
	Unaided	0.0000*	0.5951	—
Attitude towards programmed instruction	Mean	77.1430	97.5710	90.7670
	Government	—	—	—
	Aided	0.0000*	—	—
	Unaided	0.0001*	0.0739	—
Achievement motivation	Mean	29.5140	47.4290	40.0000
	Government	—	—	—
	Aided	0.0000*	—	—
	Unaided	0.0003*	0.0140*	—

*p<0.05

- The students who belong to Government and aided, Government and unaided management secondary schools differ significantly with respect to attitude towards programmed instruction at 5 per cent level of significance. It means that, the students belonging to aided secondary schools have high attitude towards programmed instruction as compared to unaided and Government schools students in conventional group.
- The students who belong to Government and aided, Government and unaided; aided and unaided management secondary schools differ significantly with respect to achievement motivation at 5 per cent level of significance. It means that, the students belonging to aided secondary schools have high achievement motivation as compared to unaided and Government schools students in conventional group

Hypothesis: There is no significant difference between different groups of achievement motivation (High and low) with respect to Pre test, post test achievement, Attitude towards physical science, Attitude towards programmed instruction, Achievement motivation of secondary schools as a whole.

To test this, the student's unpaired t-test was applied and results are presented in the following table.

Table 4.36 : Results of t Test between Groups of Achievement Motivation (High and Low) with Respect to Pre Test, Post Test Achievement, Attitude towards Physical Science, Attitude towards Programmed Instruction of Secondary Schools as a Whole

Variable	Location	Mean	SD	Unpaired t-value	P-value	Signi.
Pre-test academic achievement	Low	34.6455	10.5209	-2.5323	<0.05	S
	High	38.3889	10.2515			
Post-test academic achievement	Low	46.5545	16.1243	-7.4720	<0.05	S
	High	59.5889	4.0859			
Gain academic achievement	Low	11.9091	17.4853	-4.4358	<0.05	S
	High	21.2000	10.4249			
Attitude towards Physical science	Low	89.0364	17.2584	-15.6879	<0.05	S
	High	119.7556	7.5807			
Attitude towards progra-mmed instruction	Low	80.8727	9.3280	-15.9451	<0.05	S
	High	102.3556	9.6609			

From the above Table, it is clearly know that;

- The students of secondary schools belonging to Low and high achievement motivation differ significantly with respect to pre test of academic achievement in physical science (t=-2.5323, <0.05, S) at 5 per cent level of significance. Hence, the null hypothesis is rejected and alternative hypothesis is accepted. It means that, the students of secondary schools belonging to high achievement motivation have high pre test of academic achievement in physical science as compared to students of secondary schools with achievement motivation.

- The students of secondary schools belonging to Low and high achievement motivation differ significantly with respect to post test of academic achievement in physical science (t=-7.4720, <0.05, S) at 5 per cent level of significance. Hence, the null hypothesis is rejected and alternative hypothesis is accepted. It means that, the students of secondary schools belonging to high achievement motivation have high post test of academic achievement in physical science as compared to students of secondary schools with achievement motivation.
- The students of secondary schools belonging to Low and high achievement motivation differ significantly with respect to gain of pre and post test of academic achievement in physical science (t=-4.4358, <0.05, S) at 5 per cent level of significance. Hence, the null hypothesis is rejected and alternative hypothesis is accepted. It means that, the students of secondary schools belonging to high achievement motivation have high gain of pre and post test of academic achievement in physical science as compared to students of secondary schools with achievement motivation.
- The students of secondary schools belonging to Low and high achievement motivation differ significantly with respect to attitude towards physical science (t=-15.6879, <0.05, S) at 5 per cent level of significance. Hence, the null hypothesis is rejected and alternative

hypothesis is accepted. It means that, the students of secondary schools belonging to high achievement motivation have high attitude towards physical science as compared to students of secondary schools with achievement motivation.

- The students of secondary schools belonging to Low and high achievement motivation differ significantly with respect to attitude towards programmed instruction (t=-15.9451, <0.05, S) at 5 per cent level of significance. Hence, the null hypothesis is rejected and alternative hypothesis is accepted. It means that, the students of secondary schools belonging to high achievement motivation have high attitude towards programmed instruction as compared to students of secondary schools with achievement motivation.

Sub Hypothesis: There is no significant difference between different groups of achievement motivation (High and low) with respect to Pre test, post test achievement, Attitude towards physical science, Attitude towards programmed instruction, Achievement motivation of secondary schools in experimental group.

To test this, the student's unpaired t-test was applied and results are presented in the following table.

From the above table, it is clearly seen that;

- The students of secondary schools belonging to Low and high achievement motivation differ significantly with respect to pre test of academic achievement in physical science in experimental group (t=-2.2889, <0.05, S) at 5 per cent level of significance. Hence, the null hypothesis is rejected and alternative hypothesis is accepted. It means that, the students of secondary schools belonging to high achievement motivation have high pre test of academic achievement in physical science as compared to students of secondary schools with low achievement motivation in experimental group.

Table 4.37: Results of t-Test between Groups of Achievement Motivation (High and Low) with Respect to Pre Test, Post Test Achievement, Attitude towards Physical Science, Attitude towards Programmed Instruction of Secondary Schools in Experiment Group

Variable	Location	Mean	SD	Unpaired t-value	P-value	Sig-ni.
Pre test academic achieve-ment	Low	31.6491	10.0791	-2.2889	<0.05	S
	High	36.3721	10.3946			
Post test academic achieve-ment	Low	39.1053	13.1742	-9.8196	<0.05	S
	High	59.2791	3.1572			
Gain academic achieve-ment	Low	7.4561	16.3839	-5.4867	>0.05	S
	High	22.9070	9.7780			
Attitude towards Physical science	Low	85.7018	20.0348	-10.4737	<0.05	S
	High	118.8605	6.1667			
Attitude towards programmed instruction	Low	79.0526	11.0880	-10.8689	<0.05	S
	High	100.7442	7.9913			

- The students of secondary schools belonging to Low and high achievement motivation differ significantly with respect to post test of academic achievement in physical science in experimental group (t=-9.8196, <0.05, S) at 5 per cent level of significance. Hence, the null hypothesis is rejected and alternative hypothesis is accepted. It means that, the students of secondary schools belonging to high achievement motivation have high post test of academic achievement in physical science as compared to students of secondary schools with low achievement motivation in experimental group.

- The students of secondary schools belonging to Low and high achievement motivation differ significantly with respect to gain of pre and post test of academic achievement in physical science in experiment group (t=-5.4867, <0.05, S) at 5 per cent level of significance. Hence, the null hypothesis is rejected and alternative hypothesis is accepted. It means that, the students of secondary schools belonging to high achievement motivation have high gain of pre and post test of academic achievement in physical science as compared to students of secondary schools with low achievement motivation in experimental group.
- The students of secondary schools belonging to Low and high achievement motivation differ significantly with respect to attitude towards physical science in experimental group (t=-10.4737, <0.05, S) at 5 per cent level of significance. Hence, the null hypothesis is rejected and alternative hypothesis is accepted. It means that, the students of secondary schools belonging to high achievement motivation have high attitude towards physical science as compared to students of secondary schools with low achievement motivation in experimental group.
- The students of secondary schools belonging to Low and high achievement motivation differ significantly with respect to attitude towards programmed instruction in experimental group (t=-10.8689, <0.05, S) at 5 per cent level of significance. Hence, the null hypothesis is rejected and alternative hypothesis is accepted. It means that, the students of secondary schools belonging to high achievement motivation have high attitude towards programmed instruction as compared to students of secondary schools with low achievement motivation in experimental group.

Sub Hypothesis: There is no significant difference between different groups of achievement motivation (High and low) with respect to Pre test, post test achievement,

Attitude towards physical science, Attitude towards programmed instruction, Achievement motivation of secondary schools in conventional group.

To test this, the student's unpaired t-test was applied and results are presented in the following table.

Table 4.38 : Results of t-Test between Groups of Achievement Motivation (High and Low) with Respect to Pre Test, Post Test Achievement, Attitude towards Physical Science, Attitude towards Programmed Instruction of Secondary Schools in Conventional Group

Variable	Location	Mean	SD	Unpaired t-value	P-value	Sig-ni.
Pre-test academic achievement	Low	37.8679	10.1091	-1.1813	>0.05	NS
	High	40.2340	9.8692			
Post-test academic achievement	Low	54.5660	15.2259	-2.2894	<0.05	S
	High	59.8723	4.7986			
Gain academic achievement	Low	16.6981	17.5122	-0.9939	>0.05	NS
	High	19.6383	10.8516			
Attitude towards Physical science	Low	92.6226	12.9143	-12.5426	<0.05	S
	High	120.5745	8.6621			
Attitude towards programmed instruction	Low	82.8302	6.5155	-11.8874	<0.05	S
	High	103.8298	10.8454			

From the above Table, it is clearly seen that;

- The students of secondary schools belonging to Low and high achievement motivation do not differ significantly with respect to pre test of academic achievement in physical science in conventional group (t=-1.1813, >0.05, NS) at 5 per cent level of significance.

Hence, the null hypothesis is accepted and alternative hypothesis is rejected. It means that, the students of secondary schools belong to low and high achievement motivations have similar academic achievement in physical science in conventional group.

- The students of secondary schools belonging to Low and high achievement motivation differ significantly with respect to post test of academic achievement in physical science in conventional group (t=-2.2894, <0.05, S) at 5 per cent level of significance. Hence, the null hypothesis is rejected and alternative hypothesis is accepted. It means that, the students of secondary schools belonging to high achievement motivation have high post test of academic achievement in physical science as compared to students of secondary schools with achievement motivation in conventional group.
- The students of secondary schools belonging to Low and high achievement motivation do not differ significantly with respect to gain of pre and post test of academic achievement in physical science in conventional group (t=-0.9939, >0.05, NS) at 5 per cent level of significance. Hence, the null hypothesis is accepted and alternative hypothesis is rejected. It means that, the students of secondary schools belonging to low and high achievement motivation have similar gain of pre and post test of academic achievement in physical science in conventional group.
- The students of secondary schools belonging to Low and high achievement motivation differ significantly with respect to attitude towards physical science in conventional group (t=-12.5426, <0.05, S) at 5 per cent level of significance. Hence, the null hypothesis is rejected and alternative hypothesis is accepted. It means that, the students of secondary schools belonging to high achievement motivation have high attitude towards physical science as compared to

students of secondary schools with achievement motivation in conventional group.

- The students of secondary schools belonging to Low and high achievement motivation differ significantly with respect to attitude towards programmed instruction in conventional group (t=-11.8874, <0.05, S) at 5 per cent level of significance. Hence, the null hypothesis is rejected and alternative hypothesis is accepted. It means that, the students of secondary schools belonging to high achievement motivation have high attitude towards programmed instruction as compared to students of secondary schools with achievement motivation in conventional group.

3. Co-relational Analysis between Dependent Variable and Independent Variables: In order to investigate the relations among the dependent variable i.e. achievement and several selected independent variables like Attitude towards physical science, Attitude towards programmed instruction, Achievement motivation in both conventional and experimental groups separately. Pearson's correlation coefficient technique was applied and simple relationships were obtained. In order to test the significance of obtained 'r's the appropriate test was used.

Hypothesis: There is no significant relationship between Attitude towards physical science, Attitude towards programmed instruction, Achievement motivation and achievement in physical science of secondary school students as a whole.

To test this hypothesis, the Karl Pearson's product moment correlation coefficient test was applied and results are presented in the following table.

The above Table clearly indicated that;

- A significant and positive correlation is observed between attitude towards physical science and academic achievement in physical science of students of secondary schools (r=0.6692, <0.05, S) at 5 per cent

Table 4.39: Correlation Coefficient between Attitude towards Physical Science, Attitude towards Programmed Instruction, Achievement Motivation with Academic Achievement in Physical Science of secondary School Students as a Whole

Variables	Academic achievement in physical science				
	r-value	r^2	t-value	p-value	Signi.
Attitude towards physical science	0.6692	0.4478	12.6716	<0.05	S
Attitude towards programmed instruction	0.5617	0.3155	9.5521	<0.05	S
Achievement motivation	0.4923	0.2424	7.9585	<0.05	S

level of significance. Hence the null hypothesis is rejected and alternative hypothesis is accepted. It means that, increase in attitude towards physical science is increases in their academic achievement in physical science of students of secondary schools as a whole.

- A significant and positive correlation is observed between attitude towards programmed instruction and academic achievement in physical science of students of secondary schools (r=0.5617, <0.05, S) at 5 per cent level of significance. Hence the null hypothesis is rejected and alternative hypothesis is accepted. It means that, increase in the attitude towards programmed instruction is increases in their academic achievement in physical science of students of secondary schools as a whole.
- A significant and positive correlation is observed between achievement motivation and academic achievement in physical science of students of secondary schools (r=0.4923, <0.05, S) at 5 per cent level of significance. Hence the null hypothesis is rejected and alternative hypothesis is accepted. It means that, increase in the achievement motivation is increases in their academic achievement in physical science of students of secondary schools as a whole.

Hypothesis: There is no significant relationship between Attitude towards physical science, Attitude towards programmed instruction, Achievement motivation and achievement in physical science of secondary school students in conventional group.

To test this hypothesis, the Karl Pearson's product moment correlation coefficient test was applied and results are presented in the following table.

Table 4.40: Correlation Coefficient between Attitude towards Physical Science, Attitude towards Programmed Instruction, Achievement Motivation with Academic Achievement in Physical Science of Secondary School Students in Conventional Group

Variables	Academic achievement in physical science				
	r-value	r^2	t-value	p-value	Signi.
Attitude towards physical science	0.5760	0.3318	6.9763	<0.05	S
Attitude towards programmed instruction	0.4511	0.2035	5.0036	<0.05	S
Achievement motivation	0.2346	0.0550	2.3891	<0.05	S

The above table results clearly indicate that;

- A significant and positive correlation is observed between attitude towards physical science and academic achievement in physical science of students of secondary schools (r=0.5760, <0.05, S) at 5 per cent level of significance. Hence the null hypothesis is rejected and alternative hypothesis is accepted. It means that, increase in the attitude towards physical science is increases in their academic achievement in physical science of students of secondary schools in conventional group.
- A significant and positive correlation is observed between attitude towards programmed instruction and academic achievement in physical science of

students of secondary schools (r=0.4511, <0.05, S) at 5 per cent level of significance. Hence the null hypothesis is rejected and alternative hypothesis is accepted. It means that, increase in the attitude towards programmed instruction is increases in their academic achievement in physical science of students of secondary schools in conventional group.

- A significant and positive correlation is observed between achievement motivation and academic achievement in physical science of students of secondary schools (r=0.2346, <0.05, S) at 5 per cent level of significance. Hence the null hypothesis is rejected and alternative hypothesis is accepted. It means that, increase in the achievement motivation is increases in their academic achievement in physical science of students of secondary schools in conventional group.

Hypothesis: There is no significant relationship between attitude towards physical science, attitude towards programmed instruction, achievement motivation and achievement in physical science of secondary school boy students in conventional group.

Table 4.41: Correlation Coefficient between Attitude towards Physical Science, Attitude towards Programmed Instruction, Achievement Motivation with Academic Achievement in Physical Science of Secondary School boy Students in Conventional Group

Variables	Academic achievement in physical science of boy students with				
	r-value	r^2	t-value	p-value	Signi.
Attitude towards physical science	0.0180	0.0003	0.1245	>0.05	NS
Attitude towards programmed instruction	0.1115	0.0124	0.7775	>0.05	NS
Achievement motivation	0.3019	0.0912	2.1943	<0.05	S

To test this hypothesis, the Karl Pearson's product moment correlation coefficient test was applied and results are presented in the following table.

The above table results clearly indicate that;

- A non-significant and positive correlation is observed between attitude towards physical science and academic achievement in physical science of boys in conventional group (r=0.0180, >0.05, NS) at 5 per cent level of significance. Hence the null hypothesis is accepted and alternative hypothesis is rejected. It means that, attitude towards physical science are increases or decreases with increase or decrease in their academic achievement in physical science of boys in conventional group.
- A non-significant and positive correlation is observed between attitude towards programmed instruction and academic achievement in physical science of boys in conventional group (r=0.1115, >0.05, NS) at 5 per cent level of significance. Hence the null hypothesis is accepted and alternative hypothesis is rejected. It means that, attitude towards programmed instruction are increases or decreases with increase or decrease in their academic achievement in physical science of boy students in conventional group.
- A significant and positive correlation is observed between achievement motivation and academic achievement in physical science of boys in conventional group (r=0.3019, <0.05, S) at 5 per cent level of significance. Hence the null hypothesis is rejected and alternative hypothesis is accepted. It means that, increase in the achievement motivation is increases in their academic achievement in physical science of boys in conventional group.

Hypothesis: There is no significant relationship between attitude towards physical science, attitude towards programmed instruction, achievement motivation and achievement in physical science of secondary school girls in conventional group.

To test this hypothesis, the Karl Pearson's product moment correlation coefficient test was applied and results are presented in the following table.

Table 4.42: Correlation Coefficient between Attitude towards Physical Science, Attitude towards Programmed Instruction, Achievement Motivation with Academic Achievement in Physical Science of Secondary School girls in Conventional Group

Variables	Academic achievement in physical science				
	r-value	r^2	t-value	p-value	Signi.
Attitude towards physical science	0.8080	0.6528	9.5008	<0.05	S
Attitude towards programmed instruction	0.6256	0.3914	5.5555	<0.05	S
Achievement motivation	0.6029	0.3635	5.2356	<0.05	S

The above table results clearly indicate that;

- A significant and positive correlation is observed between attitude towards physical science and academic achievement in physical science of girls in conventional group (r=0.8080, <0.05, S) at 5% level of significance. Hence the null hypothesis is rejected and alternative hypothesis is accepted. It means that, increases in the attitude towards physical science are increases in their academic achievement in physical science of girls in conventional group.
- A significant and positive correlation is observed between attitude towards programmed instruction and academic achievement in physical science of girls in conventional group (r=0.6256, <0.05, S) at 5 per cent level of significance. Hence the null hypothesis is rejected and alternative hypothesis is accepted. It means that, increases in the attitude towards

programmed instruction are increases in their academic achievement in physical science of girls in conventional group.

- A significant and positive correlation is observed between achievement motivation and academic achievement in physical science of girls in conventional group (r=0.6029, <0.05, S) at 5 per cent level of significance. Hence the null hypothesis is rejected and alternative hypothesis is accepted. It means that, increases in the achievement motivation are increases in their academic achievement in physical science of girls in conventional group.

Hypothesis: There is no significant relationship between Attitude towards physical science, Attitude towards programmed instruction, Achievement motivation and achievement in physical science of secondary school students in experimental group.

To test this hypothesis, the Karl Pearson's product moment correlation coefficient test was applied and results are presented in the following table.

Table 4.43 : Correlation Coefficient between Attitude towards Physical Science, Attitude towards Programmed Instruction, Achievement Motivation with Academic Achievement in Physical Science of Secondary School Students in Experimental Group

Variables	Academic achievement in physical science				
	r-value	r^2	t-value	p-value	Signi.
Attitude towards physical science	0.7262	0.5274	10.4581	<0.05	S
Attitude towards programmed instruction	0.6263	0.3923	7.9533	<0.05	S
Achievement motivation	0.7664	0.5874	11.8108	<0.05	S

The above table results clearly indicate that;

- A significant and positive correlation is observed between attitude towards physical science and academic achievement in physical science of students of secondary schools (r=0.7262, <0.05, S) at 5 per cent level of significance. Hence the null hypothesis is rejected and alternative hypothesis is accepted. It means that, increase in the attitude towards physical science increase their academic achievement in physical science of students of secondary schools in experimental group.

- A significant and positive correlation is observed between attitude towards programmed instruction and academic achievement in physical science of students of secondary schools (r=0.6263, <0.05, S) at 5 per cent level of significance. Hence the null hypothesis is rejected and alternative hypothesis is accepted. It means that, increase in the attitude towards programmed instruction increases or decreases with increase in physical science of students of secondary schools in experimental group.
- A significant and positive correlation is observed between achievement motivation and academic achievement in physical science of students of secondary schools (r=0.7664, <0.05, S) at 5 per cent level of significance. Hence the null hypothesis is rejected and alternative hypothesis is accepted. It means that, increase in the achievement motivation are increases in their academic achievement in physical science of students of secondary schools in experimental group.

Hypothesis: There is no significant relationship between attitude towards physical science, attitude towards programmed instruction, achievement motivation and achievement in physical science of secondary school boy students in experimental group.

To test this hypothesis, the Karl Pearson's product moment correlation coefficient test was applied and results are presented in the following table.

Table 4.44 : Correlation Coefficient between Attitude towards Physical Science, Attitude towards Programmed Instruction, Achievement Motivation with Academic Achievement in Physical Science of Secondary School Boys in Experimental Group

Variables	Academic achievement in physical science				
	r-value	r^2	t-value	p-value	Signi.
Attitude towards physical science	0.5921	0.3506	5.0905	<0.05	S
Attitude towards programmed instruction	0.5623	0.3162	4.7108	<0.05	S
Achievement motivation	0.6687	0.4471	6.2301	<0.05	S

The above table results clearly indicate that;

- A significant and positive correlation is observed between attitude towards physical science and academic achievement in physical science of boys in experimental group (r=0.5921, <0.05, S) at 5 per cent level of significance. Hence the null hypothesis is rejected and alternative hypothesis is accepted. It means that, increase in the attitude towards physical science increase in their academic achievement in physical science of boys in experimental group.
- A significant and positive correlation is observed between attitude towards programmed instruction and academic achievement in physical science of boys in experimental group (r=0.5623, <0.05, S) at 5 per cent level of significance. Hence the null hypothesis is rejected and alternative hypothesis is accepted. It means that, increase in the attitude towards programmed instruction is increases in their academic achievement in physical science of boys in experimental group.
- A significant and positive correlation is observed between achievement motivation and academic achievement in physical science of boys in

experimental group (r=0.6687, <0.05, S) at 5 per cent level of significance. Hence the null hypothesis is rejected and alternative hypothesis is accepted. It means that, increase in the achievement motivation is increases in their academic achievement in physical science of boys in experimental group.

Hypothesis: There is no significant relationship between attitude towards physical science, attitude towards programmed instruction, achievement motivation and achievement in physical science of secondary school girls in experimental group.

To test this hypothesis, the Karl Pearson's product moment correlation coefficient test was applied and results are presented in the following table.

Table 4.45 : Correlation between Attitude towards Physical Science, Attitude towards Programmed Instruction, Achievement Motivation with Academic Achievement in Physical Science of Secondary School Girls in Experimental Group

Variables	Academic achievement in physical science				
	r-value	r^2	t-value	p-value	Signi.
Attitude towards physical science	0.8205	0.6733	9.9457	<0.05	S
Attitude towards programmed instruction	0.6982	0.4874	6.7561	<0.05	S
Achievement motivation	0.8549	0.7309	11.4178	<0.05	S

The above table results clearly indicate that;

- A significant and positive correlation is observed between attitude towards physical science and academic achievement in physical science of girl students in experiment group (r=0.8205, <0.05, S) at 5 per cent level of significance. Hence the null hypothesis is rejected and alternative hypothesis is accepted. It means that, increase in the attitude towards physical science is increases in their academic achievement in physical science of girls in experimental group.

- A significant and positive correlation is observed between attitude towards programmed instruction and academic achievement in physical science of girls in experimental group (r=0.6982, <0.05, S) at 5 per cent level of significance. Hence the null hypothesis is rejected and alternative hypothesis is accepted. It means that, increase in the attitude towards programmed instruction increase in their academic achievement in physical science of girls in experimental group.
- A significant and positive correlation is observed between achievement motivation and academic achievement in physical science of girls in experimental group (r=0.8549, <0.05, S) at 5 per cent level of significance. Hence the null hypothesis is rejected and alternative hypothesis is accepted. It means that, increase in the achievement motivation increases in their academic achievement in physical science of girls in experimental group.

Hypothesis: There is no significant relationship between attitude towards physical science, attitude towards programmed instruction, achievement motivation and achievement in physical science of secondary school boys.

Table 4.46: Correlation between Attitude towards Physical Science, Attitude towards Programmed Instruction, Achievement Motivation with Academic Achievement in Physical Science of Secondary School Boys

Variables	Academic achievement in physical science				
	r-value	r^2	t-value	p-value	Signi.
Attitude towards physical science	0.4360	0.1901	4.7955	<0.05	S
Attitude towards programmed instruction	0.4254	0.1810	4.6539	<0.05	S
Achievement motivation	0.2323	0.0540	2.3641	<0.05	S

To test this hypothesis, the Karl Pearson's product moment correlation coefficient test was applied and results are presented in the following table.

The above table results clearly indicate that;

- A significant and positive correlation is observed between attitude towards physical science and academic achievement in physical science of boys (r=0.4360, <0.05, S) at 5 per cent level of significance. Hence the null hypothesis is rejected and alternative hypothesis is accepted. It means that, increase in the attitude towards physical science increases in their academic achievement in physical science of boys.
- A significant and positive correlation is observed between attitude towards programmed instruction and academic achievement in physical science of boy students (r=0.4254, <0.05, S) at 5 per cent level of significance. Hence the null hypothesis is rejected and alternative hypothesis is accepted. It means that, increase in the attitude towards programmed instruction increases in their academic achievement in physical science of boys.
- A significant and positive correlation is observed between achievement motivation and academic achievement in physical science of boys (r=0.2323, <0.05, S) at 5 per cent level of significance. Hence the null hypothesis is rejected and alternative hypothesis is accepted. It means that, increase in the achievement motivation increases in their academic achievement in physical science of boys.

Hypothesis: There is no significant relationship between attitude towards physical science, attitude towards programmed instruction, achievement motivation and achievement in physical science of secondary school girls.

To test this hypothesis, the Karl Pearson's product moment correlation coefficient test was applied and results are presented in the following table.

Table 4.47: Correlation between Attitude towards Physical Science, Attitude towards Programmed Instruction, Achievement Motivation with Academic Achievement in Physical Science of Secondary School Girls

Variables	Academic achievement in physical science				
	r-value	r^2	t-value	p-value	Signi.
Attitude towards physical science	0.8161	0.6660	13.9801	<0.05	S
Attitude towards programmed instruction	0.6694	0.4481	8.9192	<0.05	S
Achievement motivation	0.7149	0.5111	10.1221	<0.05	S

The above table results clearly indicate that;

- A significant and positive correlation is observed between attitude towards physical science and academic achievement in physical science of girls (r=0.8161, <0.05, S) at 5 per cent level of significance. Hence the null hypothesis is rejected and alternative hypothesis is accepted. It means that, increase in the attitude towards physical science increases in their academic achievement in physical science of girls.
- A significant and positive correlation is observed between attitude towards programmed instruction and academic achievement in physical science of girls (r=0.6694, <0.05, S) at 5 per cent level of significance. Hence the null hypothesis is rejected and alternative hypothesis is accepted. It means that, increase in the attitude towards programmed instruction increases in their academic achievement in physical science of girls.
- A significant and positive correlation is observed between achievement motivation and academic achievement in physical science of girls (r=0.7149, <0.05, S) at 5 per cent level of significance. Hence the null hypothesis is rejected and alternative hypothesis

is accepted. It means that, increase in the achievement motivation increases in their academic achievement in physical science of girls.

Hypothesis: There is no significant relationship between attitude towards physical science, attitude towards programmed instruction, achievement motivation and achievement in physical science of students of urban secondary schools.

To test this hypothesis, the Karl Pearson's product moment correlation coefficient test was applied and results are presented in the following table.

Table 4.48 : Correlation between Attitude towards Physical Science, Attitude towards Programmed Instruction, Achievement Motivation with Academic Achievement in Physical Science of Students of Urban Secondary Schools

Variables	Academic achievement in physical science				
	r-value	r^2	t-value	p-value	Signi.
Attitude towards physical science	0.4380	0.1918	4.8229	<0.05	S
Attitude towards programmed instruction	0.4193	0.1758	4.5722	<0.05	S
Achievement motivation	0.2819	0.0794	2.9082	<0.05	S

The above table results clearly indicate that;

- A significant and positive correlation is observed between attitude towards physical science and academic achievement in physical science of students of urban secondary schools (r=0.4380, <0.05, S) at 5 per cent level of significance. Hence the null hypothesis is rejected and alternative hypothesis is accepted. It means that, increase in the attitude towards physical science increases in their academic achievement in physical science of students of urban secondary schools.
- A significant and positive correlation is observed between attitude towards programmed instruction

and academic achievement in physical science of students of urban secondary schools (r=0.4193, <0.05, S) at 5 per cent level of significance. Hence the null hypothesis is rejected and alternative hypothesis is accepted. It means that, increase in the attitude towards programmed instruction increases in their academic achievement in physical science of students of urban secondary schools.

- A significant and positive correlation is observed between achievement motivation and academic achievement in physical science of students of urban secondary schools (r=0.2819, <0.05, S) at 5% level of significance. Hence the null hypothesis is rejected and alternative hypothesis is accepted. It means that, increase in the achievement motivation is increases in their academic achievement in physical science of students of urban secondary schools.

Hypothesis: There is no significant relationship between attitude towards physical science, attitude towards programmed instruction, achievement motivation and achievement in physical science of students of rural secondary schools.

To test this hypothesis, the Karl Pearson's product moment correlation coefficient test was applied and results are presented in the following table.

Table 4.49: Correlation between Attitude towards Physical Science, Attitude towards Programmed Instruction, Achievement Motivation with Academic Achievement in Physical Science of Students of Rural Secondary Schools

Variables	Academic achievement in physical science				
	r-value	r^2	t-value	p-value	Signi.
Attitude towards physical science	0.8697	0.7563	17.4395	<0.05	S
Attitude towards programmed instruction	0.7371	0.5434	10.7993	<0.05	S
Achievement motivation	0.7012	0.4917	9.7359	<0.05	S

The above table results clearly indicate that;

- A significant and positive correlation is observed between attitude towards physical science and academic achievement in physical science of students of rural secondary schools (r=0.8697, <0.05, S) at 5 per cent level of significance. Hence the null hypothesis is rejected and alternative hypothesis is accepted. It means that, increase in the attitude towards physical science increases in their academic achievement in physical science of students of rural secondary schools.
- A significant and positive correlation is observed between attitude towards programmed instruction and academic achievement in physical science of students of rural secondary schools (r=0.7371, <0.05, S) at 5 per cent level of significance. Hence the null hypothesis is rejected and alternative hypothesis is accepted. It means that, increase in the attitude towards programmed instruction increases in their academic achievement in physical science of students of rural secondary schools.
- A significant and positive correlation is observed between achievement motivation and academic achievement in physical science of students of rural secondary schools (r=0.7012, <0.05, S) at 5 per cent level of significance. Hence the null hypothesis is rejected and alternative hypothesis is accepted. It means that, increase in the achievement motivation increases in their academic achievement in physical science of students of rural secondary schools.

4. Multiple Regression Analysis: The most commonly used procedure in the prediction of a continuous criterion variable is the multiple linear regression models. Weights are known, as regression coefficients are determined for each predictor variable. The resulting sum of squares on the composite of these variables will show the highest possible relationship (multiple correlations) with the criterion variable.

The most commonly applied computational procedures for multiple linear regressions, which have now been made feasible by electronic programmed instruction. In this method, multiple correlation coefficients reveal the degree of relation between linear combination of independent (or predictor) variable and respective dependent (or criterion) variable.

In this method, multiple correlations and multiple linear regressions reveal the degree to which each selected independent variable like Attitude towards physical science; Attitude towards programmed instruction, Achievement motivation is related to achievement in physical science of secondary school students. To identify this type of relationship between of independent variables on the one hand and the dependent variable on the other hand, the multiple correlations and multiple regression analysis were carried out.

Hypothesis: Attitude towards physical science, Attitude towards programmed instruction, Achievement motivations are would not be significant predictors of academic achievement in physical science of secondary school students as a whole.

Table 4.50: Summary of Linear Multiple Regression Analysis: Independent Variables i.e. Attitude towards Physical Science, Attitude towards Programmed Instruction, Achievement Motivation on Academic Achievement in Physical Science of Secondary School Students in as a Whole

Independent Variable	Reg Coeffi.	SE of Coeffi.	t-value	p-level	Signl.
Intercept	3.9097	5.6191	0.6958	>0.05	NS
Attitude towards physical science (X_1)	0.7049	0.0914	7.7152	<0.05	S
Attitude towards programmed instruction (X_2)	-0.1514	0.1201	-1.2605	>0.05	NS
Achievement motivation (X_3)	-0.2448	0.0915	-2.6760	<0.05	S

R=0.6905, R^2=0.4768, Adjusted R^2=0.4688, F=59.563 $p<0.05$, S, Std.Error of estimate: 10.102

To test or achieve this hypothesis, the multiple regression analysis was applied and results are presented in the following table.

Above Table, clearly indicated that;

- The joint effect of attitude towards physical science (X_1) on students' achievement in physical science is found to be positive and significant at 5 per cent level of significance. Hence, the null hypothesis is rejected and alternative hypothesis is accepted.
- The joint effect of achievement motivation (X_3) on students' achievement in physical science is found to be negative and significant at 5 per cent level of significance. Hence, the null hypothesis is rejected and alternative hypothesis is accepted.

Further, the multiple linear regression equation predicting the academic achievement of secondary school students (Y) in terms of attitude towards physical science (X_1), attitude towards programmed instruction (X_2) and achievement motivation (X_3) was found to be under:

Academic achievement (Y)

$$= 3.9097+0.7049X_1 -0.1514X_2 -0.2448X_3$$

The multiple R of the linear regression equation is 0.6905. For testing multiple correlation coefficients the F-ratio (59.563) was found to be significant at 0.05 per cent level. Thus, the null hypothesis is rejected and alternative hypothesis is accepted. Significant R suggests that estimation of academic achievement of secondary school students is possible on the basis of the predictors like attitude towards physical science (X_1), attitude towards programmed instruction (X_2) and achievement motivation (X_3). Further, the regression equation shows that attitude towards physical science (X_1), attitude towards programmed instruction (X_2) and achievement motivation (X_3) can be used as predictors of academic achievement of secondary school students.

The coefficient of multiple determination of R^2 is 0.4768. It can be therefore, be said that nearly 47.88 percent of the variation in academic achievement of secondary school students accounted for whatever is measured by attitude towards physical science (X_1), attitude towards programmed instruction (X_2) and achievement motivation (X_3) can taken together. The SE_{est} for the regression equation is 10.102. This means that each time the regression equation for the sample is used to predict a leadership behaviour of principals, that predicted academic achievement will not miss the actual academic achievement of secondary school students by more that ±10.102.

The relative contribution of attitude towards physical science (X_1), attitude towards programmed instruction (X_2) and achievement motivation (X_3) on academic achievement of secondary school students are presented in the following table.

Table 4.51 : Relative Contribution of Attitude towards Physical Science, Attitude towards Programmed Instruction Achievement Motivation on Achievement in Physical Science of Secondary School Students

Independent Variable	Beta	r-value	Beta × r	% of contri-bution
Attitude towards physical science (X_1)	1.0466	0.6692	0.7004	70.0355
Attitude towards programmed instruction (X_2)	-0.1561	0.5617	-0.0877	-8.7662
Achievement motivation (X_3)	-0.2758	0.4923	-0.1358 0.4769	-13.5795 47.6897

The above table presents the relative contribution of Attitude towards physical science (X_1), (Attitude towards programmed instruction (X_2), Achievement motivation (X_3) on academic achievement in physical science of secondary school students as a total are presented in the above table. The total contribution of all the three explanatory variables on academic achievement in physical science of secondary school students is found to be 47.6897 per cent. In which, the variable Attitude towards physical science (X_1) contributes maximum i.e. 70.0355 per cent followed by others.

Hypothesis: Attitude towards physical science, Attitude towards programmed instruction, Achievement motivations are would not be significant predictors of academic achievement in physical science of secondary school students in conventional group.

To test or achieve this hypothesis, the multiple regression analysis was applied and results are presented in the following table.

Table 4.52 : Summary of Linear Multiple Regression Analysis: Independent Variables i.e. Attitude towards Physical Science, Attitude towards Programmed Instruction, Achievement Motivation on Academic Achievement in Physical Science of Secondary School Students in Conventional Group

Independent Variable	Reg Coeffi.	SE of Coeffi.	t-value	p-level	Signi.
Intercept	-6.9258	6.9629	-0.9947	>0.05	NS
Attitude towards physical science (X_1)	0.8257	0.1040	7.9374	<0.05	S
Attitude towards programmed instruction (X_2)	0.0134	0.1124	0.1197	>0.05	NS
Achievement motivation (X_3)	-0.5451	0.0853	-6.3873	<0.05	S

R=0.73059, R^2=0.5337, Adjusted R^2=0.5192, F=36.636 $p<0.05$, S, Std.Error of estimate: 8.1912

The results of the above table shows that,

- The joint effect of attitude towards physical science (X_1) on students' achievement in physical science is found to be positive and significant at 5 per cent level of significance. Hence, the null hypothesis is rejected and alternative hypothesis is accepted in conventional group.
- The joint effect of achievement motivation (X_3) on students' achievement in physical science is found to be negative and significant at 5 per cent level of

significance. Hence, the null hypothesis is rejected and alternative hypothesis is accepted in conventional group.

Further, the multiple linear regression equation predicting the academic achievement of secondary school students (Y) in terms of attitude towards physical science (X_1), attitude towards programmed instruction (X_2) and achievement motivation (X_3) was found to be under:

Academic achievement (Y)

$$= -6.9258+0.8257X_1 +0.0134X_2 -0.5451X_3$$

The multiple R of the linear regression equation is 0.73059. For testing multiple correlation coefficients the F-ratio (36.636) was found to be significant at 0.05 per cent level. Thus, the null hypothesis is rejected and alternative hypothesis is accepted. Significant R suggests that estimation of academic achievement of secondary school students is possible on the basis of the predictors like attitude towards physical science (X_1), attitude towards programmed instruction (X_2) and achievement motivation (X_3). Further, the regression equation shows that attitude towards physical science (X_1), attitude towards programmed instruction (X_2) and achievement motivation (X_3) can be used as predictors of academic achievement of secondary school students in conventional group.

The coefficient of multiple determination of R^2 is 0.5337. It can be therefore, be said that nearly 53.37 percent of the variation in academic achievement of secondary school students accounted for whatever is measured by attitude towards physical science (X_1), attitude towards programmed instruction (X_2) and achievement motivation (X_3) can taken together. The SE_{est} for the regression equation is 8.1912. This means that each time the regression equation for the sample is used to predict a leadership behaviour of principals, that predicted academic achievement will not miss the actual academic achievement of secondary school students by more that ±8.1912.

The relative contribution of attitude towards physical science (X_1), attitude towards programmed instruction (X_2)

and achievement motivation (X_3) on academic achievement of secondary school students in conventional group are presented in the following table.

Table 4.53 : Relative Contribution of Attitude towards Physical Science, Attitude towards Programmed Instruction Achievement Motivation on Achievement in Physical Science of Secondary School Students in Conventional Group

Independent Variable	Beta	r-value	Beta x r	% of contri-bution
Attitude towards physical science (X_1)	1.2485	0.5760	0.7192	71.9204
Attitude towards progra-mmed instruction (X_2)	0.0156	0.4511	0.0070	0.7040
Achievement motivation (X_3)	-0.8204	0.2346	-0.1925 0.5338	-19.2475 53.3770

The above table presents the relative contribution of Attitude towards physical science (X_1), (Attitude towards programmed instruction (X_2), Achievement motivation (X_3) on academic achievement in physical science of secondary school students in conventional group are presented in the above table. The total contribution of all the three explanatory variables on academic achievement in physical science of secondary school students is found to be 53.3770 per cent. In which, the variable Attitude towards physical science (X_1) contributes maximum i.e. 71.9204 per cent followed by others.

Hypothesis: Attitude towards physical science, Attitude towards programmed instruction, Achievement motivations are would not be significant predictors of academic achievement in physical science of secondary school students in experiment group.

To test or achieve this hypothesis, the multiple regression analysis was applied and results are presented in the following table.

Table 4.54 : Summary of Linear Multiple Regression Analysis: Independent Variables i.e. Attitude towards Physical Science, Attitude towards Programmed Instruction, Achievement Motivation on Academic Achievement in Physical Science of Secondary School Students in Experimental Group

Independent Variable	Reg Coeffi.	SE of Coeffi.	t-value	p-level	Signi.
Intercept	71.7433	8.0818	8.8772	>0.05	NS
Attitude towards physical science (X_1)	0.3581	0.1190	3.0102	<0.05	S
Attitude towards programmed instruction (X_2)	-1.5603	0.1907	-8.1802	<0.05	S
Achievement motivation (X_3)	2.0070	0.2347	8.5507	<0.05	S

$R=0.8701$, $R^2=0.7571$, Adjusted $R^2=0.7495$, $F=99.771$, $p<0.05$, S, Std. Error of estimate: 7.1329

The results of the above table shows that,

- The joint effect of attitude towards physical science (X_1) on students' achievement in physical science is found to be positive and significant at 5 per cent level of significance. Hence, the null hypothesis is rejected and alternative hypothesis is accepted in experiment group.
- The joint effect of Attitude towards programmed instruction (X_2) on students' achievement in physical science is found to be negative and significant at 5 per cent level of significance. Hence, the null hypothesis is rejected and alternative hypothesis is accepted in experiment group.
- The joint effect of achievement motivation (X_3) on students' achievement in physical science is found to be positive and significant at 5 per cent level of significance. Hence, the null hypothesis is rejected and alternative hypothesis is accepted in experiment group.

Further, the multiple linear regression equation predicting the academic achievement of secondary school students (Y) in terms of attitude towards physical science (X_1), attitude towards programmed instruction (X_2) and achievement motivation (X_3) was found to be under:

Academic achievement (Y)

$$= 71.7433+0.3581X_1 -1.5603X_2 +2.0070X_3$$

The multiple R of the linear regression equation is 0.8701. For testing multiple correlation coefficients the F-ratio (99.771) was found to be significant at 0.05 per cent level. Thus, the null hypothesis is rejected and alternative hypothesis is accepted. Significant R suggests that estimation of academic achievement of secondary school students is possible on the basis of the predictors like attitude towards physical science (X_1), attitude towards programmed instruction (X_2) and achievement motivation (X_3). Further, the regression equation shows that attitude towards physical science (X_1), attitude towards programmed instruction (X_2) and achievement motivation (X_3) can be used as predictors of academic achievement of secondary school students in experiment group.

The coefficient of multiple determination of R^2 is 0.7571. It can be therefore, be said that nearly 75.71 percent of the variation in academic achievement of secondary school students accounted for whatever is measured by attitude towards physical science (X_1), attitude towards programmed instruction (X_2) and achievement motivation (X_3) can taken together. The SE_{est} for the regression equation is 7.1329. This means that each time the regression equation for the sample is used to predict a leadership behaviour of principals, that predicted academic achievement will not miss the actual academic achievement of secondary school students by more that ±7.1329.

The relative contribution of attitude towards physical science (X_1), attitude towards programmed instruction (X_2) and achievement motivation (X_3) on academic achievement of secondary school students in experiment group are presented in the following table.

Table 4.55 : Relative Contribution of Attitude towards Physical Science, Attitude towards Programmed Instruction Achievement Motivation on Achievement in Physical Science of Secondary School Students in Experimental Group

Independent Variable	Beta	r-value	Beta x r	% of contri-bution
Attitude towards physical science (X_1)	0.5704	0.7262	0.4143	41.4274
Attitude towards progra-mmed instruction (X_2)	-1.5981	0.6263	-1.0009	-100.0906
Achievement motivation (X_3)	1.7534	0.7664	1.3438 0.7572	134.3787 75.7155

The above table presents the relative contribution of Attitude towards physical science (X_1), (Attitude towards programmed instruction (X_2), Achievement motivation (X_3) on academic achievement in physical science of secondary school students in experiment group are presented in the above table. The total contribution of all the three explanatory variables on academic achievement in physical science of secondary school students is found to be 75.7155 per cent. In which, the variable Achievement motivation (X_3) contributes maximum i.e. 134.3787 per cent followed by others.

Hypothesis: Attitude towards physical science, Attitude towards programmed instruction, Achievement motivations are would not be significant predictors of academic achievement in physical science of secondary school boy students in conventional group.

To test or achieve this hypothesis, the multiple regression analysis was applied and results are presented in the following table.

The results of the above table shows that,

- The joint effect of attitude towards physical science (X_1) on boy students' achievement in physical science is found to be positive and significant at 5 per cent level of significance. Hence, the null hypothesis is rejected and alternative hypothesis is accepted in conventional group.

Table 4.56 : Summary of Linear Multiple Regression Analysis: Independent Variables i.e. Attitude towards Physical Science, Attitude towards Programmed Instruction, Achievement Motivation on Academic Achievement in Physical Science of Secondary School Boys in Conventional Group

Independent Variable	Reg Coeffi.	SE of Coeffi.	t-value	p-level	Signi.
Intercept	32.3386	8.3272	3.8835	<0.05	S
Attitude towards physical science (X_1)	0.2721	0.1035	2.6290	<0.05	S
Attitude towards programmed instruction (X_2)	0.1707	0.0951	1.7954	>0.05	NS
Achievement motivation (X_3)	-0.3805	0.0801	-4.7503	<0.05	S

R=0.5852, R^2=0.3425, Adjusted R^2=0.2996, F=7.9890 p<0.05, S, Std.Error of estimate: 5.8518

- The joint effect of achievement motivation (X_3) on boy students' achievement in physical science is found to be negative and significant at 5 per cent level of significance. Hence, the null hypothesis is rejected and alternative hypothesis is accepted in conventional group.

Further, the multiple linear regression equation predicting the academic achievement of secondary school boy students (Y) in terms of attitude towards physical science (X_1), attitude towards programmed instruction (X_2) and achievement motivation (X_3) was found to be under:

Academic achievement (Y)

$$= 32.3386+0.2721X_1 +0.1707X_2 -0.3805X_3$$

The multiple R of the linear regression equation is 0.5852. For testing multiple correlation coefficients the F-ratio (7.9890) was found to be significant at 0.05 per cent level. Thus, the null hypothesis is rejected and alternative hypothesis is accepted. Significant R suggests that estimation of academic achievement of secondary school boy students is possible on the basis of the predictors like attitude towards physical science (X_1), attitude towards programmed instruction (X_2)

and achievement motivation (X_3). Further, the regression equation shows that attitude towards physical science (X_1), attitude towards programmed instruction (X_2) and achievement motivation (X_3) can be used as predictors of academic achievement of secondary school boys in conventional group.

The coefficient of multiple determination of R^2 is 0.3425. It can be therefore, be said that nearly 34.25 percent of the variation in academic achievement of secondary school boy students accounted for whatever is measured by attitude towards physical science (X_1), attitude towards programmed instruction (X_2) and achievement motivation (X_3) can taken together. The SE_{est} for the regression equation is 5.8518. This means that each time the regression equation for the sample is used to predict a leadership behaviour of principals, that predicted academic achievement will not miss the actual academic achievement of secondary school boys by more that ±5.8518.

The relative contribution of attitude towards physical science (X_1), attitude towards programmed instruction (X_2) and achievement motivation (X_3) on academic achievement of secondary school boys in conventional group are presented in the following table.

Table 4.57 : Relative Contribution of Attitude towards Physical Science, Attitude towards Programmed Instruction Achievement Motivation on Achievement in Physical Science of Secondary School Boys in Conventional Group

Independent Variable	Beta	r-value	Beta × r	% of contri-bution
Attitude towards physical science (X_1)	0.6003	0.0180	0.0108	1.0788
Attitude towards progra-mmed instruction (X_2)	0.3079	0.1115	0.0343	3.4339
Achievement motivation (X_3)	-0.9850	-0.3019	0.2974 0.3425	29.7421 34.2547

The above table presents the relative contribution of Attitude towards physical science (X_1), (Attitude towards programmed instruction (X_2), Achievement motivation (X_3) on academic achievement in physical science of secondary school boys in conventional group are presented in the above table. The total contribution of all the three explanatory variables on academic achievement in physical science of secondary school boys is found to be 34.2547 per cent. In which, the variable Achievement motivation (X_3) contributes maximum i.e. 29.7421 per cent followed by others.

Hypothesis: Attitude towards physical science, Attitude towards programmed instruction, Achievement motivations are would not be significant predictors of academic achievement in physical science of secondary school girls in conventional group.

To test or achieve this hypothesis, the multiple regression analysis was applied and results are presented in the following table.

Table 4.58 : Summary of Linear Multiple Regression Analysis: Independent Variable i.e. Attitude towards Physical Science, Attitude towards Programmed Instruction, Achievement Motivation on Academic Achievement in Physical Science of Secondary School Girls in Conventional Group

Independent Variable	Reg Coeffi.	SE of Coeffi.	t-value	p-level	Signi.
Intercept	-5.2033	7.9819	-0.6519	>0.05	NS
Attitude towards physical science (X_1)	1.3706	0.1415	9.6869	<0.05	S
Attitude towards programmed instruction (X_2)	-0.7213	0.1737	-4.1539	<0.05	S
Achievement motivation (X_3)	-0.3835	0.1246	-3.0788	<0.05	S

$R=0.8967$, $R^2=0.8041$, Adjusted $R^2=0.7913$, $F=62.942$ $p<0.05$, S,Std.Error of estimate: 6.4926

The results of the above table shows that,

- The joint effect of attitude towards physical science (X_1) on girls achievement in physical science is found to be positive and significant at 5 per cent level of significance. Hence, the null hypothesis is rejected and alternative hypothesis is accepted in conventional group.

- The joint effect of Attitude towards programmed instruction (X_2) on girls achievement in physical science is found to be negative and significant at 5 per cent level of significance. Hence, the null hypothesis is rejected and alternative hypothesis is accepted in conventional group.
- The joint effect of achievement motivation (X_3) on girls achievement in physical science is found to be negative and significant at 5 per cent level of significance. Hence, the null hypothesis is rejected and alternative hypothesis is accepted in conventional group.

Further, the multiple linear regression equation predicting the academic achievement of secondary school girls (Y) in terms of attitude towards physical science (X_1), attitude towards programmed instruction (X_2) and achievement motivation (X_3) was found to be under:

Academic achievement (Y)

$$= -5.2033+1.3706X_1 -0.7213X_2 -0.3835X_3$$

The multiple R of the linear regression equation is 0.8967. For testing multiple correlation coefficients the F-ratio (62.942) was found to be significant at 0.05 per cent level. Thus, the null hypothesis is rejected and alternative hypothesis is accepted. Significant R suggests that estimation of academic achievement of secondary school girls is possible on the basis of the predictors like attitude towards physical science (X_1), attitude towards programmed instruction (X_2) and achievement motivation (X_3). Further, the regression equation shows that attitude towards physical science (X_1), attitude towards programmed instruction (X_2) and achievement motivation (X_3) can be used as predictors of academic achievement of secondary school girls in conventional group.

The coefficient of multiple determination of R^2 is 0.8041. It can be therefore, be said that nearly 80.41 percent of the variation in academic achievement of secondary school girls accounted for whatever is measured by attitude towards physical science (X_1), attitude towards programmed instruction (X_2) and achievement motivation (X_3) can taken together. The SE_{est} for the regression equation is 6.4926. This means that each time the regression equation for the sample is used to predict a leadership behaviour of principals, that predicted academic achievement will not miss the actual academic achievement of secondary school girls by more that ±6.4926.

The relative contribution of attitude towards physical science (X_1), attitude towards programmed instruction (X_2) and achievement motivation (X_3) on academic achievement of secondary school girls in conventional group are presented in the following table.

Table 4.59 : Relative Contribution of Attitude towards Physical Science, Attitude towards Programmed Instruction Achievement Motivation on Achievement in Physical Science of Secondary School Girls in Conventional Group

Independent Variable	Beta	r-value	Beta × r	% of contribution
Attitude towards physical science (X_1)	1.9296	0.8080	1.5591	155.9065
Attitude towards programmed instruction (X_2)	-0.7517	0.6256	-0.4703	-47.0279
Achievement motivation (X_3)	-0.4722	0.6029	-0.2847 0.8041	-28.4675 80.41

The above table presents the relative contribution of Attitude towards physical science (X_1), (Attitude towards programmed instruction (X_2), Achievement motivation (X_3) on academic achievement in physical science of secondary school girl students in conventional group are presented in the above table. The total contribution of all the three explanatory variables on academic achievement in physical science of secondary school girls is found to be 80.4111 per cent. In which, the variable Attitude towards physical science

(X_1)) contributes maximum i.e. 155.9065 per cent followed by others.

Hypothesis: Attitude towards physical science, Attitude towards programmed instruction, Achievement motivations are would not be significant predictors of academic achievement in physical science of secondary school boys in experimental group.

To test or achieve this hypothesis, the multiple regression analysis was applied and results are presented in the following table.

Table 4.60 : Summary of Linear Multiple Regression Analysis: Independent Variables i.e. Attitude towards Physical Science, Attitude towards Programmed Instruction, Achievement Motivation on Academic Achievement in Physical Science of Secondary School Boys in Experimental Group

Independent Variable	Reg Coeffi.	SE of Coeffi.	t-value	p-level	Signi.
Intercept	58.2818	12.3550	4.7173	<0.05	S
Attitude towards physical science (X_1)	0.0849	0.1722	0.4931	>0.05	NS
Attitude towards progra-mmed instruction (X_2)	-0.8426	0.3127	-2.6948	<0.05	S
Achievement motivation (X_3)	1.4576	0.3476	4.1931	<0.05	S

$R=0.7281$, $R^2=0.5301$, Adjusted $R^2=0.4995$, $F=17.304$ $p<0.05$, S, Std.Error of estimate: 8.0889

The results of the above table shows that,

- The joint effect of Attitude towards programmed instruction (X_2) on boy students' achievement in physical science is found to be negative and significant at 5 per cent level of significance. Hence, the null hypothesis is rejected and alternative hypothesis is accepted in experimental group.
- The joint effect of achievement motivation (X_3) on boys' achievement in physical science is found to be negative and significant at 5 per cent level of

significance. Hence, the null hypothesis is rejected and alternative hypothesis is accepted in experimental group.

Further, the multiple linear regression equation predicting the academic achievement of secondary school boys (Y) in terms of attitude towards physical science (X_1), attitude towards programmed instruction (X_2) and achievement motivation (X_3) was found to be under:

Academic achievement (Y)

$$= 58.2818+0.0849X_1 -0.8426X_2 +1.4576X_3$$

The multiple R of the linear regression equation is 0.7281. For testing multiple correlation coefficients the F-ratio (17.304) was found to be significant at 0.05 per cent level. Thus, the null hypothesis is rejected and alternative hypothesis is accepted. Significant R suggests that estimation of academic achievement of secondary school boys is possible on the basis of the predictors like attitude towards physical science (X_1), attitude towards programmed instruction (X_2) and achievement motivation (X_3). Further, the regression equation shows that attitude towards physical science (X_1), attitude towards programmed instruction (X_2) and achievement motivation (X_3) can be used as predictors of academic achievement of secondary school boys in experimental group.

The coefficient of multiple determination of R^2 is 0.5301. It can be therefore, be said that nearly 53.01 percent of the variation in academic achievement of secondary school boys accounted for whatever is measured by attitude towards physical science (X_1), attitude towards programmed instruction (X_2) and achievement motivation (X_3) can taken together. The SE_{est} for the regression equation is 8.0889. This means that each time the regression equation for the sample is used to predict a leadership behaviour of principals, that predicted academic achievement will not miss the actual academic achievement of secondary school boys s by more that ±8.0889.

The relative contribution of attitude towards physical science (X_1), attitude towards programmed instruction (X_2) and achievement motivation (X_3) on academic achievement of secondary school boys in experimental group are presented in the following table.

Table 4.61 : Relative Contribution of Attitude towards Physical Science, Attitude towards Programmed Instruction Achievement Motivation on Achievement in Physical Science of Secondary School Boys in Experimental Group

Independent Variable	Beta	r-value	Beta x r	% of contri-bution
Attitude towards physical science (X_1)	0.1613	0.5921	0.0955	9.5530
Attitude towards progra-mmed instruction (X_2)	-1.1120	0.5623	-0.6252	-62.5249
Achievement motivation (X_3)	1.5851	0.6687	1.0599 0.5302	105.9913 53.0193

The above table presents the relative contribution of Attitude towards physical science (X_1), (Attitude towards programmed instruction (X_2), Achievement motivation (X_3) on academic achievement in physical science of secondary school boys in experimental group are presented in the above table. The total contribution of all the three explanatory variables on academic achievement in physical science of secondary school boys is found to be 53.0193 per cent. In which, the variable Attitude towards physical science (X_1)) contributes maximum i.e. 105.9913 per cent followed by others.

Hypothesis: Attitude towards physical science, Attitude towards programmed instruction, Achievement motivations are would not be significant predictors of academic achievement in physical science of secondary school girls in experimental group.

To test or achieve this hypothesis, the multiple regression analysis was applied and results are presented in the following table.

Table 4.62 : Summary of Linear Multiple Regression Analysis: Independent Variables i.e. Attitude towards Physical Science, Attitude towards Programmed Instruction , Achievement Motivation on Academic Achievement in Physical Science of Secondary School Girls in Experimental Group

Independent Variable	Reg Coeffi.	SE of Coeffi.	t-value	p-level	Signi.
Intercept	83.2770	7.5517	11.0276	<0.05	S
Attitude towards physical science (X_1)	0.4643	0.1374	3.3782	<0.05	S
Attitude towards programmed instruction (X_2)	-2.0195	0.1742	-11.5959	<0.05	S
Achievement motivation (X_3)	2.4585	0.2482	9.9067	<0.05	S

$R=0.9656$, $R^2=0.9325$, Adjusted $R^2=0.9281$, $F=212.04$ $p<0.05$, S, Std.Error of estimate: 4.4352

The results of the above table shows that,

- The joint effect of Attitude towards physical science (X_1) on girl students' achievement in physical science is found to be positive and significant at 5 per cent level of significance. Hence, the null hypothesis is rejected and alternative hypothesis is accepted in experimental group.
- The joint effect of Attitude towards programmed instruction (X_2) on girls achievement in physical science is found to be negative and significant at 5 per cent level of significance. Hence, the null hypothesis is rejected and alternative hypothesis is accepted in experimental group.
- The joint effect of achievement motivation (X_3) on girls' achievement in physical science is found to be positive and significant at 5 per cent level of significance. Hence, the null hypothesis is rejected and alternative hypothesis is accepted in experimental group.

Further, the multiple linear regression equation predicting the academic achievement of secondary school girls (Y) in terms of attitude towards physical science (X_1), attitude towards programmed instruction (X_2) and achievement motivation (X_3) was found to be under:

Academic achievement (Y)

$$= 83.2770+0.4643X_1 -2.0195X_2 +2.4585X_3$$

The multiple R of the linear regression equation is 0.9656. For testing multiple correlation coefficients the F-ratio (212.04) was found to be significant at 0.05 per cent level. Thus, the null hypothesis is rejected and alternative hypothesis is accepted. Significant R suggests that estimation of academic achievement of secondary school girls is possible on the basis of the predictors like attitude towards physical science (X_1), attitude towards programmed instruction (X_2) and achievement motivation (X_3). Further, the regression equation shows that attitude towards physical science (X_1), attitude towards programmed instruction (X_2) and achievement motivation (X_3) can be used as predictors of academic achievement of secondary school girls in experimental group.

The coefficient of multiple determination of R^2 is 0.9325. It can be therefore, be said that nearly 93.25 percent of the variation in academic achievement of secondary school girls accounted for whatever is measured by attitude towards physical science (X_1), attitude towards programmed instruction (X_2) and achievement motivation (X_3) can taken together. The SE_{est} for the regression equation is 4.4352. This means that each time the regression equation for the sample is used to predict a leadership behaviour of principals, that predicted academic achievement will not miss the actual academic achievement of secondary school girls by more that ±4.4352.

The relative contribution of attitude towards physical science (X_1), attitude towards programmed instruction (X_2) and achievement motivation (X_3) on academic achievement of secondary school girls in experimental group are presented in the following table.

Table 4.63 : Relative Contribution of Attitude towards Physical Science, Attitude towards Programmed Instruction Achievement Motivation on Achievement in Physical Science of Secondary School Girls in Experimental Group

Independent Variable	Beta	r-value	Beta x r	% of contri-bution
Attitude towards physical science (X_1)	0.6671	0.8205	0.5474	54.7402
Attitude towards progra-mmed instruction (X_2)	-1.7354	0.6982	-1.2116	-121.1567
Achievement motivation (X_3)	1.8677	0.8549	1.5967 0.9326	159.6728 93.2563

The above table presents the relative contribution of Attitude towards physical science (X_1), (Attitude towards programmed instruction (X_2), Achievement motivation (X_3) on academic achievement in physical science of secondary school girls in experimental group are presented in the above table. The total contribution of all the three explanatory variables on academic achievement in physical science of secondary school girls is found to be 93.2563 per cent. In which, the variable Attitude towards physical science (X_1)) contributes maximum i.e. 54.7402 per cent followed by others.

5. Path Analysis: In simple, multiple regression analysis, emphasis was on the study of the extent to which the dependent variable(s) get affected by the contribution of the independent variable(s) on original scales measurements being standardized for comparison of the studies being carried out by others with the same variables(s). The regression coefficients obtained carrying out simple, multiple regression analysis was found to get affected by the unit of measurement. In other words, the values of the regression coefficients of the variables get affected with the change of unit of measurement of the variable(s). In order to understand the true relation between the dependent and independent variables it becomes necessary to have regression coefficients independent of the unit of measurement of the variables. This is achieved by both the dependent and the independent variables being standardized as: Z=(X-m)/s with m and s being the mean and the standard deviation of the variable X. It is evident that the standardized variable Z has meant zero (0) and standard deviation (1) (Garrett, 1981). With the standardized variables, the regression coefficients will be having the same values as that of the corresponding correlation coefficients. The regression coefficients are directional in the sense that they indicate the direction of the direction in the form of independent variable as the cause of the corresponding dependent variable. Thus, the regression coefficients in the regression models of the standardized variables have come to be named path (directional) coefficients, with the path (direction) being from an independent variable towards the corresponding dependent variable. Hence the regression analysis carried out with the help of standardized variables has come to be known as path analysis. It is worth nothing that, one value of the path coefficients as regression coefficients of the standardized variables are the same in their values as those of the corresponding correlation coefficients. In the magnitude, the path coefficients are directional, but correlation coefficients are not directional, though both are independent of the units of measurement of the corresponding variables.

Added advantage of path analysis over multiple linear regression analysis is that of finding the direct and indirect effects of the independent variables on the corresponding dependent variable. In general, a variable can have its effect being revealed by the magnitude and the direction of the path coefficient of the independent variable. It can also have an effect on the dependent variable by the virtue of its relation with another independent variable. Thus, the effect of an independent variable on a dependent variable as received by the path coefficient of the independent variable is known as direct effect of the independent variable. On the other hand, the effect of an independent variable through another variable is termed as indirect effect of the independent variable on the dependent variable.

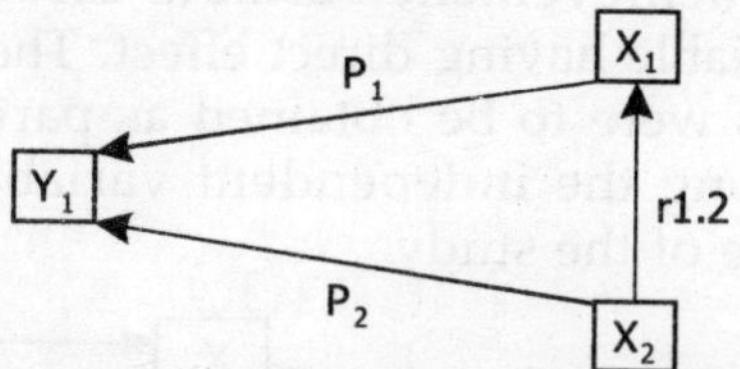

Fig. 4.6: Indirect paths through variables

In the above figure, P1 is the direct effect of X_1 on Y, r $_{.2}$ P_1 is the indirect effect of X_1 on Y through X_2 and p_2 is direct effect of X_2 on Y

A variable not exerting direct effect on the dependent variable may exert indirect effect on the dependent variable through an independent variable. Such a phenomenon holds good in many situations.

In the above figure X_1, X_2, and X_3 are the independent variables each having direct effect as well as indirect effect on the dependent variables Y. The variables u_1, u_2, u_3, v_1, and v_2 are also the independent variables with only indirect effect on Y through some or all of the independent variables X_1, X_2, and X_3 as indicated in the figure 2. In such situations the variables X_1, X_2, and X_3 are called the intermediately variables between Y and u_1, u_2, u_3, v_1, and v_2.

From the above narration it is evident that a variable can have only direct effect, only indirect effect and both direct and indirect effects on a dependent variable or variables.

The details of selected significant direct and indirect, independent variables and achievement of secondary school students in physical science with their interrelations is given in the following table and figures:

6. Direct and Indirect Paths from Independent Variables to Achievement Variables: Multiple regression analysis of standardized independent and achievement variable was carried out to identify direct and indirect paths (effects) from each of the independent variables to the achievement variable. The regression coefficient of independent variable having significant direct path with an achievement variable was considered as indirect path from the source independent variable to the achievement variable through the other independent variable having direct effect. The actual values of indirect paths were to be obtained as partial correlation coefficients among the independent variables but it was beyond the scope of the study.

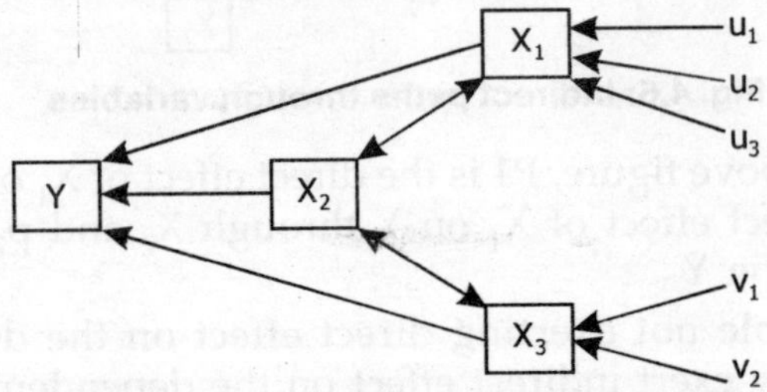

Fig. 4.7 : Indirect paths through variables

Hypothesis: There is no significant direct and indirect effect of attitude towards physical science, attitude towards programmed instruction, achievement motivation test on achievement in physical science of secondary school students as a whole.

To achieve this hypothesis, the linear multiple regression analysis was applied and the results are presented in the following table.

Table 4.64 : The Direct and Indirect Path Coefficients of Independent Variables (Attitude towards Physical Science, Attitude towards Programmed Instruction, Achievement Motivation Test) Achievement in Physical Science of Secondary School Students

Independent Variable	Direct effects	Indirect effects through		
		X_1	X_2	X_3
Attitude towards physical science (X_1)	0.7049*	—	0.3611*	0.3239*
Attitude towards programmed instruction (X_2)	-0.1514	-0.1341*	—	-0.0461*
Achievement motivation (X_3)	-0.2448*	-0.1127*	-0.0432*	—

* Indicates significant at 5% level of significance

The results of the above table reveal that,

- The direct effect of Attitude towards physical science (X_1) and Achievement motivation (X_3) on achievement of students in physical science is found to be significant as a total.
- The indirect effect of Attitude towards physical science (X_1) through Attitude towards programmed instruction (X_2) and Achievement motivation (X_3) on achievement of students in physical science is found to be significant as a total.
- The indirect effect of Attitude towards programmed instruction (X_2) through Attitude towards physical science (X_1) and Achievement motivation (X_3) on achievement of students in physical science is found to be significant as a whole.
- The indirect effect of Achievement motivation (X_3) through Attitude towards physical science (X_1) and Attitude towards programmed instruction (X_2) on achievement of students in physical science is found to be significant as a whole.

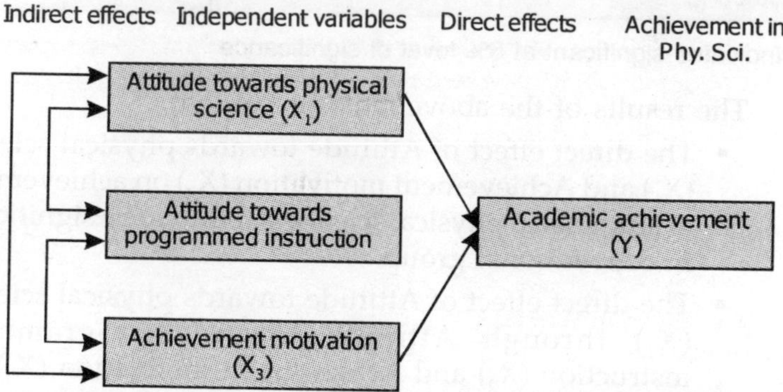

Fig. 4.8 : The direct and indirect path coefficients of Attitude towards physical science, Attitude towards programmed instruction and Achievement motivation test on achievement in physical science of secondary school students as a whole

Hypothesis: There is no significant direct and indirect effect of attitude towards physical science, attitude towards programmed instruction, achievement motivation test on achievement in physical science of secondary school students in conventional group.

To achieve this hypothesis, the linear multiple regression analysis was applied and the results are presented in the following table.

Table 4.65 : The Direct and Indirect Path Coefficients of Independent Variables (Attitude towards Physical Science, Attitude towards Programmed Instruction, Achievement Motivation Test) Achievement in Physical Science of Secondary School Students in Conventional Group

Independent Variable	Direct effects	Indirect effects through		
		X_1	X_2	X_3
Attitude towards physical science (X_1)	0.8257*	—	0.4518*	0.5776*
Attitude towards programmed instruction (X_2)	0.0135	0.0086*	—	0.0028
Achievement motivation (X_3)	-0.5451*	-0.2566*	-0.0644	—

* Indicates significant at 5% level of significance

The results of the above table reveal that,

- The direct effect of Attitude towards physical science (X_1) and Achievement motivation (X_3) on achievement of students in physical science is found to be significant in conventional group.
- The direct effect of Attitude towards physical science (X_1) through Attitude towards programmed instruction (X_2) and Achievement motivation (X_3) on achievement of students in physical science is found to be significant in conventional group.
- The indirect effect of Attitude towards programmed instruction (X_2) through Attitude towards physical science (X_1) on achievement of students in physical science is found to be significant in conventional group.

- The indirect effect of Achievement motivation (X_3) through Attitude towards physical science (X_1) on achievement of students in physical science is found to be significant in conventional group.

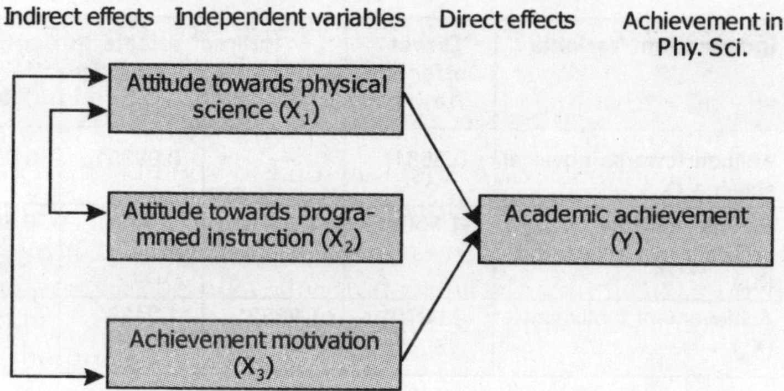

Fig. 4.9 : The Direct and Indirect Path Coefficients of Attitude towards Physical Science, Attitude towards Programmed Instruction and Achievement Motivation Test on Achievement in Physical Science of Secondary School Students in Conventional Group

Hypothesis: There is no significant direct and indirect effect of attitude towards physical science, attitude towards programmed instruction, achievement motivation test on achievement in physical science of secondary school students in experimental group.

To achieve this hypothesis, the linear multiple regression analysis was applied and the results are presented in the following table.

The results of the above table reveal that,

- The direct effect of Attitude towards physical science (X_1), Attitude towards programmed instruction (X_2) and Achievement motivation (X_3) on achievement of students in physical science is found to be significant in experimental group.
- The direct effect of Attitude towards physical science (X_1) through Attitude towards programmed instruction (X_2) and Achievement motivation (X_3) on achievement of students in physical science is found to be significant in experimental group.

Table 4.66 : The Direct and Indirect Path Coefficients of Independent Variables (Attitude towards Physical Science, Attitude towards Programmed Instruction, Achievement Motivation Test) Achievement in Physical Science of Secondary School Students in Experimental Group

Independent Variable	Direct effects	Indirect effects through		
		X_1	X_2	X_3
Attitude towards physical science (X_1)	0.3581*	—	0.0935*	0.0910*
Attitude towards programmed instruction (X_2)	-1.5603*	-1.0470*	—	-0.6893*
Achievement motivation (X_3)	2.0070*	1.9852*	1.3428*	—

* Indicates significant at 5% level of significance

- The indirect effect of Attitude towards programmed instruction (X_2) through Attitude towards physical science (X_1) and Achievement motivation (X_3) on achievement of students in physical science is found to be significant in experimental group.

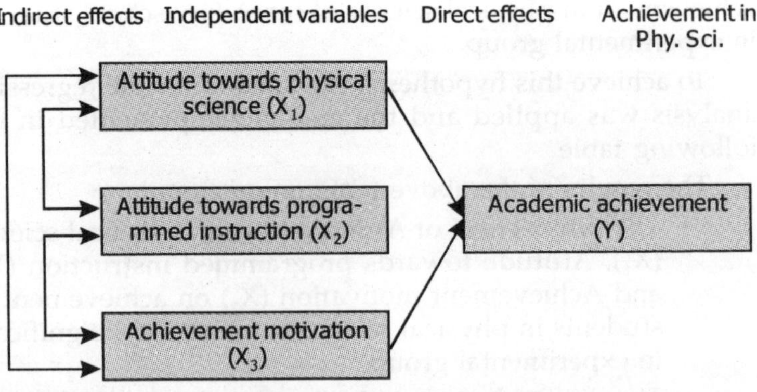

Fig. 4.10 : The Direct and Indirect Path Coefficients of Attitude towards Physical Science, Attitude towards Programmed Instruction and Achievement Motivation Test on Achievement in Physical Science of Secondary School Students in Experimental Group.

- The indirect effect of Achievement motivation (X_3) through Attitude towards physical science (X_1) and Achievement motivation (X_3) on achievement of students in physical science is found to be significant in experimental group.

Hypothesis: There is no significant direct and indirect effect of attitude towards physical science, attitude towards programmed instruction, achievement motivation test on achievement in physical science of secondary school boys in conventional group.

To achieve this hypothesis, the linear multiple regression analysis was applied and the results are presented in the following table.

Table 4.67 : The Direct and Indirect Path Coefficients of Independent Variables (Attitude towards Physical Science, Attitude towards Programmed Instruction, Achievement Motivation Test) Achievement in Physical Science of Secondary School Boys in Conventional Group

Independent Variable	Direct effects	Indirect effects through		
		X_1	X_2	X_3
Attitude towards physical science (X_1)	0.2721*	—	0.1290*	0.2347*
Attitude towards programmed instruction (X_2)	0.1707	0.0684*	—	0.0269
Achievement motivation (X_3)	-0.3805*	-0.1966*	-0.0426*	—

* Indicates significant at 5% level of significance

The results of the above table reveal that,

- The direct effect of Attitude towards physical science (X_1) and Achievement motivation (X_3) on achievement of boy students in physical science is found to be significant in conventional group.
- The direct effect of Attitude towards physical science (X_1) through Attitude towards programmed

instruction (X_2) and Achievement motivation (X_3) on achievement of boy students in physical science is found to be significant in conventional group.

- The indirect effect of Attitude towards programmed instruction (X_2) through Attitude towards physical science (X_1) on achievement of boy students in physical science is found to be significant in conventional group.
- The indirect effect of Achievement motivation (X_3) through Attitude towards physical science (X_1) on achievement of boy students in physical science is found to be significant in conventional group.

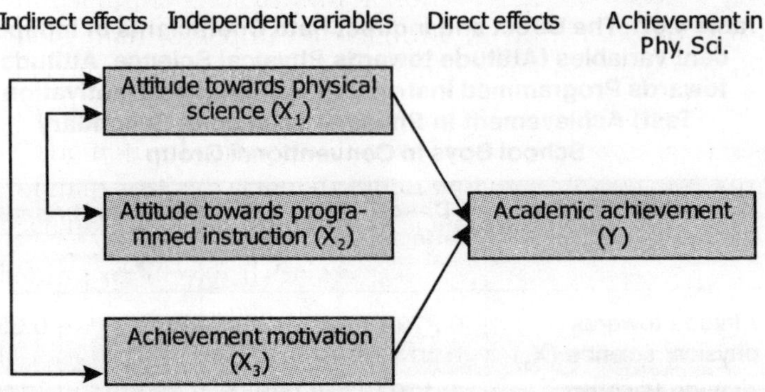

Fig. 4.11 : The Direct and Indirect Path Coefficients of Attitude towards Physical Science, Attitude towards Programmed Instruction and Achievement Motivation Test on Achievement in Physical Science of Secondary School Boys in Conventional Group

Hypothesis: There is no significant direct and indirect effect of attitude towards physical science, attitude towards programmed instruction, achievement motivation test on achievement in physical science of secondary school girls in conventional group.

To achieve this hypothesis, the linear multiple regression analysis was applied and the results are presented in the following table.

Table 4.68 : The Direct and Indirect Path Coefficients of Independent Variables (Attitude towards Physical Science, Attitude towards Programmed Instruction, Achievement Motivation Test) Achievement in Physical Science of Secondary School Girls in Conventional Group

Independent Variable	Direct effects	Indirect effects through		
		X_1	X_2	X_3
Attitude towards physical science (X_1)	1.3706*	—	0.7453*	0.7431*
Attitude towards programmed instruction (X_2)	-0.7213*	-0.5909*	—	-0.2554
Achievement motivation (X_3)	-0.3835*	-0.1611*	-0.0699	—

* Indicates significant at 5% level of significance

The results of the above table reveal that,

- The direct effect of Attitude towards physical science (X_1), Attitude towards programmed instruction (X_2) and Achievement motivation (X_3) on achievement of girls in physical science is found to be significant in conventional group.
- The direct effect of Attitude towards physical science (X_1) through Attitude towards programmed instruction (X_2) and Achievement motivation (X_3) on achievement of girls in physical science is found to be significant in conventional group.
- The indirect effect of Attitude towards programmed instruction (X_2) through Attitude towards physical science (X_1) on achievement of girl students in physical science is found to be significant in conventional group.
- The indirect effect of Achievement motivation (X_3) through Attitude towards physical science (X_1) on achievement of girls in physical science is found to be significant in conventional group.

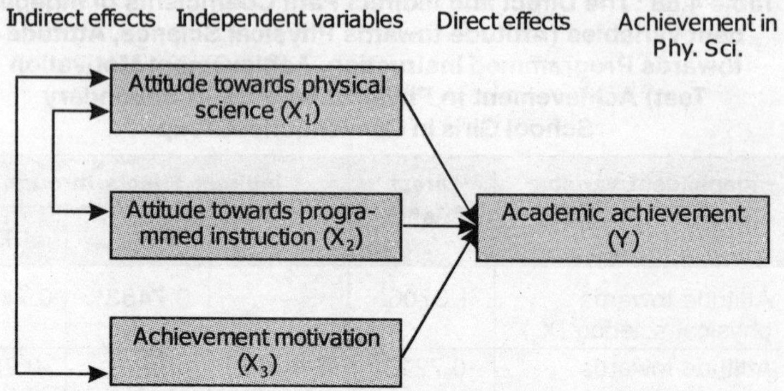

Fig. 4.12: The Direct and Indirect Path Coefficients of Attitude towards Physical Science, Attitude towards Programmed Instruction and Achievement Motivation Test on Achievement in Physical Science of Secondary School Girls in Conventional Group

Hypothesis: There is no significant direct and indirect effect of attitude towards physical science, attitude towards programmed instruction, achievement motivation test on achievement in physical science of secondary school boys in experimental group.

To achieve this hypothesis, the linear multiple regression analysis was applied and the results are presented in the following table.

The results of the above table reveal that,

- The direct effect of Attitude towards programmed instruction (X_2) and Achievement motivation (X_3) on achievement of boys in physical science is found to be significant in experimental group.
- The direct effect of Attitude towards physical science (X_1) through Attitude towards programmed instruction (X_2) and Achievement motivation (X_3) on achievement of boys in physical science is found to be significant in experimental group.
- The indirect effect of Attitude towards programmed instruction (X_2) through Attitude towards physical science (X_1) on achievement of boys in physical science is found to be significant in experimental group.

Table 4.69: The Direct and Indirect Path Coefficients of Independent Variable (Attitude towards Physical Science, Attitude towards Programmed Instruction, Achievement Motivation Test) Achievement in Physical Science of Secondary School Boys in Experimental Group

Independent Variable	Direct effects	Indirect effects through		
		X_1	X_2	X_3
Attitude towards physical science (X_1)	0.0849	—	0.0227*	0.0126*
Attitude towards programmed instruction (X_2)	-0.8426*	-0.7436*	—	-0.4957
Achievement motivation (X_3)	1.4576*	0.8835*	1.0601	—

* Indicates significant at 5% level of significance

- The indirect effect of Achievement motivation (X_3) through Attitude towards physical science (X_1) on achievement of boy students in physical science is found to be significant in experiment group.

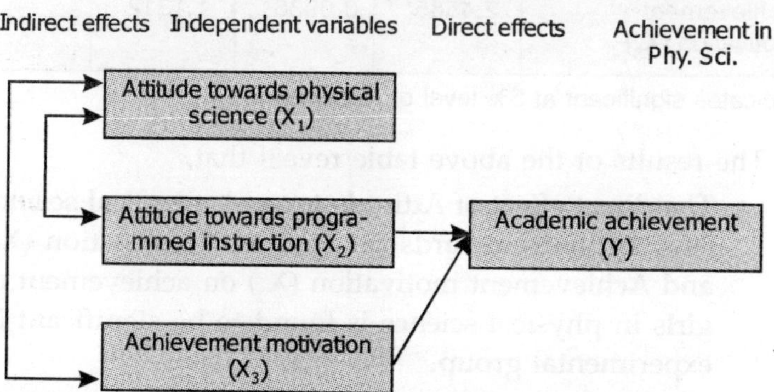

Fig. 4.13 : The Direct and Indirect Path Coefficients of Attitude towards Physical Science, Attitude towards Programmed Instruction and Achievement Motivation Test on Achievement in Physical Science of secondary School Boys in Experimental Group

Hypothesis: There is no significant direct and indirect effect of attitude towards physical science, attitude towards programmed instruction, achievement motivation test on achievement in physical science of secondary school girls in experimental group.

To achieve this hypothesis, the linear multiple regression analysis was applied and the results are presented in the following table.

Table 4.70: The Direct and Indirect Path Coefficients of Independent Variable (Attitude towards Physical Science, Attitude towards programmed instruction, Achievement Motivation Test Achievement in Physical Science of Secondary School Girls Experimental Group

Independent Variable	Direct effects	Indirect effects through		
		X_1	X_2	X_3
Attitude towards physical science (X_1)	0.4643*	—	0.1570*	0.1792*
Attitude towards programmed instruction (X_2)	-2.0195*	-1.0967*	—	-0.4576
Achievement motivation (X_3)	2.4585*	3.0936*	1.1312	—

* Indicates significant at 5% level of significance

The results of the above table reveal that,

- The direct effect of Attitude towards physical science (X_1), Attitude towards programmed instruction (X_2) and Achievement motivation (X_3) on achievement of girls in physical science is found to be significant in experimental group.
- The direct effect of Attitude towards physical science (X_1) through Attitude towards programmed instruction (X_2) and Achievement motivation (X_3) on achievement of girls in physical science is found to be significant in experimental group.

- The indirect effect of Attitude towards programmed instruction (X_2) through Attitude towards physical science (X_1) on achievement of girls in physical science is found to be significant in experimental group.
- The indirect effect of Achievement motivation (X_3) through Attitude towards physical science (X_1) on achievement of girls in physical science is found to be significant in experimental group.

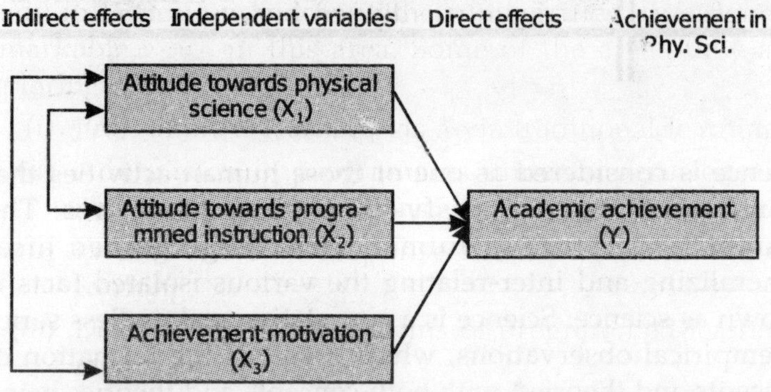

Fig. 4.14 : The Direct and Indirect Path Coefficients of Attitude towards Physical Science, Attitude towards Programmed Instruction and Achievement Motivation Test on Achievement in Physical Science of Secondary School Girls in Experimental Group.

Summary, Findings and Suggestions

Science is considered as one of those human activities that man has created to satisfy his needs and desires. The systematized store of human knowledge gained after generalizing and inter-relating the various isolated facts is known as science. Science is a cumulative and endless series of empirical observations, which result in the formation of concepts and theories, with both concepts and theories being subject to modification in the light of further empirical (practical) observations. Science is both a body of knowledge and the process of acquiring it. Science is accumulated and systematized learning in general usage restricted to natural phenomenon. The progress of science is not marked not only by an accumulation of fact, but by the emergence of scientific method and of the scientific attitude.

The purpose of physical science teaching in secondary schools is to enable students to grasp systematically the basic knowledge of physical science needed for the further study of modern science and technology and to understand its applications. In addition, it should help them to acquire experiment skills, develop the ability to think and to use mathematics to solve physical problems, cultivate a dialectical material First view point and make them aware of need to study haul and to struggle for the modernization, along socialist lines, of industry, agriculture, national defense and science and technology. For teaching physical science more effectively, we need more advanced teaching strategies along with the traditional ones. One such is programmed instruction.

Programmed institution is the process of arranging the material to be learned into a series of sequential steps, usually it moves the student from a familiar background into a complex and new set of concepts, principles and understanding (Smith and More, 1962). A programme is a sequence of small steps of institutional material (called frames), most of which requires a response to be made by completing a blank space in a sentence. To ensure that required responses are given, a system of cuing is applied, and each response is verified by the provision of immediate knowledge of results. Such a sequence is intended to be worked at the learners 'own pace as individualized self-instruction (Leith, 1966). Programmed learning is the first application of laboratory technique utilized in the study of the learning process to the practical problems of education (Skinner, 1954). Programmed learning as popularly understood is a method of giving individualized instruction, in which the student is active and proceeds at his own pace and is provided with immediate knowledge of results. The teacher is not physically present (Gulati and Gulati, 1976). The programmer, while developing programmed material has to follow the laws of behaviour and validate his strategy in terms of student learning.

The problem selected for the study is "A Study of the Effectiveness of Programmed Instruction as an Instructional Strategy in Physical Science".

The objectives identified keeping different aspects of the study in view were: 1. To study the difference between pre and post test scores of academic achievement in physical science of secondary school students in experimental and conventional groups. 2. To study the difference between experimental and conventional groups with respect to pre test, post test and their gain scores of academic achievement in physical science of secondary school students. 3. To study the difference between experimental and conventional groups with respect to pre test, post test and their gain scores of academic achievement in physical science of secondary school boys. 4. To study the difference between experimental and conventional groups with respect to pre test, post test and their gain scores of academic achievement in physical science of secondary school girl students. 5. To study the difference between experimental and conventional groups with respect to attitude towards attitude towards programmed instruction, achievement motivation scores of secondary schools students. 6. To study the difference between experimental and conventional groups with respect to attitude towards attitude towards programmed instruction, achievement motivation scores of secondary schools boys. 7. To study the difference between experimental and conventional groups with respect to attitude towards attitude towards programmed instruction, achievement motivation scores of secondary schools girl students. 8. To study the difference between boys and girls students of secondary schools with respect to pre test scores of academic achievement in physical science as a whole. 9. To study the difference between boys and girls students of secondary schools with respect to attitude towards attitude towards programmed instruction, achievement motivation scores (both experiment and conventional). 10. To study the difference between urban and rural secondary school students with respect to pre test scores of academic achievement in physical science as a whole. 11. To study the difference between urban and rural secondary school students with respect to attitude towards attitude towards programmed instruction, achievement motivation scores (both experiment and conventional). 12. To study the difference between different types of management (government, aided and unaided) with respect to pre test and post test academic achievement in physical science scores of secondary school students as a whole. 13. To study the difference between different types of managements (government, aided and unaided) with respect to attitude towards attitude towards programmed instruction, achievement motivation of secondary school students as a whole. 14. To study the difference between different groups of achievement motivation (high and low) with respect to pre-test scores, post-test achievement scores, attitude towards programmed instruction, and achievement motivation scores of secondary school students as a whole.

The Experimental method was used in the present study.

The variables considered in the study were: (A) *Control Variables*: Intelligence, and Treatment of Method of Teaching; (B) *Dependent Variable*: Achievement and Retention in Physical Science; (C) *Independent Variables*: Conventional Method, Programmed Instruction, Attitude towards Physical Science, Attitude towards Programmed Instruction, and Achievement Motivation

The null hypotheses formulated for the investigation were: *1. Hypothesis:* There is no significant difference between pre and post test of academic achievement in physical science of secondary school students in experimental and conventional groups. *1A. Sub-Hypothesis:* There is no significant difference between pre and post test of academic achievement in physical science of secondary school boys in experimental and conventional groups. *1B. Sub-Hypothesis:* There is no significant difference between pre and post test of academic achievement in physical science of secondary school girls in experimental group and conventional group. *2. Hypothesis:* There is no significant difference between experimental and conventional groups with respect to pre test, post test and their gain of academic achievement in physical science of secondary school students. *3. Hypothesis:* There is no significant difference between experimental and conventional groups with respect to pre test, post test and their gain of academic achievement in physical science of secondary school boys. *4. Hypothesis:* There is no significant difference between experimental and conventional groups with respect to pre test, post test and their gain of academic achievement in physical science of secondary school girls. *5. Hypothesis:* There is no significant difference between experimental and conventional groups with respect to attitude towards physical science, attitude towards programmed instruction, achievement motivation of secondary schools students. 6. *Hypothesis:* There is no significant difference between experimental and conventional groups with respect to attitude towards physical science, attitude towards programmed instruction, achievement motivation of secondary school boys. 7. *Hypothesis:* There is no significant difference between experimental and conventional groups with respect to attitude towards physical science, attitude towards programmed instruction, achievement motivation of secondary schools girls. 8. *Hypothesis:* There is no significant difference between boys and girls of secondary schools with respect to pre test of academic achievement in physical science as a whole. *8A. Sub-Hypothesis:* There is no significant difference between boys and girls of secondary schools with respect to pre test of academic achievement in physical science in experimental group. *8B. Sub-Hypothesis:* There is no significant difference between boys and girls of secondary schools with respect to pre test of academic achievement in physical science in conventional group. 9. *Hypothesis:* There is no significant difference between boys and girls of secondary schools with respect to attitude towards physical science, attitude towards programmed instruction, achievement motivation (both experimental and conventional). *9A. Sub-Hypothesis:* There is no significant difference between boys and girls of secondary schools with respect to attitude towards physical science, attitude towards programmed instruction, achievement motivation in experimental group. *9B. Sub-Hypothesis:* There is no significant difference between boys and girls of secondary schools with respect to attitude towards physical science, attitude towards programmed instruction, achievement motivation in conventional group. *10. Hypothesis:* There is no significant difference between urban and rural secondary school students with respect to pre test of academic achievement in physical science as a whole. *10A. Sub-Hypothesis:* There is no significant difference between urban and rural secondary school students with respect to pre test of academic achievement in physical science in experimental group. *10B. Sub-Hypothesis:* There is no significant difference between urban and rural secondary school students with respect to pre test of academic achievement in physical science in conventional group. *11. Hypothesis:* There is no significant difference between urban and rural secondary school students with respect to attitude towards physical science, attitude towards programmed instruction, achievement motivation (both experimental and conventional). *11A. Sub-Hypothesis:* There is no significant difference between urban and rural secondary school students with respect to attitude towards physical science, attitude towards programmed instruction, achievement motivation in experimental group. *11B. Sub-Hypothesis:* There is no significant difference between urban and rural secondary school students with respect to attitude towards physical science, attitude towards programmed instruction, achievement motivation in conventional group. *12. Hypothesis:* There is no significant difference between different types of management (government, aided and unaided) with respect to pre test and post test academic achievement in physical science of secondary schools as a whole. *12A. Sub-Hypothesis:* There is no significant difference between different types of management (government, aided and unaided) with respect to pre test and post test academic achievement in physical science of secondary schools in experimental group. *12B. Sub-Hypothesis:* There is no significant difference between different types of management (government, aided and unaided) with respect to pre test and post test academic achievement in physical science of secondary schools in conventional group. *13. Hypothesis:* There is no significant difference between different types of managements (government, aided and unaided) with respect to attitude towards physical science, attitude towards programmed instruction, achievement motivation of secondary schools as a whole. *13A. Sub-Hypothesis:* There is no significant difference between different types of managements (government, aided and unaided) with respect to attitude towards physical science, attitude towards programmed instruction, achievement motivation of secondary schools in experimental group. *13B. Sub-Hypothesis:* There is no significant difference between different types of managements (government, aided and unaided) with respect to attitude towards physical science, attitude towards programmed instruction, achievement motivation of secondary schools in conventional group. *14. Hypothesis:* There is no significant difference between different groups of achievement motivation (High and low) with respect to pre test, post test achievement, Attitude towards physical science, Attitude towards programmed instruction, Achievement motivation of secondary schools as a whole. *14A. Sub-Hypothesis:* There is no significant difference between different groups of achievement motivation (high and low) with respect to pre test, post test achievement, Attitude towards physical science, Attitude towards programmed instruction, Achievement motivation of secondary schools in experimental group. *14B. Sub-Hypothesis:* There is no significant difference between different groups of achievement motivation (high and low) with respect to Pre test, post test achievement, Attitude towards physical science, Attitude towards programmed instruction, Achievement motivation of secondary schools in conventional group. *15. Hypothesis:* There is no significant relationship between Attitude towards physical science, Attitude towards programmed instruction, Achievement motivation and achievement in physical science of secondary school students as a whole. *16. Hypothesis:* There is no significant relationship between Attitude towards physical science, Attitude towards programmed instruction, Achievement motivation and achievement in physical science of secondary school students in conventional group. *17. Hypothesis:* There is no significant relationship between attitude towards physical science, attitude towards programmed instruction, achievement motivation and achievement in physical science of secondary school boys in conventional group. *18. Hypothesis:* There is no significant relationship between attitude towards physical science, attitude towards programmed instruction, achievement motivation and achievement in physical science of secondary school girls in conventional group. *19. Hypothesis:* There is no significant relationship between Attitude towards physical science, Attitude towards programmed instruction, Achievement motivation and achievement in physical science of secondary school students in experimental group. *20. Hypothesis:* There is no significant relationship between attitude towards physical science, attitude towards programmed instruction, achievement motivation and achievement in physical science of secondary school boys in experimental group. *21. Hypothesis:* There is no significant relationship between attitude towards physical science, attitude towards programmed instruction, achievement motivation and achievement in physical science of secondary school girls in experimental group. *22. Hypothesis:* There is no significant relationship between attitude towards physical science, attitude towards programmed instruction, achievement motivation and achievement in physical science of secondary school boys. *23. Hypothesis:* There is no significant relationship between attitude towards physical science, attitude towards programmed instruction, achievement motivation and achievement in physical science of secondary school girls. *24. Hypothesis:* There is no significant relationship between attitude towards physical science, attitude towards programmed instruction, achievement motivation and achievement in physical science of students of urban secondary schools. *25. Hypothesis:* There is no significant relationship between attitude towards physical science, attitude towards programmed instruction, achievement motivation and achievement in physical science of students of rural secondary schools. *26. Hypothesis:* Attitude towards physical science, Attitude towards programmed instruction, Achievement motivations are would not be significant predictors of academic achievement in physical science of secondary school students as a whole. *27. Hypothesis:* Attitude towards physical science, Attitude towards programmed instruction, Achievement motivations are would not be significant predictors of academic achievement in physical science of secondary school students in conventional group. *28. Hypothesis:* Attitude towards physical science, Attitude towards programmed instruction, Achievement motivations are would not be significant predictors of academic achievement in physical science of secondary school students in experimental group. *29. Hypothesis:* Attitude towards physical science, Attitude towards programmed instruction, Achievement motivations are would not be significant predictors of academic achievement in physical science of secondary school boys in conventional group. *30. Hypothesis:* Attitude towards physical science, Attitude towards programmed instruction, Achievement motivations are would not be significant predictors of academic achievement in physical science of secondary school girls in conventional group. *31. Hypothesis:* Attitude towards physical science, Attitude towards programmed instruction, Achievement motivations are would not be significant predictors of academic achievement in physical science of secondary school boys in experimental group. *32. Hypothesis:* Attitude towards physical science, Attitude towards programmed instruction, Achievement motivations are would not be significant predictors of academic achievement in physical science of secondary school girls in experimental group. *33. Hypothesis:* There is no significant direct and indirect effect of attitude towards physical science, attitude towards programmed instruction, achievement motivation test on achievement in physical science of secondary school students as a whole. *34. Hypothesis:* There is no significant direct and indirect effect of attitude towards physical science, attitude towards programmed instruction, achievement motivation test on achievement in physical science of secondary school students in conventional group. *35. Hypothesis:* There is no significant direct and indirect effect of attitude towards physical science, attitude towards programmed instruction, achievement motivation test on achievement in physical science of secondary school students in experimental group. *36. Hypothesis:* There is no significant direct and indirect effect of attitude towards physical science, attitude towards programmed instruction, achievement motivation test on achievement in physical science of secondary school boys in conventional group. *37. Hypothesis:* There is no significant direct and indirect effect of attitude towards physical science, attitude towards programmed instruction, achievement motivation test on achievement in physical science of secondary school girls in conventional group. *38. Hypothesis:* There is no significant direct and indirect effect of attitude towards physical science, attitude towards programmed instruction, achievement motivation test on achievement in physical science of secondary school boys in experimental group. *39. Hypothesis:* There is no significant direct and indirect effect of attitude towards physical science, attitude towards programmed instruction, achievement motivation test on achievement in physical science of secondary school girls in experimental group.

The present study focused on a sample of 100 in two groups, namely, Conventional or Traditional Instruction Group and Programmed Instruction Group containing both boys and girls of different Socio-Economic and Educational Background.

The tools used for the collection of the data were: 1. Construction of Achievement Test in Physical Science for IX Standard Students, 2. Achievement Motivation Test (ACMT), 3. Preparation of Lesson Plans for Conventional Instructions, 4. Development of the Programme Instruction Package (PI), 5. Programmed Instruction Attitude Scale (PIAS), and 6. Attitude Scale to Measure Attitude towards Physical Science.

The statistical techniques used for the data analyses were Descriptive Statistics, Differential Analysis, Correlation Coefficient, Regression Analysis, and Path Analysis.

Findings of the Study

The following were the findings of the present research on the 'study of effectiveness of programmed instruction as an instructional strategy in physical science'.

1. Finding of Differential Analysis

1. The post-test scores of academic achievement in physical science secondary school students are high as compared to pre-test of academic achievement in physical science experimental group students.
2. The post-test academic achievement in physical science of secondary school students is high as compared to pre-test academic achievement in physical science of secondary school conventional group students.
3. The post-test academic achievement in physical science of secondary school students is high as compared to pre-test of academic achievement in physical science of secondary school experimental group boys.
4. The post-test academic achievement in physical science of secondary school boys is high as compared to pre-test academic achievement in physical science of secondary school conventional group students.
5. The post-test academic achievement in physical science of secondary school students is high as compared to pre-test academic achievement in physical science of secondary school experimental group girls.
6. The post-test academic achievement in physical science of secondary school girls is high as compared to pre-test academic achievement in physical science of secondary school conventional group students.
7. The post-test academic achievement in physical science of secondary school students is high in experimental group as compared to conventional group.
8. The gain of pre- and post-test of academic achievement in physical science of secondary school students is high in experimental group as compared to conventional group.
9. The post-test of academic achievement in physical science of secondary school students is high in experimental group as compared to conventional group.

10. The gain of pre- and post-test of academic achievement in physical science of secondary school students is high in experimental group as compared to conventional group.
11. The pre-test of academic achievement in physical science of secondary school boys is high in experimental group as compared to conventional group.
12. The post-test of academic achievement in physical science of secondary school boys is high in experimental group as compared to conventional group.
13. The gain of pre- and post-test of academic achievement in physical science of secondary school boys is high in experimental group as compared to conventional group.
14. The pre-test of academic achievement in physical science of secondary school girls is high in experimental group as compared to conventional group.
15. The post-test of academic achievement in physical science of secondary school girls is high in experimental group as compared to conventional group.
16. The attitude towards physical science of secondary school students is high in experimental group as compared to conventional group.
17. The attitude towards programmed instruction of secondary school students is high in experimental group as compared to conventional group.
18. The achievement motivation of secondary school students is high in experimental group as compared to conventional group.
19. The achievement motivation of secondary school girls is high in experimental group as compared to conventional group.

20. The secondary school boys are high in post-test academic achievements in physical science as compared to girls of secondary schools.
21. The secondary school boys have high in post-test academic achievements in physical science as compared to secondary school girls in experimental group.
22. The urban and rural secondary school students have different post-test academic achievements in physical science.
23. The urban and rural secondary school experimental group students have different post-test academic achievements in physical science.
24. The urban secondary school conventional group students have high in post-test academic achievement in physical science than the post-test academic achievement in physical science.
25. The urban and rural secondary school conventional group students have different gain of pre-test and post-test academic achievements in physical science.
26. The urban and rural secondary school students have different levels attitude towards physical science.
27. The urban and rural secondary school students have different levels of attitude towards programmed instruction.
28. The urban and rural secondary school students have different levels of achievement motivation.
29. The urban secondary school experiment group students have high on attitude towards physical science when compared to rural secondary school students.
30. The urban secondary school experiment group students have high on attitude towards programmed instruction when compared to rural secondary school students.
31. The urban secondary school students have high on attitude towards programmed instruction in conventional group when compared to rural secondary school students.

32. The urban secondary school conventional group students have high achievement motivation as compared to rural secondary school students.
33. The students of aided secondary schools have high academic achievement in physical sciences in post-test as compared to unaided and government school students.
34. The students of aided secondary schools have high gain in academic achievement in pre- and post-tests in physical sciences as compared to unaided and government school students.
35. The students of aided secondary schools have high in academic achievement in physical sciences in post-test as compared to unaided and government school conventional group students.
36. The students of aided secondary schools have high gain academic achievement in pre- and post-tests in physical sciences as compared to unaided and government schools conventional group students.
37. The students of aided secondary schools have high attitude towards physical science as compared to unaided and government school students.
38. The students of aided secondary schools have high attitude towards programmed instruction as compared to unaided and government school students.
39. The students of aided secondary schools have high in achievement motivation as compared to unaided and government school students.
40. The students of aided secondary schools have high attitude towards physical science as compared to unaided and government school conventional group students.
41. The students of aided secondary schools have high in attitude towards programmed instruction as compared to unaided and government school conventional group students.

42. The students of aided secondary schools have high in achievement motivation as compared to unaided and government school conventional group students.
43. The secondary school students belonging to high achievement motivation have high academic achievement in physical science in pre-test as compared to secondary school students in achievement motivation.
44. The secondary school students belonging to high achievement motivation have high academic achievement in physical science in post-test as compared to secondary school students having lower academic achievement.
45. The secondary school students of belonging to high achievement motivation have high gain of pre- and post-test of academic achievement in physical science as compared to secondary school students with low achievement motivation.
46. The secondary school students belonging to high achievement motivation have high attitude towards physical science as compared to secondary school students with low achievement motivation.
47. The secondary school students belonging to high achievement motivation have high attitude towards programmed instruction as compared to secondary school students with low achievement motivation.
48. The secondary school students belonging to high achievement motivation have high academic achievement in physical science in pre-test as compared to secondary school experiment group students with low achievement motivation.
49. The secondary school students belonging to high achievement motivation have high academic achievement in physical science in post-test as compared to secondary school experimental group students with low achievement motivation.

50. The secondary school students belonging to high achievement motivation have high gain in academic achievement in physical science in pre- and post-test as compared to secondary school experimental group students with low achievement motivation.
51. The secondary school students belonging to high achievement motivation have high attitude towards physical science as compared to secondary school experimental group students with low achievement motivation.
52. The secondary school students belonging to high achievement motivation have high attitude towards programmed instruction as compared to secondary school experimental group student with low achievement motivation.
53. The secondary school students belonging to high achievement motivation have high post-test academic achievement in physical science as compared to secondary school conventional group students with low achievement motivation.
54. The secondary school students belonging to high achievement motivation have high attitude towards physical science as compared to secondary school conventional group students with low achievement motivation.
55. The secondary school students belonging to high achievement motivation have high attitude towards programmed instruction as compared to secondary school conventional group students with achievement motivation.

2. *Findings of Correlation Analysis*

56. Increase in attitude towards physical science increases their academic achievement in physical science of secondary school students as a whole.
57. Increase in the attitude towards programmed instruction increases their academic achievement in

physical science of secondary school students as a whole.

58. Increase in the achievement motivation increases their academic achievement in physical science of secondary school students as a whole.
59. Increase in the attitude towards physical science increases their academic achievement in physical science of secondary school conventional group students.
60. Increase in the attitude towards programmed instruction increases their academic achievement in physical science of secondary schools conventional group students.
61. Increase in the achievement motivation increases their academic achievement in physical science of secondary school conventional group students.
62. Increase in the achievement motivation increases their academic achievement in physical science of secondary school conventional group boys.
63. Increase in the attitude towards physical science increases their academic achievement in physical science of secondary school conventional group girls.
64. Increase in the attitude towards programmed instruction increases their academic achievement in physical science of secondary school conventional group girls.
65. Increase in the achievement motivation increases their academic achievement in physical science of secondary school conventional group girls.
66. Increase in the attitude towards physical science increases their academic achievement in physical science of secondary school experimental group students.
67. Increase in the attitude towards programmed instruction increases or decreases with increase in physical science of secondary school experimental group students.

68. Increase in the achievement motivation increases their academic achievement in physical science of secondary school experimental group students.
69. Increase in the attitude towards physical science increases their academic achievement in physical science of secondary school experimental group boys.
70. Increase in the attitude towards programmed instruction increases their academic achievement in physical science of secondary school experimental group boys.
71. Increase in the achievement motivation increases their academic achievement in physical science of secondary school experimental group boys.
72. Increase in the attitude towards physical science increases their academic achievement in physical science of secondary school experimental group girls.
73. Increase in the attitude towards programmed instruction increases their academic achievement in physical science of secondary school experimental group girls.
74. Increase in the achievement motivation increases their academic achievement in physical science of secondary school experimental group girls.
75. Increase in the attitude towards physical science increases their academic achievement in physical science of secondary school boys.
76. Increase in the attitude towards programmed instruction increases their academic achievement in physical science of secondary school boys.
77. Increase in the achievement motivation increases in their academic achievement in physical science of secondary school boys.
78. Increase in the attitude towards physical science increases their academic achievement in physical science of girls.
79. Increase in the attitude towards programmed instruction increases their academic achievement in physical science of secondary school girls.

80. Increase in the achievement motivation increases their academic achievement in physical science of secondary school girls.
81. Increase in the attitude towards physical science increases their academic achievement in physical science of urban secondary school students.
82. Increase in the attitude towards programmed instruction increases their academic achievement in physical science of urban secondary school students.
83. Increase in the achievement motivation increases their academic achievement in physical science of urban secondary school students.
84. Increase in the attitude towards physical science increases their academic achievement in physical science of rural secondary school students.
85. Increase in the attitude towards programmed instruction increases their academic achievement in physical science of rural secondary school students.
86. Increase in the achievement motivation increases their academic achievement in physical science of rural secondary school students.

3. *Findings of Multiple Regression Analysis*

87. The variable attitude towards physical science contributes maximum followed by others.
88. The variable achievement motivation contributes maximum followed by others.
89. The variable attitude towards physical science contributes maximum followed by others.

4. *Findings of Path Analysis*

90. The dependent and independent variables and achievement of secondary school students in physical science have significant interrelations
91. The direct effect of attitude towards physical science and achievement motivation on achievement of secondary school students in physical science is found to be significant as a total.

92. The indirect effect of attitude towards physical science through attitude towards programmed instruction and achievement motivation on achievement of secondary school students in physical science is found to be significant as a total.
93. The indirect effect of attitude towards programmed instruction through attitude towards physical science and achievement motivation on achievement of secondary school students in physical science is found to be significant as a whole.
94. The indirect effect of achievement motivation through attitude towards physical science and attitude towards programmed instruction on achievement of secondary school students in physical science is found to be significant as a whole.
95. The direct effect of attitude towards physical science and achievement motivation on achievement of secondary school students in physical science is found to be significant in conventional group.
96. The direct effect of attitude towards physical science through attitude towards programmed instruction and achievement motivation on achievement of secondary school students in physical science is found to be significant in conventional group.
97. The indirect effect of attitude towards programmed instruction through attitude towards physical science on achievement of secondary school students in physical science is found to be significant in conventional group.
98. The indirect effect of achievement motivation through attitude towards physical science on achievement of secondary school students in physical science is found to be significant in conventional group.
99. The direct effect of attitude towards physical science, attitude towards programmed instruction and achievement motivation on achievement of secondary

school students in physical science is found to be significant in experimental group.

100. The direct effect of attitude towards physical science through attitude towards programmed instruction and achievement motivation on achievement of secondary school students in physical science is found to be significant in experimental group.
101. The indirect effect of attitude towards programmed instruction through attitude towards physical science and achievement motivation on achievement of secondary school students in physical science is found to be significant in experimental group.
102. The indirect effect of achievement motivation through attitude towards physical science and achievement motivation on achievement of secondary school students in physical science is found to be significant in experimental group.
103. The direct effect of attitude towards physical science and achievement motivation on achievement of secondary school boys in physical science is found to be significant in conventional group.
104. The direct effect of attitude towards physical science through Attitude towards programmed instruction and achievement motivation on achievement of secondary school boys in physical science is found to be significant in conventional group.
105. The indirect effect of attitude towards programmed instruction through attitude towards physical science on achievement of secondary school boys in physical science is found to be significant in conventional group.
106. The indirect effect of achievement motivation through attitude towards physical science on achievement of secondary school boys in physical science is found to be significant in conventional group.
107. The direct effect of attitude towards physical science, attitude towards programmed instruction and

achievement motivation on achievement of secondary school girls in physical science is found to be significant in conventional group.

108. The direct effect of attitude towards physical science through attitude towards programmed instruction and achievement motivation on achievement of secondary school girls in physical science is found to be significant in conventional group.
109. The indirect effect of attitude towards programmed instruction through attitude towards physical science on achievement of secondary school girls in physical science is found to be significant in conventional group.
110. The indirect effect of achievement motivation through attitude towards physical science on achievement of secondary school girls in physical science is found to be significant in conventional group.
111. The direct effect of attitude towards programmed instruction and achievement motivation on achievement of secondary school boys in physical science is found to be significant in experimental group.
112. The direct effect of attitude towards physical science through attitude towards programmed instruction and achievement motivation on achievement of secondary school boys in physical science is found to be significant in experimental group.
113. The indirect effect of attitude towards programmed instruction through attitude towards physical science on achievement of secondary school boys in physical science is found to be significant in experimental group.
114. The indirect effect of achievement motivation through attitude towards physical science on achievement of secondary school boys in physical science is found to be significant in experimental group.
115. The direct effect of attitude towards physical science, attitude towards programmed instruction and

achievement motivation on achievement of secondary school girls in physical science is found to be significant in experimental group.

116. The direct effect of attitude towards physical science through attitude towards programmed instruction and achievement motivation on achievement of secondary school girls in physical science is found to be significant in experimental group.
117. The indirect effect of attitude towards programmed instruction through attitude towards physical science on achievement of secondary school girls in physical science is found to be significant in experimental group.
118. The indirect effect of achievement motivation through attitude towards physical science on achievement of secondary school girls in physical science is found to be significant in experimental group.

Educational Implications

The following are the educational implications of the present study.

1. Research evidence suggests that the Programmed Instruction (PI) improves the student performance in physical sciences, particularly if used in combination with the other techniques.
2. Immediate feedback helps the students verify their learning.
3. Self-pacing is possible, if the tutorial mode is used.
4. The higher cognitive abilities are achievable with the right mode.
5. Programmed instruction is more successful in critical sagacity (discerment) of the logic of various subjects and inspires the student in creative thinking and judgment making.
6. Good teachers are freed from the humdrum of routine class-room activity and they are in a position to devote their time to more creative activities.

7. Some educationists fear that the programmed instruction will deteriorate the quality of instruction. On the other hand, the use of it has improved the quality of education in general.
8. The use of programmed instruction has brought a revolution in the social setting of the classroom. Many emotional and social problems have been eliminated and problems of discipline have been automatically solved.
9. Programmed instruction is a great thrust in the direction of individualized instruction. A well-organized programmed instructional device is tailored to cater to the needs of individual students of the class.
10. Programmed instruction helps the teacher to diagnose the problems of the individual learner.
11. By presenting the material in small segments of information (i.e., in small frames), it makes the learning as an interesting game in which the learner is challenged by his own capabilities.

Suggestions for Further Research

1. It can be studied further as a big project to prepare planned programmed instruction for all the units of IX standard physical science in the form of Programmed Instruction Package.
2. It can be taken as a study to prepare planned programmed instruction for all the units of VIII, IX and X standards in physical science.
3. Similar studies can also be undertaken for other programmed instruction studies in languages, social sciences, general and applied sciences.
4. A comparative study of Programmed Instruction to the self study through the text may be undertaken.
5. A comparative study of Programmed Instruction for the self study may be undertaken.
6. Similar studies can be taken as a programme for vivid and individualistic approach of teaching different subjects at secondary school level.

7. Programmed Instruction can be converted into Data Base programmed in future.
8. In the modern scientific and technological age, more programmed instruction based packages can be developed through extensive educational research.
9. To create awareness among school students about the programmed instruction and its uses in teaching–learning process, research studies on programmed instruction may be taken up at all levels of education.

Bibliography

Aggarwal, J. C. (1996). *Essentials of Educational Technology*. New Delhi: Vikas Publishing House.

Aggarwal, J. C. (2003). Essentials of Educational Technology: Teaching Learning. New Delhi: Vikas Publishing House.

Wajiha, A. H. (2002). *Factors effecting Academic achievement of IX Std. Students in Mathematics*. Unpublished Ph.D. Thesis in Education, Karnatak University, Dharwad.

Ananth Krishnan, K. R. (1971). *Construction of programmed learning Material in Statistics for B.Ed. Students and Comparison of its Effectiveness with the Traditional Method of Teaching*. Unpublished M.Ed. Dissertation, Karnatak University, Dharwad.

Annett, J. (1994). *Programmed Learning*. London: Sweet and Maxwell.

Association for Educational Communications and Technology (1977). *Educational Technology: Definition and Glossary of Terms* (Vol.1). Washington, D.C.: Association for Educational Communications and Technology.

Best, J. W. (1989). *Research in Education*. New Delhi: Prentice Hall of India Private Ltd.

Bhagwat, S. A. (1992). *To prepare a package of divergent production type problems in mathematics and to study the effectiveness of the package against levels of intelligence and sex differences for standard VIII students in Pune City*. Unpublished Ph.D. Thesis in Education. Shrimati Nathibai Damodar Thackersey Women's University, Bombay.

Bialo, E. and Sivin, J. (1980). *Report on the effectiveness of Micro computers and schools*. Washington: Software Publishers Association.

Bigger, M. L. (1982). *Learning Theories for Teachers*. New York: Harper and Row.

Buch, M. B., Editor (1979). *Second Survey of Research in Education.* Baroda: The Society for Educational Research and Development.

Buch, M. B., Vhief Editor (1992). Fifth survey of Research in Education. New Delhi: NCERT.

Burns P. K. and Bozeman W.C. (1981). Computer Assisted Instruction and Mathematics achievement: Is there a Relationship. *Educational Technology*, 32-39.

Carpenter, Thomas P. and Lehrer, Richard (1996) Teaching and Learning Mathematics with understanding. *Psychological Abstracts*, 86(7), p-2896.

Chauhan, S. S. (1983). *Innovations in Educational Technology*. New Delhi: Sterling Publishers.

Christmann, E., Badgett, J. and Lucking, R. (1997). Progressive comparison of the effects of computer-assisted instruction on the academic achievement of secondary students. *Journal of Research on Computing in Education*, 29(4), 325-337.

Wener, C. (1973). The Principles of Programmed Learning in Relation to Behavioural Psychology. *Education*, Pp.66-77.

D' Souza Fiosy, C.R. (2000). *Computer assisted instruction (CAI) an effective strategy to individualized instruction.* Paper presented at second refresher course in education. Academic Staff College, University of Calicutta, Calcutta.

Dandapani C. *Dimensions of Effective teaching of Mathematics.* Unpublished Ph.D. Thesis in Education. Annamalai University, Annamalainagar.

Dasgupta, Dipti (1988). Teaching School Economics by the Personalized System of Instruction (PSI). New Delhi: *Fifth survey of Research in Education*, NCERT.

Dash, P.C. (1996). *Effects of Instructional Strategies on the Situation Process of Primary School Children in Arithmetical Problems.* Independent study. Bhubaneswar: Regional Institute of Education (DPEP Study).

Dececco, P. J. (1964). *Educational Technology: Readings in Programmed Instructions.* San Francisco: Halt Ranehart and Winston.

Dececco, J. B. (1977). *The Psychology of Learning and Instruction.* New Delhi: Prentice Hall of India Pvt. Ltd.

Dedeo, Michelle R. (2002) Improving Pass rates in Mathematics using interactive computer software. *Psychological Abstracts*, 89 (1).

Desai, K.V. (1988). An Investigation into efficacy of different instructional media in the teaching of science in the pupils of class VII and relation to certain variables. In Buch, *Fourth Survey of Research in Education*. New Delhi: NCERT.

Desmukh, V. (1997). *An Experiments in the use of Educational Technology for Teaching Mathematics Concepts. Textbook and Curriculum Research: Annual Research Report.* Pune: Maharashtra State Bureau of Text book Production and Curricula Research.

Devies, I. K. (1972). *Contributions to an Educational Technology.* London: Butterworth and Co. Ltd.

Dhamija, N. (1985). A Comparative study of the Effectiveness of three approaches of instructions – Conventional, Radio vision and modular approach on achievement of students in social studies. In Buch, *Fourth Survey of Research in Education*. New Delhi: NCERT.

Doshi, P.C. (1989). A Study of Achievement and Cognitive Preference Styles in Mathematics of Class X Students. In Buch, *Fifth Survey of Research in Education*. New Delhi: NCERT,

DSERT (2003). 9th Std. *Physical Science Text Book* (Kannada and English version). Bangalore: Directorate of Text Books.

Dunn, C.A. (2002). *An investigation of the effects of computer assisted reading instruction versus traditional reading instruction on selected high school freshmen.* Unpublished Dissertation, Loyola University, Chicago.

Durga Prasad, R. (1989), Programmed Instruction. *Educational India* (1), pp. 17-19.

Ebel, L. (1969). *Encyclopedia of Educational Research.* London: The Macmillan Company.

Edwards J, Norton, Tyalor. S., Weiss M. and Dusseldor, P.R. (1975). How effective is CAI? Review the Research. *Educational Leadership*, 33/2, pp.147-153.

Edwards, A.L. (1979). *Techniques of Attitude Scale Construction.* Bombay: Viakils, Feffer and Simons Ltd.

Ferguson, A. (1971). *Statistical Analysis in Psychology and Education.* New York: McGraw-Hill Book Co.

Garett, H.E. (1965). *Statistics in Psychology and Education.* Bombay: Vakils, Feffer and Simons Pvt. Ltd.

Goel, S.K. *(1996). A Study of Mathematical Language Needs of Students of Class I and II for Smooth Transaction from Concrete to Abstract Stage of Comprehension of Mathematics Teaching.* Independent study. Bhuvaneshwar: Regional Institute of Education, (DPEP Study).

Golani T.P. (1982). The use of AV-aids in the Secondary Schools of District. In Buch, *Third Survey of Research in Education.* New Delhi: NCERT.

Goldsmith, M. (1963). *Mechanization in the Classroom: An Introduction to Teaching Machines and Programmed Learning.* London: Souvenir Press.

Good, H.S. (1973). *Dictionary of Education.* New York: McGraw Hill Publishing Company Limited.

Guilford, J.P. (1954). *Psychometric Methods.* New Delhi: McGraw Hill Publishing Co. Ltd.

Hariharan, D. (1992). Attitude of High School Students towards Home Work and their Achievement in Physical Science. In Buch, *Fifth Survey of Research in Education.* New Delhi: NCERT.

Harneek, S. K. and Kaur, M. (1990), Achievement Motivation in Relation to Over and under Achievement in Science and Mathematics. *Journal of Experiments in Education*, XVIII (4), pp. 111-114

Hassan, M. M., and Amna, K. (1999), Sex differences in Science achievement across 10 Academic years among high school students in the United Arab Emirates. Psychological Abstracts, 86(9), p. 3725.

Hasselbring, T. (1984). *Effectiveness of Computer Based Instruction.* A Review Technical Report No. 84.1.3. Nashville, T.N.: George Peabody College for Teachers, Learning Technology Centre (Ed 262 754).

Hawley, D.E., Fletcher, J.D. and Piele, P.K. (1986). *Costs Effects and utility of Micro Computer Assisted Instruction.* Eugene. Oregon: University of Oregon.

Husen, T. (1988). *The International Encyclopedia of Education,* Sixth Volume. New York: Pergamon Press.

Huxford, D.E. (1999). *The Relative Efficacy of Computer Assisted Instruction.* Unpublished Thesis, West Virginia University.

Iyer, K.K. (1977). Some Factors Related to Achievement in Mathematics of Secondary School. In Buch, *Third Survey of Educational Research in Education.* New Delhi: NCERT.

Mohanty, J. (2003). *Modern Trends in Educational Technology.* Hyderabad: Neelkamal Publications, pp. 285-306.

Jeyamani. P. (1991). Effectiveness of the Simulation model of teaching through CAI. In Buch, *Fifth Survey of Educational Research in Education.* New Delhi: NCERT.

Joel. William J. (2002). A Problem solving based computer use for Non majors. *Psychological Abstracts,* 89, p. 375.

Singh, J. and Singh, K. (2003). *Computer Education.* Ludhiana: Tandon Publications.

John, L. and Manoharan, R. (2004). A Qualitative Analysis on diagnostic Assessment in effective teaching of Mathematics. *Edutracks,* pp. 8-10.

Joshi, V. (1987). A Study of the effectiveness of school television programmes in science at the secondary school level. In Buch, *Fifth Survey of Educational Research in Education.* New Delhi: NCERT.

Joshi, M. (1988). A study of the effect of Test anxiety and Intelligence on the performance of high school students in a segment of science, followed programmed instruction in linear and Branching styles. In Buch, *Fifth Survey of Educational Research in Education*. New Delhi: NCERT.

Kapadia, G. G. (1974). A Study of Relationship between Personality Variables and Achievement on Programmed Learning Material. *Quest in Education*, pp. 97-111.

Komoski, P. K. (1968). Technology and the Classroom. *Educational Leadership*, p. 736.

Kulkarni, L. R. (1981). *Construction and Evaluation of Programmed Learning material on Introduction and classification of organic compounds for Xth standard students*. Unpublished M.Ed. Dissertation, Karnatak University, Dharwad.

Kulkarni, S. S. (1982). *A Hand Book of Programmed Learning*. Baroda: T.A.P.L. Publication.

Kulkarni, S. S. (1970), The Psychology and Sociological Basis of Programmed Learning. *Journal of Education and Psychology*, pp. 27-31.

Kulkarni, S. S. (1982). *An Introduction to Programmed Instruction*. New Delhi: NCERT.

Kumari, S..K. (1972). *Development of Programmed Learning with Reference to a Unit of Physical Geography and Experimental Evaluation of its Effectiveness*. Unpublished M.Ed. Dissertation, Karnatak University, Dharwad.

Mahithi, S. (2001). *Free Computer Education Programme for High School Children of Karnataka*. New Delhi: DSERT.

Manager, T. (1996). Gender differences in Mathematical achievement at the Norwegian Elementary school level. *Psychological Abstracts*, 83(3), p. 1255.

Mangal S. K. (1988). General Psychology. New Delhi: Sterling Publishers.

Mangal S. K. (2006). *Teaching of Mathematics*. Ludhiana: Tandon Publications.

Mann, B.,S. (1981), An experimental study of the effect of unit tests on retention following programmed instruction material in a segment of physics. In Buch, *Third Survey of Research in Education*. New Delhi: NCERT.

Ediger, M. and Rao, Digumarti Bhaskara (2003). *Teaching Mathematics in Elementary Schools.* New Delhi: Discovery Publishing House.

Mary, K. B. (1977). *Construction of Programmed Learning Material in Magnetism for S.S.L.C. Students and Comparison of its Effectiveness with the Traditional Method of Teaching.* Unpublished M.Ed. Dissertation. Dharwad: Karnataka University.

Math, S. (1980). *Construction and Evaluation of Programmed Learning Material on Animal Tissue for VIII standard students.* Unpublished M.Ed. Dissertation, Karnatak University, Dharwad.

Mehta, J. M. (1985), Construction of different types of programmes on the unit of interest in Mathematics of Std. IX and study of relative efficiency of these. In Buch, *Fourth Survey of Research in Education.* New Delhi: NCERT.

Merchant, H. (1978). *The Construction and Evaluation of Programmed Modules for short course in Tropical Parasitology, Aspect of Educational Technology.* New York: Pitman Publishing House.

Mevarech, A. R. and Rich (1985), Effects of Computer Assisted Mathematical Instruction on disadvantaged pupils' cognitive and Affective development. *Journal of Educational Research,* 79(1) pp. 5-11.

Ministry of Human Resource Development (1986). *National Policy on Education.* New Delhi: Government of India

Ministry of Human Resource Development (1993). *Learning without Burden.* New Delhi. Government of India

Misra, C. H. K. (1970), Development of Programmed Material. Journal of Education and Psychology, pp. 14-18.

Mohanty, J. (1974), Educational Explosion and Educational Technology. *The Education Quarterly,* pp.-14.

Nagar, N. (1988). *Effectiveness of Computers in teaching Mathematics in schools.* Unpublished M.Phil. Dissertation. University of Delhi, Delhi.

Narayan, Shankara B.L. (1997), Achievement in mathematics under guided discovery learning an reception learning conditions. In Buch, *Fifth Survey of Educational Research in Education*. New Delhi: NCERT

Parameswaran, E. G. and Beena, C. (2004). *An Invitation to Psychology*. Hyderabad: Neelkamal Publications Pvt. Ltd.

Debasis, P. (1996), A Comparative study of Mathematical achievement of boys and girls at secondary level. *Journal of Centre for Pedagogical Studies in Mathematics*, pp. 6-8.

Passi, B.K. (1976). *Becoming Better Teacher.* Ahmadabad: Sahitya Mudranalaya.

Patel, A. S. (1970), Programmed Instruction: Its Psychological Basis and Evaluation. *Journal of Education and Psychology*, pp. 35-48.

Patel, I. J. (1972). *A Hand Book of Programmed Learning*. Baroda: Indian Association of Programmed Learning.

Perfect Practice Series (2011*). Mathematics-I, Work Books (Part-I and II) (Based on Karnataka State Syllabus*. Mumbai: Jeevan Deep Prakashan Pvt. Ltd.

Peterson, P.L. (1985), Effective Teaching Students Engagement in classroom Activities and Sex related Difference in Learning Mathematics. *American Educational Research Journal*, 22 (3).

Prabha, Rashmi (1992*). An Investigation in to the Effectiveness of Programmed Method in Relation to Some Socio-Academic Variables.* Unpublished Ph.D. Thesis in Education. Patna: University of Patna.

Raghavan, S.S. *Development of a training Package for teachers based on the Identification of Teaching-Learning difficulties in Mathematics in Class –I of Tamil-Nadu Schools.*

, Independent Study. Mysore: Regional Institute of Education. (DPEP Study).

Rajput, A. S. (1984). Study of Academic Achievement of Students in Mathematics in Relation to their Intelligence, Achievement Motivation and Socio Economic Status. In Buch, *Fifth Survey of Educational Research*. New Delhi: NCERT.

Rangaraj, K. R. (1997), Effectiveness of Computer assisted instruction in teaching physics at higher secondary stage. *Indian Educational Abstracts*, 4, pp. 47-48.

Rao, T. R. (1993). *A Comparative Study of Programmed Learning and Conventional Learning Methods Instruction of Mathematics – A Psychological Approach*. Unpublished Ph.D. Thesis in Education. Osmania University, Hyderabad.

Rapaport, P. and Savard, W. (1980). *CAI Topic Summary Report*. Portland.

Roberts, V. A. and Madhere, S. (1990). Chapter I *Resource Laboratory Programme for CAI* (1989-90). Evaluation report for the District of Columbia Public Schools, Washington, DC.

Rosaly, A. (1992). *The Relationship between Attitude of Students towards Mathematics and Achievement*. Unpublished M.Phil. Dissertation. Madurai Kamaraj University, Madurai.

Rose, Antony Stella, V. (1992). Effectiveness of CAI with special reference to under achievers. In Buch, *Fifth Survey of Educational Research*. New Delhi: NCERT.

Rupe, V. S. (1986). *A Study of CAI: Its Uses Effects, Advantages and Limitations*. South Bend IN: Indiana university.

Shah, G. B. (1973), A Conspectus of Studies in Programmed Learning. *Indian Educational Review*, pp. 79-97.

Shah, G. B. (1970), Developing Programmed Learning Courses in Colleges of Education. *Journal of Education and Psychology*, pp. 19-26.

Sharma, M. M. (1968). *A Comparative Study of the Outcome of Teaching Algebra by Conventional Classroom Methods and Programmed Instruction*. New Delhi: I.A.P.L.

Singh, M. (2004). *Modern Teaching of Mathematics*. New Delhi: Anmol Publications Pvt. Ltd.

Skinner, B. F. (1968). *Technology of Teaching*. New York: Appleton Century Crofts.

Srivastava, H. S. (1978), Trends in Examination Reforms in India. *NIE Journal*, VI, p. 17.

Sukhia, S. P. (1974). *Elements of Educational Research*. New Delhi: Allied Publishers Pvt. Ltd.

Traweak, M. W. (1964), Relationship between Personality Variables and Achievement through Programmed Instruction. *Journal of Educational Research*, 15, pp. 215-220.

Vanaja, M. and Rajashekhar, S. (2010). *Educational Technology and Computer Education*. Hyderabad: Neelkamal Publication Pvt. Ltd.

Varma, M. N. (1977). *The Effect of Schedules of Reinforcement and Extroversion on Programmed Instruction*. Unpublished Ph.D. Thesis in Education, University of Baroda, Baroda.

Vijayaratharaj, D. (1980). *Construction and Evaluation of a Programme on Kinds of Sets*. Unpublished M.Ed. Dissertation, Karnatak University, Dharwad.

Websites

http://www.npc.gov.np/introduction/ndc/index.jsp

http://arunmehta.freeyellow.com/page120.htm

www.ask.com

www.google.com

http://www.undp.org.in/programme/education/edusub.htm

http://www.lib.umd.edu/MCK/tesol.html

http://shikshanic.nic.in

www.infoline.com

Additional Reading

Bhaskara Rao, Digumarti (1994). *Scientific Aptitude*. New Delhi: Ashish Publishing House. ISBN 81-7024-658-X.

Bhaskara Rao, Digumarti (1995). *Animal Kingdom*. New Delhi: Discovery Publishing House. ISBN 81-7141-274-2.

Bhaskara Rao, Digumarti (1995). *Batracology*. New Delhi : Discovery Publishing House. ISBN 81-7141-279-3.

Bhaskara Rao, Digumarti (1997). *Scientific Attitude*. New Delhi: Discovery Publishing House. ISBN 81-7141-381-1.

Bhaskara Rao, Digumarti (1996). *Scientific Attitude vis-à-vis Scientific Aptitude.* New Delhi : Discovery Publishing House. ISBN 81-7141-308-0.

Bhaskara Rao, Digumarti (2004). *Scientific Attitude, Scientific Aptitude and Achievement.* New Delhi : Discovery Publishing House. ISBN 81-7141-781-7.

Bhaskara Rao, Digumarti (2004). *Educational Administration.* New Delhi : Discovery Publishing House. ISBN 81-7141-842-2.

Bhaskara Rao, Digumarti (2004). *Issues in School Education.* New Delhi : Discovery Publishing House. ISBN 81-8356-025-3.

Bhaskara Rao, Digumarti, editor (1996). *Encyclopaedia of Education For All,* 5 volumes. New Delhi : APH Publishing Corporation. ISBN 81-7024-759-4 (set).

Vol. I *Education For All : The World Conference.* ISBN 81-7024-760-8

Vol. II *Education For All : The EPA-9 Summit.* ISBN 81-7024-761-6

Vol. II *Education For All : Quality Education For All.* ISBN 81-7024-762-6.

Vol. IV *Education For All : Planning and Monitoring.* ISBN 81-7024-763-4.

Vol. V *Education For All : The Indian Scenario.* ISBN 81-7024-764-0.

Bhaskara Rao, Digumarti, editor (1999). *International Encyclopaedia of AIDS,* 11 volumes. New Delhi: Discovery Publishing House. ISBN 81-7141-522-6 (set).

Vol. 1 *Introduction to HIV/AIDS.* ISBN 81-7141-523-7.

Vol. 2 *HIV/AIDS – Issues and Challenges,* 2 parts. ISBN 81-7141-524-5.

Vol. 3 *HIV/AIDS – Socio Economic Realities.* ISBN 81-7141-524-3.

Vol. 4 *HIV/AIDS – Law Ethics and Human Rights,* 2 parts. ISBN 81-7141-526-1.

Vol. 5 *AIDS and NGOs.* ISBN 81-7141-527-X.

Vol. 6 *AIDS and Home Care*. ISBN 81-7141-528-8.

Vol. 7 *STD Case Management*. ISBN 81-7141-529-6.

Vol. 8 *HIV/AIDS Prevention and Care – Teaching Modules for Nurses and Midwives*. ISBN 81-7141-530-X.

Vol. 9 *HIV Prevention Education for Educational Institutions*. ISBN 81-7141-531-8.

Vol.10 *Instructional Modules for AIDS Education*. ISBN 81-7141-532-6.

Vol.11 *School Health Education to prevent AIDS and STD – A Package for Curriculum Planners*. ISBN 81-7141-533-4.

Bhaskara Rao, Digumarti, editor (2000). *International Encyclopaedia of Human Rights*, 7 volumes in 13 parts. New Delhi : Discovery Publishing House. ISBN 81-7141-567-9 (set).

Vol. 1 *International Instruments of Human Rights*, 2 parts. ISBN 81-7141-569-4.

Vol. 2 *Regional Instruments of Human Rights*. ISBN 81-7141-604-7.

Vol. 3 *Human Rights and the United Nations*, 2 parts. ISBN 81-7141-605-5.

Vol. 4 *Fact Files of Human Rights*, 3 parts. ISBN 81-7141-606-3.

Vol. 5 *Study Stories of Human Rights*, 3 parts. ISBN 81-7141-607-3.

Vol. 6 *International Meetings on Human Rights*, 2 parts. ISBN 81-714-608-X.

Vol. 7 *Professional Training in Human Rights*. ISBN 81-7141-609-8.

Bhaskara Rao, Digumarti, editor (2000). *International Encyclopaedia of Science and Technology Education*, 11 volumes. New Delhi : Discovery Publishing House. ISBN 81-7141-548-2 (set).

Vol. 1 *Science and Technology Education*. ISBN 81-7141-568-7.

Vol. 2 *Science Education in Developing Countries.* ISBN 81-7141-569-9.

Vol. 3 *Organizational Structure of Science.* ISBN 81-7141-570-9.

Vol. 4 *Science Education in Asia and the Pacific.* ISBN 81-7141-571-7

Vol. 5 *Science and Technology Education For All.* ISBN 81-7141-572-5.

Vol. 6 *Values, Ethics, Talent and Girls in Science and Technology Education.* ISBN 81-7141-573-3.

Vol. 7 *Popularization of Science and Technology Education.* ISBN 81-7141-574-1.

Vol. 8 *Science, Power and Society.* ISBN 81-7141- 575-X.

Vol. 9 *Information Technology.* ISBN 81-7141-576-8.

Vol.10 *Teacher Training in Science and Technology Education.* ISBN 81-7142-577-6.

Vol.11 *Teacher Training in Science and Technology : A Curriculum Framework.* ISBN 81-7141-578-4.

Bhaskara Rao, Digumarti, editor (2000). *Education For All : Achieving the Goal*, 3 volumes. New Delhi : APH Publishing Corporation. ISBN 81-7648-152-1 (set).

Vol. I *The Global Consensus.* ISBN 81-7648-155-6.

Vol. II *Mid-Decade Review Reports of Regional Seminars.* ISBN 81-7648-154-8.

Vol. III *Issues and Trends.* ISBN 81-7648-155-6.

Bhaskara Rao, Digumarti, editor (2004). *International Encyclopaedia of Learning to Live Together*, 4 volumes. New Delhi : Discovery Publishing House. ISBN 81-7141-848-1.

Vol. 1 *International Conference on Learning to Live Together.*

Vol. 2 *Globalization and Living Together.*

Vol. 3 *Curriculum for Learning to Live Together.*

Vol. 4 *Science Education for the Contemporary Society .*

Bhaskara Rao, Digumarti, editor (2005). *Encyclopaedia of Education For All*, 3 volumes. New Delhi : Discovery Publishing House. ISBN 81-7141-647-0 (set).

Bhaskara Rao, Digumarti, editor (2007). *Encyclopaedia of Teacher Education*, 4 volumes. New Delhi : Discovery Publishing House. ISBN 81-8356-306-6 (set).

Bhaskara Rao, Digumarti, editor (2007). *Encyclopaedia of Edeucation for Living Together*, 4 volumes. New Delhi : Discovery Publishing House. ISBN 81-7141-848-1 (set).

Bhaskara Rao, Digumarti, editor (1996). *National Policy on Education*, 2 volumes. New Delhi: Anmol Publications Pvt. Ltd. ISBN 81-7488-323-1.

Bhaskara Rao, Digumarti, editor (1996). *Global Perceptions on Peace Education*, 3 volumes. New Delhi : Discovery Publishing House. ISBN 81-7141-319-6.

Bhaskara Rao, Digumarti, editor (1997). *Education for the 21st Century.* New Delhi : Discovery Publishing House. ISBN 81-7141-389-7.

Bhaskara Rao, Digumarti, editor (1997). *Reflections on Scientific Attitude.* New Delhi : Discovery Publishing House. ISBN 81-7141-319-6.

Bhaskara Rao, Digumarti, editor (1997). *Success Story of a Primary Education Project.* New Delhi : APH Publishing Corporation. ISBN 81-7024-850-7

Bhaskara Rao, Digumarti, editor (1997). *World Food Summit.* New Delhi : Discovery Publishing House. ISBN 81-7141-386-2.

Bhaskara Rao, Digumarti, editor (1997). *Care the Child*, 2 volumes. New Delhi: Discovery Publishing House. ISBN 81-7141-394-3.

Bhaskara Rao, Digumarti, editor (1998). *Earth Summit*, 2 volumes. New Delhi : Discovery Publishing House. ISBN 81-7141-435-4.

Bhaskara Rao, Digumarti, editor (1998). *Adolescence Education.* New Delhi : Discovery Publishing House. ISBN 81-7141-432-X.

Bhaskara Rao, Digumarti, editor (1998). *Community and School Nutrition Education.* New Delhi : Discovery Publishing House. ISBN 81-7141-435-4.

Bhaskara Rao, Digumarti, editor (1998). *District Primary Education Programme.* New Delhi: Discovery Publishing House. ISBN 81-7141-396-X.

Bhaskara Rao, Digumarti, editor (1998). *National Policy on Education : Towards an Enlightened and Humane Society.* New Delhi : Discovery Publishing House. ISBN 81-7141-426-5.

Bhaskara Rao, Digumarti, editor (1998). *Reforming School Education.* New Delhi : Discovery Publishing House. ISBN 81-7141-403-6.

Bhaskara Rao, Digumarti, editor (1998). *Teacher Education in India.* New Delhi : Discovery Publishing House. ISBN 81-7141-406-0.

Bhaskara Rao, Digumarti, editor (1998). *World Summit for Social Development.* New Delhi : Discovery Publishing House. ISBN 81-7141-420-6.

Bhaskara Rao, Digumarti, editor (2001). *Nuclear Materials : Issues and Concerns,* 2 volumes. New Delhi : Discovery Publishing House. ISBN 81-7141-611-X.

Bhaskara Rao, Digumarti, editor (2001). *Distance Education in Different Countries.* New Delhi : APH Publishing Corporation. ISBN 81-7648-229-3.

Bhaskara Rao, Digumarti, editor (2001). *Decentralised Management of Education : Management of Education in Panchayati Raj and Municipal Bodies.* New Delhi : Discovery Publishing House. ISBN 81-7141-617-9.

Bhaskara Rao, Digumarti, editor (2001). *Electrochemistry for Environmental Protection.* New Delhi: Discovery Publishing House. ISBN 81-7141-619-5.

Bhaskara Rao, Digumarti, editor (2001). *Global Educational Studies.* New Delhi : Discovery Publishing House. ISBN 81-7141-616-0.

Bhaskara Rao, Digumarti, editor (2001). *Global Synthesis of Educational Assessment.* New Delhi : Discovery Publishing House. ISBN 81-7141-613-6.

Bhaskara Rao, Digumarti, editor (2001). *Jomtein Decade of Education.* New Delhi : Discovery Publishing House. ISBN 81-7141-618-7.

Bhaskara Rao, Digumarti, editor (2001). *World Conference on Education for All.* New Delhi: APH Publishing Corporation. ISBN 81-7141-274-9.

Bhaskara Rao, Digumarti, editor (2001). *World Conference on Higher Education.* New Delhi : Discovery Publishing House. ISBN 81-7141-610-1.

Bhaskara Rao, Digumarti, editor (2001). *World Conference on Science.* New Delhi : Discovery Publishing House. ISBN 81-7141-612-8.

Bhaskara Rao, Digumarti, editor (2003). *Inspiring Experiences in Teacher Education.* New Delhi : Discovery Publishing House. ISBN 81-7141-656-X.

Bhaskara Rao, Digumarti, editor (2003). *International Studies in Education,* 3 volumes. New Delhi : Discovery Publishing House. ISBN 81-7141-647-0.

Bhaskara Rao, Digumarti, editor (2003). *Military Conversion : Impact on Science and Technology.* New Delhi : Discovery Publishing House. ISBN 81-7141-578-4.

Bhaskara Rao, Digumarti, editor (2003). *United Nations Millennium Summit.* New Delhi : Discovery Publishing House. ISBN 81-7141-632-2.

Bhaskara Rao, Digumarti, editor (2003). *World Assembly on Aging.* New Delhi : Discovery Publishing House. ISBN 81-7141-637-3.

Bhaskara Rao, Digumarti, editor (2003). *World Conference on Human Rights.* New Delhi: Discovery Publishing House. ISBN 81-7141-661-6.

Bhaskara Rao, Digumarti, editor (2003). *World Education Forum.* New Delhi: Discovery Publishing House. ISBN 81-7141-639-X.

Bhaskara Rao, Digumarti, editor (2003). *Education, Employment and Human Resource Development.* New Delhi : Discovery Publishing House. ISBN 81-7141- 681-0.

Bhaskara Rao, Digumarti, editor (2003). *Successful Schooling.* New Delhi : Discovery Publishing House. ISBN 81-7141-677-2.

Bhaskara Rao, Digumarti, editor (2003). *European Education and Teachers.* New Delhi: Discovery Publishing House. ISBN 81-7141-702-7.

Bhaskara Rao, Digumarti, editor (2003). *Teachers in a Changing World.* New Delhi : Discovery Publishing House. ISBN 81-7141-694-2.

Bhaskara Rao, Digumarti, editor (2004). *International Guidelines on Open and Distance Teacher Education.* New Delhi: Discovery Publishing House. ISBN 81-7141-777-9.

Bhaskara Rao, Digumarti, editor (2004). *Adult Learning in the 21st Century.* New Delhi: Discovery Publishing House. ISBN 81-7141-797-3.

Bhaskara Rao, Digumarti, editor (2004). *Educational Practices : Research and Recommendations.* New Delhi: Discovery Publishing House. ISBN 81-7141-835-X

Bhaskara Rao, Digumarti, editor (2004). *General Secondary Education In the 21st Century.* New Delhi: Discovery Publishing House.

Bhaskara Rao, Digumarti, editor (2004). *Reforming Secondary Education.* New Delhi: Discovery Publishing House. ISBN 81-7141-843-0.

Bhaskara Rao, Digumarti, editor (2004). *Human Rights Education.* New Delhi : Discovery Publishing House. ISBN 81-7141-882-1.

Bhaskara Rao, Digumarti, editor (2004). *United Nations Decade for Human Rights Education.* New Delhi : Discovery Publishing House. ISBN 81-7141- 887-2.

Bhaskara Rao, Digumarti, editor (2004). *Technical and Vocational Education and Training in the 21st Century.* New Delhi : Discovery Publishing House. ISBN 81-7141- 984-4.

Bhaskara Rao, Digumarti, editor (2005). *Encyclopaedia of Education For All,* 3 volumes. New Delhi : Discovery Publishing House.

Bhaskara Rao, Digumarti, editor (2011). *Right to Education.* Hyderabad : Neel Kamal Publishers. ISBN 81-7648-470-9. 978-81-8316-284-5

Bhaskara Rao, Digumarti, editor (2011). *International Encyclopaedia of Educational Policies*. Hyderabad : Neel Kamal Publishers.

Bhaskara Rao, Digumarti, editor (2011). *International Encyclopaedia of Educational Practices*. Hyderabad : Neel Kamal Publishers.

Bhaskara Rao, Digumarti and B.S.V. Dutt, editors (2003). *Education : Programmes and Policies*. New Delhi : APH Publishing Corporation. ISBN 81-7648-470-9.

Bhaskara Rao, Digumarti, C.A.P. Swamy and B.S.V. Dutt (1997). *Self-Evaluation in Student Teaching*. New Delhi : Discovery Publishing House. ISBN 81-7141-374-9.

Bhaskara Rao, Digumarti and C. D. Swarna Lattha, editors (2006). *Encyclopaedia of Biotechnology*, 5 volumes. New Delhi : Discovery Publishing House. ISBN 81-8356-168-3 (set).

Bhaskara Rao, Digumarti, C. Sridevi and K. Vijaya (1995). *Achievement in Social Studies*. New Delhi: Discovery Publishing House. ISBN 81-7141-281-5.

Bhaskara Rao, Digumarti and D. Naresh Kumar (2004). *School Teacher Effectiveness*. New Delhi : Discovery Publishing House. ISBN 81-7141-

Bhaskara Rao, Digumarti and D. Sridhar (2002). *Job Satisfaction of School Teachers*. New Delhi : Discovery Publishing House. ISBN 81-7141-652-7.

Bhaskara Rao, Digumarti and Digumarti Pushpa Latha, editors (1998). *International Encyclopaedia of Women*, 5 volumes. New Delhi : Discovery Publishing House. ISBN 81-7141-410-9 (set).

Vol. 1 *Status of World's Women*. ISBN 81-7141- 494-X.

Vol. 2 *Women, Education and Empowerment*. ISBN 81-7141-498-1.

Vol. 3 *Women Challenges and Advancement*. ISBN 81-7141-497-4.

Vol. 4 *Women and Family Health*. ISBN 81-7141- 497-4.

Vol. 5 *Women and International Action*. ISBN 81-7141-498-2.

Bhaskara Rao, Digumarti and Digumarti Pushpa Latha (1994). *Achievement in Biology.* New Delhi : Discovery Publishing House. ISBN 81-7141-264-5.

Bhaskara Rao, Digumarti and Digumarti Pushpa Latha (1995). *Achievement in English.* New Delhi : Discovery Publishing House. ISBN 81-7141-283-1.

Bhaskara Rao, Digumarti and Digumarti Pushpa Latha (1994). *Achievement in Science.* New Delhi : Discovery Publishing House. ISBN 81-7141-280-70.

Bhaskara Rao, Digumarti and Digumarti Pushpa Latha (1995). *Achievement in Mathematics.* New Delhi : Discovery Publishing House. ISBN 81-7141-278-5.

Bhaskara Rao, Digumarti and Digumarti Pushpa Latha (2004). *Education for Women.* New Delhi : Discovery Publishing House. ISBN 81-7141-873-2.

Bhaskara Rao, Digumarti, Digumarti Pushpa Latha and Digumarthi Harshitha, editors (2001). *Biological Warfare.* New Delhi: Discovery Publishing House. ISBN 81-7141-597-0.

Bhaskara Rao, Digumarti, Digumarti Pushpa Latha and Digumarthi Harshitha, editors (2001). *Women as Educators.* New Delhi: Discovery Publishing House. ISBN 81-7141-602-0.

Bhaskara Rao, Digumarti and Digumarthi Harshitha (2004). *Adjustment of Adolescents.* New Delhi: APH Publishing House. ISBN 81-7648-836-8.

Bhaskara Rao, Digumarti and Digumarthi Harshitha, editors (2001). *Education in India.* New Delhi: APH Publishing House. ISBN 81-7648-207-2.

Bhaskara Rao, Digumarti, Digumarti Pushpa Latha and Digumarthi Harshitha, editors (2001). *Assessing Learning Achievement.* New Delhi : Discovery Publishing House. ISBN 81-7141-601-2.

Bhaskara Rao, Digumarti, Digumarti Pushpa Latha and Digumarthi Harshitha, editors (2001). *Energy Security.* New Delhi : Discovery Publishing House. ISBN 81-7141-598-9.

Bhaskara Rao, Digumarti, Digumarthi Harshitha and K.R.S. Sambasiva Rao, editors (1999). *Advanced Biotechnology.* New Delhi : Discovery Publishing House. ISBN 81-7141-516-4.

Bhaskara Rao, Digumarti and K.R.S. Sambasiva Rao, editors (1996). *Current Trends in Indian Education.* New Delhi : Discovery Publishing House. ISBN 81-7141-311-0.

Bhaskara Rao, Digumarti and D. Naresh Kumar (2004). *School Teacher Effectiveness.* New Delhi : Discovery Publishing House. ISBN 81-7141-782-5.

Bhaskara Rao, Digumarti and E. Sreekanth Babu (2004). *Educational Interests of School Students.* New Delhi : Discovery Publishing House. ISBN 81-7141-837-6.

Bhaskara Rao, Digumarti and K. Vijaya (1995). *A Text Book Evaluation.* Ambala Cantt : The Associated Publishers.

Bhaskara Rao, Digumarti and M.A. Fayaz (2004). *Problems of Primary School Drop-outs.* New Delhi : Discovery Publishing House. ISBN 81-7141- 834-1.

Bhaskara Rao, Digumarti and N.V.M. Mohana Rao (2002). *Problems of Mentally Handicapped Children.* New Delhi : Discovery Publishing House. ISBN 81-7141- 645-4.

Bhaskara Rao, Digumarti and S. Chandra Mohan (2002). *Sports Management.* New Delhi : APH Publishing House. ISBN 81-7648-467-9.

Bhaskara Rao, Digumarti and S.A. Khader (2004). *Problems of Private School Teachers.* New Delhi : Discovery Publishing Corporation. ISBN 81-7141-838-4.

Bhaskara Rao, Digumarti and S.A. Khader (2004). *School Education in India.* New Delhi : Discovery Publishing Corporation. ISBN 81-7141-849-X.

Bhaskara Rao, Digumarti and Sk. Johni Basha (2004). *Teachers' Population Education Awareness.* New Delhi : Discovery Publishing House. ISBN 81-7141-832-5.

Bhaskara Rao, Digumarti, V.V. Rao, V.V. Lakshmi and V.V. Krishna, editors (1999). *Status and Advancement of Women.* New Delhi: APH Publishing Corporation. ISBN 81-7648-169-6.

Appala Naidu, P.Ch., author and Digumarti Bhaskara Rao, editor (2007). *Student Feedback Methods.* New Delhi : Discovery Publishing House.

Babu, P.C., author and Digumarti Bhaskara Rao, editor (2004). *Flowers of Wisdom.* New Delhi : Discovery Publishing House. ISBN 81-7141-695-0.

Babu, P.C., author and Digumarti Bhaskara Rao, editor (2008). *Worlds of Wisdom.* New Delhi: Discovery Publishing House.

Bujji Babu, K., author and Digumarti Bhaskara Rao, editor (2007). *Teaching Aptitude of Primary School Teachers.* New Delhi: Sonali Publications. ISBN 81-8411-083-9.

Amala, P. A. and Anupama, P., authors and Digumarti Bhaskara Rao, editor (2004). *History of Education.* New Delhi: Discovery Publishing House. ISBN 81-7141-860-0.

Bhagya Lakshmi, L., author and Digumarti Bhaskara Rao, editor (2000). *Reading and Comprehension.* New Delhi : Discovery Publishing House. ISBN 81-7141-543-1.

Bhasha, S.A., author and Digumarti Bhaskara Rao, editor (2004). *Methods of Teaching Geography.* New Delhi : Discovery Publishing House. ISBN 81-7141-807-4.

Bhuvaneswara Lakshmi, Gadde, author and Digumarti Bhaskara Rao, editor(2000). *Attitude Towards Science.* New Delhi : Discovery Publishing House. ISBN 81-7141-541-6.

Bhuvaneswara Lakshmi, G., author and Digumarti Bhaskara Rao, editor (2004). *Methods of Teaching Life Science.* New Delhi : Discovery Publishing House. ISBN 81-7141-804-X.

Bhuvaneswara Lakshmi, G. and K. Subba Rao, authors and Digumarti Bhaskara Rao, editor (2004). *Methods of Teaching Biology.* New Delhi : Discovery Publishing House. ISBN 81-7141-914-3.

Chary, K.V.N.B., author and Digumarti Bhaskara Rao, editor (2006). *Techniques of Teaching Physics.* New Delhi : Sonali Publications. ISBN 81-8411-046-4.

Chowdary, S.B.J.R. and Naga Raju, authors and Digumarti Bhaskara Rao, editor (2004). *Mastery of Teaching Skills.* New Delhi : Discovery Publishing House.

Dayakara Reddy, V. and Digumarti Bhaskara Rao, editors (2006). *Value-Oriented Education.* New Delhi : Discovery Publishing House.

Devraj, T.A.S., author and Digumarti Bhaskara Rao, editor (1997). *Trace Analysis of Uranium and Thorium.* New Delhi : Discovery Publishing House. ISBN 81-7141-375-7.

Durga Rani, K., author and Digumarti Bhaskara Rao, editor (2000). *Educational Aspirations and Scientific Attitudes.* New Delhi : Discovery Publishing House. ISBN 81-7141-555-5.

Dutt, B.S.V. and Digumarti Bhaskara Rao (2001). *Empowering Primary Teachers.* New Delhi : Discovery Publishing House. ISBN 81-7141-615-2.

Dutt, B.S.V., author and Digumarti Bhaskara Rao, editor (2004). *Comparative Education.* New Delhi: Discovery Publishing House. ISBN 81-7141-912-7.

Ediger, Marlow and Digumarti Bhaskara Rao, editors (2006). *Encyclopaedia of School Education,* 5 volumes. New Delhi : Discovery Publishing House. ISBN 81-8356-308-2 (set).

Ediger, Marlow and Digumarti Bhaskara Rao, editors (2006). *Encyclopaedia of School Administration,* 4 volumes. New Delhi: Discovery Publishing House. ISBN 81-8356-307-4 (set).

Ediger, Marlow and Digumarti Bhaskara Rao, editors (2007). *Encyclopaedia of School Curriculum,* 10 volumes. New Delhi: Discovery Publishing House. ISBN 81-8356-305-8 (set).

Ediger, Marlow and Digumarti Bhaskara Rao, editors (2007). *Encyclopaedia of Teaching,* 8 volumes. New Delhi : Discovery Publishing House. ISBN 81-8356-305-8 (set).

Marlow Ediger and Digumarti Bhaskara Rao, editors (2006). *Encyclopaedia of School Education,* 5 volumes. New Delhi : Discovery Publishing House. ISBN 81-8356-308-2 (set).

Marlow Ediger and Digumarti Bhaskara Rao, editors (2006). *Encyclopaedia of School Administration,* 4 volumes. New Delhi: Discovery Publishing House. ISBN 81-8356-307-4 (set).

Marlow Ediger and Digumarti Bhaskara Rao, editors (2007). *Encyclopaedia of School Curriculum*, 10 volumes. New Delhi : Discovery Publishing House. ISBN 81-8356-305-8 (set).

Marlow Ediger and Digumarti Bhaskara Rao, editors (2007). *Encyclopaedia of Teaching*, 8 volumes. New Delhi : Discovery Publishing House. ISBN 81-8356-305-8 (set).

Ediger, Marlow and Digumarti Bhaskara Rao (1996). *Science Curriculum*. New Delhi: Discovery Publishing House. ISBN 81-7141-321-8.

Ediger, Marlow and Digumarti Bhaskara Rao (2000). *Teaching Mathematics Successfully*. New Delhi : Discovery Publishing House. ISBN 81-7141-552-0.

Ediger, Marlow and Digumarti Bhaskara Rao (2001). *Teaching Science Successfully*. New Delhi : Discovery Publishing House. ISBN 81-7141-600-4.

Ediger, Marlow and Digumarti Bhaskara Rao (2001). *Teaching Social Studies Successfully*. New Delhi : Discovery Publishing House. ISBN 81-7141-596-2.

Ediger, Marlow and Digumarti Bhaskara Rao (2002). *Philosophy and Curriculum*. New Delhi: Discovery Publishing House. ISBN 81-7141-631-4.

Ediger, Marlow and Digumarti Bhaskara Rao (2002). *Improving School Administration*. New Delhi : Discovery Publishing House. ISBN 81-7141-633-0

Ediger, Marlow and Digumarti Bhaskara Rao (2002). *Elementary Curriculum*. New Delhi : Discovery Publishing House. ISBN 81-7141-658-6.

Ediger, Marlow and Digumarti Bhaskara Rao (2003). *Language Arts Curriculum*. New Delhi : Discovery Publishing House. ISBN 81-7141-657-8.

Ediger, Marlow and Digumarti Bhaskara Rao (2003). *Psychology and Curriculum*. New Delhi : Discovery Publishing House. ISBN 81-7141-691-8.

Ediger, Marlow and Digumarti Bhaskara Rao (2003). *Teaching Language Arts Successfully*. New Delhi : Discovery Publishing House. ISBN 81-7141-

Ediger, Marlow and Digumarti Bhaskara Rao (2003). *School Curriculum and Administration.* New Delhi : Discovery Publishing House. ISBN 81-7141-709-4.

Ediger, Marlow and Digumarti Bhaskara Rao (2003). *Teaching Mathematics in Elementary Schools.* New Delhi : Discovery Publishing House. ISBN 81-7141-687-X.

Ediger, Marlow and Digumarti Bhaskara Rao (2003). *Teaching Science in Elementary Schools.* New Delhi: Discovery Publishing House. ISBN 81-7141-698-5.

Ediger, Marlow and Digumarti Bhaskara Rao (2003). *School Curriculum and Administration.* New Delhi : Discovery Publishing House. ISBN 81-7141-709-4.

Ediger, Marlow and Digumarti Bhaskara Rao (2003). *Elementary Curriculum Improvement.* New Delhi : Discovery Publishing House. ISBN 81-7141-740-X.

Ediger, Marlow and Digumarti Bhaskara Rao (2004). *School Organisation.* New Delhi : Discovery Publishing House. ISBN 81-7141-843-0.

Ediger, Marlow and Digumarti Bhaskara Rao (2004). *Relevancy in Elementary Curriculum.* New Delhi : Discovery Publishing House. ISBN 81-7141-845-9.

Ediger, Marlow and Digumarti Bhaskara Rao (2005). *Quality School Education.* New Delhi : Discovery Publishing House. ISBN 81-8356-022-9.

Ediger, Marlow and Digumarti Bhaskara Rao (2006). *Successful School Education.* New Delhi : Discovery Publishing House. ISBN 81-8356-054-7.

Ediger, Marlow and Digumarti Bhaskara Rao (2006). *Successful School Administration.* New Delhi : Discovery Publishing House. ISBN 81-8356-046-6.

Ediger, Marlow and Digumarti Bhaskara Rao (2006). *Issues in School Curruculum.* New Delhi : Discovery Publishing House. ISBN 81-8356-052-0.

Ediger, Marlow and Digumarti Bhaskara Rao (2006). *Community College – Curriculum and Teaching.* New Delhi : Discovery Publishing House. ISBN 81-8356-053-9.

... Marlow and Digumarti Bhaskara Rao (2006). *...ministration of Schools.* New Delhi : Discovery Publishing H... use.

Ediger, Marlow and Digumarti Bhaskara Rao (2006). *Reading Curriculum and Instruction.* New Delhi : Discovery Publishing House.

Ediger, Marlow and Digumarti Bhaskara Rao (2006). *Curriculum Organisation.* New Delhi: Discovery Publishing House.

Ediger, Marlow and Digumarti Bhaskara Rao (2006). *Curriculum of School Subjects.* New Delhi : Discovery Publishing House.

Ediger, Marlow, B.S.V. Dutt and Digumarti Bhaskara Rao (2003). *Teaching English Successfully.* New Delhi : Discovery Publishing House. ISBN 81-7141-707-8.

Ediger, Marlow and Digumarti Bhaskara Rao (2007). *School Science Education.* New Delhi : Discovery Publishing House. ISBN 81-8356-352-X.

Ediger, Marlow and Digumarti Bhaskara Rao (2007). *Language Arts Education.* New Delhi : Discovery Publishing House. ISBN 81-8356-333-3.

Ediger, Marlow and Digumarti Bhaskara Rao (2010). *Effective Schooling.* New Delhi : Discovery Publishing House. ISBN 978-81-8356-613-1.

Ediger, Marlow and Digumarti Bhaskara Rao (2010). *Effective School Curriculum.* New Delhi : Discovery Publishing House. ISBN 978-81-8356-585-1.

Ediger, Marlow and Digumarti Bhaskara Rao (2010). *Essays on Teaching Science.* New Delhi : Discovery Publishing House.

Ediger, Marlow and Digumarti Bhaskara Rao (2010). *Essays on Teaching Social Studies.* New Delhi : Discovery Publishing House.

Ediger, Marlow and Digumarti Bhaskara Rao (2010). *Essays on Teaching Reading.* New Delhi : Discovery Publishing House

Ediger, Marlow and Digumarti Bhaskara Rao (2010). *Essays on Teaching Mathematics.* New Delhi : Discovery Publishing House.

Ediger, Marlow and Digumarti Bhaskara Rao (2010). *Essays on Teaching.* New Delhi : Discovery Publishing House.

Elizabeth, M.E.S., author and Digumarti Bhaskara Rao, editor (2004). *Methods of Teaching English.* New Delhi : Discovery Publishing House. ISBN 81-7141-809-0.

Elizabeth, M.E.S., author and Digumarti Bhaskara Rao, editor (2004). *Acquisition of English Vocabulary.* New Delhi : Discovery Publishing House. ISBN 81-7141- .

Fatima, Sk. author and Digumarti Bhaskara Rao, editor (2007). *Reasoning Ability of School Students.* New Delhi : Discovery Publishing House. ISBN 81-8356-330-9.

Fatima, Sk. and Digumarti Bhaskara Rao (2008). *Reasoning Ability of Adolescent Students.* New Delhi : Sonali Publications.

Gopala Krishna, M., author and Digumarti Bhaskara Rao, editor (2007). *Techniques of Teaching Physical Education.* New Delhi : Sonali Publications. ISBN 81-8411-044-8.

Gopala Krishna, M., author and Digumarti Bhaskara Rao, editor (2007). *Techniques of Teaching Education.* New Delhi : Sonali Publications. ISBN 81-8411-062-6.

Harshitha, Digumarthi, author and Digumarti Bhaskara Rao, editor (2004). *Methods of Teaching Information Technology.* New Delhi : Discovery Publishing House. ISBN 81-7141-805-8.

Harshitha, Digumarthi, author and Digumarti Bhaskara Rao, editor (2007). *Techniques of Teaching Computer Science.* New Delhi : Sonali Publications. ISBN 81-8411-036-7.

Indira Devi, author and J. Prasanth Kumar and Digumarti Bhaskara Rao, editors (2004). *Values in Language Text Books.* New Delhi : APH Publishing Corporation. ISBN 81-7648-

Jalaja Kumari, C., author and Digumarti Bhaskara Rao, editor (2004). *Methods of Teaching Educational Technology.* New Delhi: Discovery Publishing House. ISBN 81-7141-810-4.

Jalaja Kumari, C., author and Digumarti Bhaskara Rao, editor (2007). *Job Satisfaction of Teachers.* New Delhi : Discovery Publishing House.

Janardhan Reddy, B., author and Digumarti Bhaskara Rao, editor (2006). *Techniques of Teaching Sociology.* New Delhi : Sonali Publications. ISBN 81-8411-042-1.

Jayasree, K., author and Digumarti Bhaskara Rao, editor (1999). *Correlates of Socialisation.* New Delhi : Discovery Publishing House. ISBN 81-7141-517-2.

Jayasree, K., author and Digumarti Bhaskara Rao, editor (2004). *Methods of Teaching Science.* New Delhi : Discovery Publishing House. ISBN 81-7141-801-5.

John Babu, C., author and T.J.R. Prasad, G.M. Madhukar and Digumarti Bhaskara Rao, editors (2004). *Problem Solving in Mathematics.* New Delhi : APH Publishing Corporation. ISBN 81-7648-273-0.

Joseph Raju, B and G.A. Anitha, authors and Digumarti Bhaskara Rao, editor (2004). *Population Education.* New Delhi : Sonali Publications. ISBN 81-88836-31-3.

Jyosthana, M., author and Digumarti Bhaskara Rao, editor (2011). *Achievement Motivation and Achievement in English of School Students.* New Delhi : Discovery Publishing House.

Lalitha, T., author and K.S. Prabhakaram, D.S.N. Sastry and Digumarti Bhaskara Rao, editors (2004). *Educational Philosophic Beliefs.* New Delhi: Discovery Publishing House. ISBN 81-7141-765-5.

Krishna, G., author and Digumarti Bhaskara Rao, editor (2006). *Techniques of Teaching Physical Education.* New Delhi : Discovery Publishing House. ISBN 81-8411-044-8.

Kumar Raja, G., author and Digumarti Bhaskara Rao, editor (2007). *Principles of Primary School.* New Delhi : Sonali Publications. ISBN 81-8411-054-5.

Lakshmi Kumari, V., author and Digumarti Bhaskara Rao, editor (2006). *Techniques of Teaching Home Science.* New Delhi : Discovery Publishing House. ISBN 81-8411-048-0.

Madhava, K., author and Digumarti Bhaskara Rao, editor (2008). *Personality of Adolescent Students.* New Delhi: Sonali Publications.

Madhu Bala, Jampala, author and Digumarti Bhaskara Rao, editor (2004). *Methods of Teaching Exceptional Children.* New Delhi: Discovery Publishing House. ISBN 81-7141-802-3.

Mallikarjuna Reddy, V., author and Digumarti Bhaskara Rao, editor (2011). *Teaching Aptitude, Social Adjustment and Job Satisfaction of Science Teachers.* New Delhi: Discovery Publishing House.

Mallikarjun C. Kankatte., author and Digumarti Bhaskara Rao, editor (2012). *Effectiveness of Programmed Instruction.* New Delhi: Discovery Publishing House.

Marja, Talvi and Digumarti Bhaskara Rao, editors (1996). *Educational Leadership and Social Changes.* New Delhi : Discovery Publishing House. ISBN 81-7141-320-X.

Naga Kumari, U., author and Digumarti Bhaskara Rao, editor (2008). *Science Process Skills of School Students.* New Delhi : Sonali Publications.

Nageswara Rao, S. and M. Srihari, authors and Digumarti Bhaskara Rao, editor (2004). *Guidance and Counselling.* New Delhi : Discovery Publishing House. ISBN 81-7141-840-6.

Nageswara Rao, S., author and Digumarti Bhaskara Rao, editor (2006). *Techniques of Teaching Psychology.* New Delhi : Discovery Publishing House. ISBN 81-8411-040-5.

Nageswara Rao, S. and P. Sridhar, authors and Digumarti Bhaskara Rao, editor (2004). *Methods and Techniques of Teaching.* New Delhi : Sonali Publications. ISBN 81-88836-33-8.

Nirmala Jyothi, M., author and Digumarti Bhaskara Rao, editor (2003). *Non-detention System in School Education.* New Delhi : Discovery Publishing House. ISBN 81-7141-654-3.

Padma Tulasi, G., author and Digumarti Bhaskara Rao, editor (2004). *Methods of Teaching Elementary Science.* New Delhi : Discovery Publishing House. ISBN 81-7141-871-6.

Pala Prasada Rao, V., author and K. N. Rani and D. Bhaskara Rao, editors (2004). *India Pakistan : Partition Perspectives in Indo English Novels.* New Delhi: Discovery Publishing House. ISBN 81-7141-871-6.

Pala Prasada Rao, V., author and D. Bhaskara Rao, editors (2008). *Functioning of Autonomous Colleges.* New Delhi : Sonali Publications.

Pitchi Reddy, M., author and Digumarti Bhaskara Rao, editor (2007). *Techniques of Teaching Social Sciences.* New Delhi : Sonali Publications. ISBN 81-8411-066-X.

Prasad Babu, B., author and P. Madhu and Digumarti Bhaskara Rao, editors (2006). *Psychological Adjustment and Well-being.* New Delhi: Discovery Publishing House. ISBN 81-8356-204-3.

Prasad Babu, B., author and M.V.R. Raju and Digumarti Bhaskara Rao, editors (2006). *Behavioural Problems of School Children.* New Delhi: Discovery Publishing House. ISBN 81-8356-206-X.

Prabhakaram, K.S., author and Digumarti Bhaskara Rao, editors (1998). *Concept Attainment Model in Mathematics Teaching.* New Delhi : Discovery Publishing House. ISBN 81-7141-424-9.

Prasanth Kumar, J., author and Digumarti Bhaskara Rao, editor (1998). *Effectiveness of Distance Education System.* New Delhi: Discovery Publishing House. ISBN 81-7141-437-0.

Prasanth Kumar, J., author and Digumarti Bhaskara Rao, editor (2004). *Methods of Teaching Civics.* New Delhi : Discovery Publishing House. ISBN 81-7141-806-6.

Prasanth Kumar, J., author and G. Sundara Rao and Digumarti Bhaskara Rao, editors (2000). *Open University Student Support Services.* New Delhi : Discovery Publishing House. ISBN 81-7141-550-4.

Raja Kumari, M.A. and D.R.S. Sundari, authors and Digumarti Bhaskara Rao, editor (2004). *Special Education.* New Delhi: Discovery Publishing House. ISBN 81-7141-846-5.

Raja Kumari, M.A. and D.R.S. Sundari, authors and Digumarti Bhaskara Rao, editor (2004). *Methods of Teaching Educational Psychology.* New Delhi : Discovery Publishing House. ISBN 81-7141-

Ramatulasamma, K., author and Digumarti Bhaskara Rao, editor (2002). *Job Satisfaction of Teacher Educators.* New Delhi: Discovery Publishing House. ISBN 81-7141-655-1.

Rama Krishnaiah, D., author and Digumarti Bhaskara Rao, editor (1998). *Job Satisfaction of College Teachers.* New Delhi: Discovery Publishing House. ISBN 81-7141-438-9.

Rama Kumar Ratnam, M.V., author and Digumarti Bhaskara Rao, editor (1998). *Dukkha : Suffering in Early Buddhism.* New Delhi: Discovery Publishing House. ISBN 81-7141-653-5.

Rama Krishna Prasad and P. Vide Sagar, authors and Digumarti Bhaskara Rao, editor (2004). *Methods of Teaching Physical Education.* New Delhi : Discovery Publishing House.

Rama Seshaiah, P. author and Digumarti Bhaskara Rao, editor (2004). *Methods of Teaching Home Science.* New Delhi : Discovery Publishing House. ISBN 81-7141-916-X.

Rama Swamy, K., author and Digumarti Bhaskara Rao, editor (2007). *Techniques of Teaching Environmental Science.* New Delhi : Sonali Publications. ISBN 81-8411-035-9.

Ramesh, A.R., author and Digumarti Bhaskara Rao, editor (2006). *Techniques of Teaching Commerce.* New Delhi : Sonali Publications. ISBN 81-8411-043-X.

Ramesh, Ghanta and Digumarti Bhaskara Rao, editors (1998). *Environmental Education : Problems and Prospects.* New Delhi: Discovery Publishing House. ISBN 81-7141-423-0.

Ranga Rao, B., author and Digumarti Bhaskara Rao, editor (2007). *Techniques of Teaching Economics.* New Delhi : Sonali Publications. ISBN 81-8411-056-1..

Ranga Rao, R., author and Digumarti Bhaskara Rao, editor (2004). *Methods of Teacher Teaching.* New Delhi : Discovery Publishing House. ISBN 81-7141-812-0.

Rani, S.S., author and Digumarti Bhaskara Rao, editor (2006). *Techniques of Teaching Botany.* New Delhi : Discovery Publishing House. ISBN 81-8411-037-5.

Rathaiah, Lavu and Digumarti Bhaskara Rao, editors (1996), *International Innovations in Education.* New Delhi : Discovery Publishing House. ISBN 81-7141-359-5.

Rathaiah, Lavu and Digumarti Bhaskara Rao (1997). *Achievement Correlates.* New Delhi: Discovery Publishing House. ISBN 81-7141- 385-4.

Ravi Krishna, M., author and Digumarti Bhaskara Rao, editor (2004). *Examination System.* New Delhi : Discovery Publishing House. ISBN 81-7141-824-4.

Ravi Kumar, M., author and Digumarti Bhaskara Rao, editor (2004). *Methods of Teaching Computer Science.* New Delhi : Discovery Publishing House. ISBN 81-7141-823-6.

Rudramamba, B., author and Digumarti Bhaskara Rao, editor (2003). *Problems of Teaching.* New Delhi : APH Publishing Corporation. ISBN 81-7648-462-8.

Rudramamba, B. and V. Lakshmi Kumari, authors and Digumarti Bhaskara Rao, editor (2004). *Methods of Teaching Economics.* New Delhi : Discovery Publishing House. ISBN 81-7141-900-3.

Sambasiva Rao, P., author and Digumarti Bhaskara Rao, editor (2007). *Techniques of Teaching Psychology.* New Delhi : Sonali Publications. ISBN 81-8411-040-5.

Sanjeeva Rao, P.C., author and Digumarti Bhaskara Rao, editor (1996). *A Text Book of Geology.* New Delhi : Discovery Publishing House. ISBN 81-7141-313-7.

Santhanam, T., B. Prasad Babu and S. Sugandhi, authors and Digumarti Bhaskara Rao, editor (2007). *Children with Learning Disabilities.* New Delhi : Sonali Publications. ISBN 81-8411-077-4.

Santhanam, T., B. Prasad Babu and S. Sugandhi, authors and Digumarti Bhaskara Rao, editor (2008). *Learning Disabilities and Remedial Programmes.* New Delhi : Discovery Publishing House.

Sarala, M.M.O., author and Digumarti Bhaskara Rao, editor (2006). *Techniques of Teaching English.* New Delhi : Sonali Publications. ISBN 81-8411-047-2.

Satya Narayana, G., author and Digumarti Bhaskara Rao, editor (2008). *Attitude towards Social Studies and Achievement in Social Studies.* New Delhi : Sonali Publications.

Satya Narayana, V., author and Digumarti Bhaskara Rao, editor (2001). *Physical Education, Social Attitudes and Leadership Qualities.* New Delhi : Discovery Publishing House. ISBN 81-7141-593-8.

Satya Narayana, P.V.V. and G. Krishna, authors and Digumarti Bhaskara Rao, editor (2004). *Curriculum Development and Management.* New Delhi : Discovery Publishing House. ISBN 81-7141-813-9.

Shamsuddin, Sk. and V. Dayakara Reddy, authors and Digumarti Bhaskara Rao, editor (2007). *Academic Achievement and Values.* New Delhi : Discovery Publishing House.

Singh, Y.C., author and Digumarti Bhaskara Rao, editor (2006). *Techniques of Teaching Science.* New Delhi : Sonali Publications. ISBN 81-8411-041-3.

Sirisha Rani, S., author and Digumarti Bhaskara Rao, editor (2007). *Techniques of Teaching Botany.* New Delhi : Sonali Publications. ISBN 81-8411-037-5.

Sivaratnam Reddy, M., author and Digumarti Bhaskara Rao, editor (2004). *Creativity in College Students.* New Delhi : Discovery Publishing House. ISBN 81-7141-697-7.

Siva Lakshmi, G.V. and G.L. Subbaiah, authors and Digumarti Bhaskara Rao, editor (2004). *Methods of Teaching Environmental Science.* New Delhi: Discovery Publishing House. ISBN 81-7141-839-2.

Srinivas, G. and Digumarti Bhaskara Rao (2007). *Anxiety of Prospective Teachers.* New Delhi : Sonali Publications. ISBN 81-8411-084-7.

Srinivas, G. and Digumarti Bhaskara Rao (2011). *Intelligence and Personality of Prospective Teachers.* New Delhi : Discovery Publishing House.

Srinivas, M. and I. Prasada Rao, authors and Digumarti Bhaskara Rao, editor (2004). *Methods of Teaching History.* New Delhi : Discovery Publishing House.

Srinivas Rao, P., author and Digumarti Bhaskara Rao, editor (2007). *Principles of Secondary School.* New Delhi : Sonali Publications. ISBN 81-8411-058-8.

Srinivasulu, K., author and Digumarti Bhaskara Rao, editor (2011). *Achievement Motivation and Academic Achievement of Alcoholic and Non-alcoholic College Students.* New Delhi : Discovery Publishing House.

Srinivasulu, Kopperla and Digumarti Bhaskara Rao (2011). *Achievement Motivation, Academic Achievement and Alcoholism.* Saarbrucken, Germany : LAMBERT Academic Publishing GmbH & Co. KG. ISBN 978-3-8465-9296-0

Srinivasulu Reddy, M. and K.R.S. Sambasiva Rao, authors and Digumarti Bhaskara Rao, editor (1999). *A Text Book of Aquaculture.* New Delhi : Discovery Publishing House. ISBN 81-7141-482-6.

Srinivasa Rao, Mandalapu, author and Digumarti Bhaskara Rao, editor (2003). *Achievement Motivation and Achievement in Mathematics.* New Delhi : Discovery Publishing House. ISBN 81-7141-674-8.

Srihari, M., author and Digumarti Bhaskara Rao, editor (2003). *Values of Prospective Teachers.* New Delhi : Discovery Publishing House. ISBN 81-8356-328-7.

Subba Rao, K., author and Digumarti Bhaskara Rao, editor (2007). *School Education Policy.* New Delhi : Discovery Publishing House. ISBN 81-8356-285-X.

Subba Rao, K., author and Digumarti Bhaskara Rao, editor (2007). *Education Planning.* New Delhi : Sonali Publications. ISBN 81-8411-053-7.

Subramanyam, N.R., author and Digumarti Bhaskara Rao, editor (2011). *Effectiveness of In-service Training Programmes.* New Delhi : Discovery Publishing House.

Sudhakar Reddy, Y., author and Digumarti Bhaskara Rao, editor (2003). *Creativity in Adolescents.* New Delhi : Discovery Publishing House. ISBN 81-7141-659-4.

Sunil Kumar, K. and K. Rama Krishana, authors and Digumarti Bhaskara Rao, editor (2004). *Methods of Teaching Chemistry.* New Delhi : Discovery Publishing House. ISBN 81-7141-913-5.

Suneetha, G., author and Digumarti Bhaskara Rao, editor (2004). *Environmental Awareness of School Students.* New Delhi: Sonali Publications. ISBN 81-8411-085-5.

Sunita, E. and R. Sambasiva Rao, authors and Digumarti Bhaskara Rao, editor (2004). *Methods of Teaching Mathematics.* New Delhi : Discovery Publishing House. ISBN 81-7141-915-1.

Surya Madhava, I., author and Digumarti Bhaskara Rao, editor (2006). *Techniques of Teaching Geography.* New Delhi : Discovery Publishing House. ISBN 81-8411-034-0.

Surya Madhava, I., author and Digumarti Bhaskara Rao, editor (2007). *Techniques of Teaching Political Science.* New Delhi : Discovery Publishing House. ISBN 81-8411-061-8.

Swamy, K.R., author and Digumarti Bhaskara Rao, editor (2006). *Techniques of Teaching Environmental Science.* New Delhi : Discovery Publishing House. ISBN 81-8411-035-9.

Swarna Jyothi, K., author and Digumarti Bhaskara Rao, editor (2007). *Educational Research.* New Delhi : Sonali Publications. ISBN 81-8411-063-4.

Swarna Latha, C.D., and Digumarti Bhaskara Rao, editors (2006). *Encyclopaedia of Biotechnology,* 5 volumes. New Delhi : Discovery Publishing House. ISBN 81-8356-168-3.

Swarupa Rani, T. and J.R. Priyadarshini, authors and Digumarti Bhaskara Rao, editor (2004). *Educational Measurement and Evaluation.* New Delhi : Discovery Publishing House. ISBN 81-7141-859-7.

Vanaja, M., author and Digumarti Bhaskara Rao, editor (1999). *Inquiry Training Model.* New Delhi : Discovery Publishing House. ISBN 81-7141-515-6.

Vanaja, M., author and Digumarti Bhaskara Rao, editor (2004). *Methods of Teaching Physics.* New Delhi : Discovery Publishing House. ISBN 81-7141-867-8

Vanaja, M. and N. Sneha Latha, authors and Digumarti Bhaskara Rao, editor (2004). *Student Shyness.* New Delhi : APH Publishing Corporation. ISBN 81-7648-

Valeri V. Koustiouk, author and Digumarti Bhaskara Rao, editor (2002). *A Text Book of Cryogenics.* New Delhi : Discovery Publishing House. ISBN 81-7141-642-X.

Vamsi Krishna, V., author and Digumarti Bhaskara Rao, editor (2004). *School Psychology.* New Delhi: Discovery Publishing House. ISBN 81-7141-880-5.

Veena Kumari, Balusu and Digumarti Bhaskara Rao (1996). *Operation Black Board.* New Delhi : APH Publishing Corporation. ISBN 81-7024-711-X.

Veena Kumari, Balusu, author and Digumarti Bhaskara Rao, editor (2004). *Methods of Teaching Social Studies.* New Delhi: Discovery Publishing House. ISBN 81-7141-899-6.

Veena Kumari, Balusu, author and Digumarti Bhaskara Rao, editor (2000). *Psycho-Social Correlates of Achievement.* New Delhi : Discovery Publishing House. ISBN 81-7141-547-4.

Venkata Rao, B., author and Digumarti Bhaskara Rao, editor (2007). *Techniques of Teaching Chemistry.* New Delhi : Sonali Publications. ISBN 81-8411-057-X.

Venkata Rao, P. and Digumarti Bhaskara Rao (1989). *A Text Book of Zoology – Junior Intermediate.* Guntur : Vignan Publishers.

Venkata Rao, P. and Digumarti Bhaskara Rao (1989). *A Text Book of Zoology – Senior Intermediate.* Guntur : Vignan Publishers.

Venkateswara Rao, V., author and Digumarti Bhaskara Rao, editor (2004). *Problems of Education.* New Delhi : Discovery Publishing House. ISBN 81-7141-841-4.

Venkateswara Rao, V., V. Vijaya Lakshmi and V. Vamsi Krishna, authors and Digumarti Bhaskara Rao, editor (2004). *Education For All.* New Delhi : Sonali Publications. ISBN 81-88836-30-3.

Venkateswara Rao, V., V. Vijaya Lakshmi and V. Vamsi Krishna, authors and Digumarti Bhaskara Rao, editor (2004).

Education in India. New Delhi : Sonali Publications. ISBN 81-88836-858-9.

Venkateswara Reddy, L. and Narayana, M. L., authors and Digumarti Bhaskara Rao, editor (2004). *Education for Dalits*. New Delhi : Discovery Publishing House. ISBN 81-7141-872-4.

Venkateswara Reddy, L. and Narayana, M. L, authors and Digumarti Bhaskara Rao, editor (2004). *Methods of Teaching Rural Sociology*. New Delhi : Discovery Publishing House. ISBN 81-7141-811-2.

Venkateswarlu, K. and S.J. Basha, authors and Digumarti Bhaskara Rao, editor (2004). *Methods of Teaching Commerce*. New Delhi : Discovery Publishing House. ISBN 81-7141-808-2.

Venugopala Rao, K., author and Digumarti Bhaskara Rao, editor (2000). *Teacher Morale in Secondary Schools*. New Delhi: Discovery Publishing House. ISBN 81-7141-551-2.

Venugopala Rao, K., author and Digumarti Bhaskara Rao, editor (2007). *Techniques of Teaching history*. New Delhi : Sonali Publications. ISBN 81-8411-059-6.

Vidya, C., author and Digumarti Bhaskara Rao, editor (1996). *A Text Book of Nutrition*. New Delhi : Discovery Publishing House. ISBN 81-7141-309-9.

Vimala, T.D., B. Prasad Babu and Digumarti Bhaskara Rao, editors (2007). *Stress, Coping and Management*. New Delhi: Sonali Publications. ISBN 81-8411-086-3.

Vijaya Bharathi, D., author and Digumarti Bhaskara Rao, editor (2000). *Educational Philosophies of Swami Vivekananda and John Dewey*. New Delhi : APH Publishing House. ISBN 81-7648-309-9.

Vijaya Bharathi, D., author and Digumarti Bhaskara Rao, editor (2005). *Educational Philosophy of John Dewey*. New Delhi : Discovery Publishing House. ISBN 81-8356-024-5.

Vijaya Bharathi, D., author and Digumarti Bhaskara Rao, editor (2005). *Educational Philosophy of Swami Vivekananda*. New Delhi : Discovery Publishing House. ISBN 81-8356-023-7.

Vijaya Lakshmi, D., author and Digumarti Bhaskara Rao, editor (2004) *Basic Education.* New Delhi : Discovery Publishing House. ISBN 81-7141-881-3.

Vijaya Lakshmi, V., author and Digumarti Bhaskara Rao, editor (2006). *Techniques of Teaching Music.* New Delhi : Discovery Publishing House. ISBN 81-8411-038-3.

Vijaya Kumar, S.J., author and Digumarti Bhaskara Rao, editor (2006). *Techniques of Teaching Mathematics.* New Delhi : Sonali Publications. ISBN 81-8411-039-1.

Visalakshi, V., author and Digumarti Bhaskara Rao, editor (2006). *Techniques of Teaching Biology.* New Delhi : Sonali Publications. ISBN 81-8411-045-6.

Visalakshi, V., author and Digumarti Bhaskara Rao, editor (2007). *Techniques of Teaching Zoology.* New Delhi : Sonali Publications. ISBN 81-8411-055-3.

Books in Telugu Language

Bhaskara Rao, Digumarti (1986). *Dhrushya Sravana Bodhanapakaranalu* (Audio Visual Teaching Aids). Guntur : Nagarjuna Publishers.

Bhaskara Rao, Digumarti (1993). *Jeevasashtra Bodhana* (Teaching of Biology). Guntur : Nagarjuna Publishers.

Bhaskara Rao, Digumarti (1995). *Vignanasasthra Bodhana* (Teaching of science) Guntur : Nagarjuna Publishers.

Bhaskara Rao, Digumarti (1994). *Vidya Manovignana Sastram* (Educational Psychology). Guntur : Nagarjuna Publishers.

Bhaskara Rao, Digumarti (1997). *Vidya Manovignana Sastram* (Educational Psychology). Guntur : Creative Press.

Bhaskara Rao, Digumarti (1998). *DSC Study Material.* Guntur: Nagarjuna Publishers.

Bhaskara Rao, Digumarti (1998). *Upadhyayudu Vidya.* (Teacher and Education) Guntur : Nagarjuna Publishers.

Bhaskara Rao, Digumarti (1998). *Vidya Drukpadalu* (Perspectives of Education). Guntur : Nagarjuna Publishers.

Bhaskara Rao, Digumarti (1999). *EdCET Teaching Aptitude.* Guntur : Nagarjuna Publishers.

Bhaskara Rao, Digumarti (2001). *Bharata Samajamulo Upadyayudu Vidhya* (Teacher and Education in Emerging Indian Society). Guntur : Sri Nagarjuna Publishers.

Bhaskara Rao, Digumarti (2001). *Bhoutika Sastra Bodhana Padhatulu* (Methods of Teaching Physical Science). Guntur: Sri Nagarjuna Publishers.

Bhaskara Rao, Digumarti (2001). *Jeeva Sastra Bodhana Padhatulu* (Methods of Teaching Biology).Guntur : Sri Nagarjuna Publishers.

Bhaskara Rao, Digumarti (2001). *Vidya Manovignana Sastram* (Educational Psychology). Guntur : Sri Nagarjuna Publishers.

Bhaskara Rao, Digumarti (2003). *Patasala Yajamanyam / Paripalana* (School Management and Administration). Guntur : Sri Nagarjuna Publishers.

Bhaskara Rao, Digumarti and M. Srihari (2009). *Vardamana Bharata Desamulo Vidya* (Education in Emerging India). Guntur : Sri Nagarjuna Publishers.

Bhaskara Rao, Digumarti and B. Prasad Babu (2009). *Vidya Manovignana Sastram* (Educational Psychology). Guntur : Sri Nagarjuna Publishers.

Bhaskara Rao, Digumarti and B. Prasad Babu (2009). *Pradhamika Vidya mariyu Vileena Vidya Dhrukpadhalu* (Perspectives in Primary Education and Inclusive Education). Guntur : Sri Nagarjuna Publishers.

Bhaskara Rao, Digumarti and K. Subba Rao (2009). *Elementary Vidya, Pranalika, Yajamanyam, Upadyaya Kartavyalu* (Elementary Education, Planning, Management and Teacher Functions). Guntur : Sri Nagarjuna Publishers.

Bhaskara Rao, Digumarti and G. Prasanthi (2009). *Samardya Nirmanamu* (Capacity Building). Guntur : Sri Nagarjuna Publishers.

Bhaskara Rao, Digumarti and A. Jagadish (2009). *Vignansastra Bodhana Padhatulu* (Methods of Teaching Science).Guntur: Sri Nagarjuna Publishers.

Bhaskara Rao, Digumarti, editor (2010). *Vardamana Bharata Desamulo Vidya – Question Bank* (D.Ed. Education in Emerging India). Guntur : Sri Nagarjuna Publishers.

Bhaskara Rao, Digumarti, editor (2010). *Vidya Manovignana Sastram – Question Bank* (D.Ed. Educational Psychology). Guntur : Sri Nagarjuna Publishers.

Bhaskara Rao, Digumarti, editor (2010). *Pradhamika Vidya mariyu Vileena Vidya Dhrukpadhalu – Question Bank* (D.Ed. Perspectives in Primary Education and Inclusive Education). Guntur : Sri Nagarjuna Publishers.

Bhaskara Rao, Digumarti, Editor (2010). *Elementary Vidya, Pranalika, Yajamanyam, Upadyaya Kartavyalu – Question Bank* (D.Ed. Elementary Education, Planning, Management and Teacher Functions). Guntur : Sri Nagarjuna Publishers.

Bhaskara Rao, Digumarti, editor (2010). *Samardya Nirmanamu – Question Bank* (D.Ed. Capacity Building). Guntur : Sri Nagarjuna Publishers.

Bhaskara Rao, Digumarti, editor (2010). *Ganithasastra Bodhana Padhatulu – Question Bank* (D.Ed. Methods of Teaching Science).Guntur : Sri Nagarjuna Publishers.

Bhaskara Rao, Digumarti, editor (2010). *Vignansastra Bodhana Padhatulu – Question Bank* (D.Ed. Methods of Teaching Science).Guntur : Sri Nagarjuna Publishers.

Bhaskara Rao, Digumarti, editor (2010). *Sanghikasastra Bodhana Padhatulu – Question Bank* (D.Ed. Methods of Teaching Social Studies).Guntur : Sri Nagarjuna Publishers.

Bhaskara Rao, Digumarti, editor (2010). *Telugu Bodhana Padhatulu – Question Bank* (D.Ed. Methods of Teaching Social Studies).Guntur : Sri Nagarjuna Publishers.

Bhaskara Rao, Digumarti, editor (2010). *Methods of Teaching English – Question Bank*. (D.Ed.) Guntur : Sri Nagarjuna Publishers.

Bhaskara Rao, Digumarti, editor (2011). *Vidya Adhralu – Question Bank* (B.Ed. Philosophical Foundations of Education). Guntur : Sri Nagarjuna Publishers.

Bhaskara Rao, Digumarti, editor (2011). *Vidya Manovignana Sastram – Question Bank* (B.Ed. Educational Psychology). Guntur : Sri Nagarjuna Publishers.

Bhaskara Rao, Digumarti, editor (2011). *Vidya Sanketika Sastrm – Computer Vidya – Question Bank* (B.Ed. Educational Technology and Computer Vidya). Guntur : Sri Nagarjuna Publishers.

Bhaskara Rao, Digumarti, Editor (2011). *School Management – Systems of Education – Question Bank* (B.Ed. School Management and Systems of Education). Guntur : Sri Nagarjuna Publishers.

Bhaskara Rao, Digumarti, editor (2011). *Personality Development and Communicative English – Question Bank* (B.Ed. Personality Development and Communicative English). Guntur : Sri Nagarjuna Publishers.

Bhaskara Rao, Digumarti, editor (2011). *Ganithasastra Bodhana Padhatulu – Question Bank* (B.Ed. Methods of Teaching Science). Guntur : Sri Nagarjuna Publishers.

Bhaskara Rao, Digumarti, editor (2011). *Bhoutikasastra Bodhana Padhatulu – Question Bank* (B.Ed. Methods of Teaching Physical Science).Guntur : Sri Nagarjuna Publishers.

Bhaskara Rao, Digumarti, editor (2011). *Jeevasastra Bodhana Padhatulu – Question Bank* (B.Ed. Methods of Teaching Biological Science). Guntur : Sri Nagarjuna Publishers.

Bhaskara Rao, Digumarti, editor (2011). *Sanghikasastra Bodhana Padhatulu – Question Bank* (B.Ed. Methods of Teaching Social Studies). Guntur : Sri Nagarjuna Publishers.

Bhaskara Rao, Digumarti, editor (2011). *Telugu Bodhana Padhatulu – Question Bank* (B.Ed. Methods of Teaching Social Studies). Guntur : Sri Nagarjuna Publishers.

Bhaskara Rao, Digumarti, editor (2011). *Methods of Teaching English – Question Bank.* (B.Ed.) Guntur : Sri Nagarjuna Publishers.

Bhaskara Rao, Digumarti, N. Saraja, J. Lalitha and V. Mrunalini, Translators (2008). *Vidya – Samajam (Education - Society). Hyderabad* : Dr. B. R. Ambedkar Open University.

Gopala Krishna, G., A. Rama Krishna, K. Subba Rao and Bhaskara Rao, Digumarti (2004). *Jeevasashtra Bodhana Padhatulu* (Methods of Teaching of Biological science). Guntur : Sri Nagarjuna Publishers.

Krishna Murthy, V., K.S. Sudheer Reddy and Digumarti Bhaskara Rao (2004). *Vidya Manovignana Sastra Adharalu* (Foundations of Educational Psychology). Guntur : Sri Nagarjuna Publishers.

Lalini, V., V. Dayakara Reddy, M. Srihari and Digumarti Bhaskara Rao (2004). *Vidya Adharalu* (Foundations of Education). Guntur : Sri Nagarjuna Publishers.

Sastry, G.E.P. and G. Satya Narayana, authors, Bhaskara Rao, Digumarti, editor (2009). *Sanghikasastra Bodhana Padhatulu* (Methods of Teaching Social Studies).Guntur : Sri Nagarjuna Publishers.

Subba Rao, K.P., P. Ayodhya and Digumarti Bhaskara Rao (2004). *Patasala Yajamanyam – Vidhya Vyavasthalu* (School Management and Systems of Education). Guntur : Sri Nagarjuna Publishers.

Sudhakar, V., B. Ravindra Babu, D.S. Kumar and Digumarti Bhaskara Rao (2004). *Vidya Sanketika Sastram - Computer Vidhya* (Educational Technology and Computer Education). Guntur : Sri Nagarjuna Publisher.

Gopala Krishna, G. & Rama Krishna & Subba Rao and Bhaskara Rao Digumarti (2011). *Jeevasastra Bodhana Paddhatulu* (Methods of Teaching of Biological Sciences). Guntur: Sri Nagarjuna Publishers.

Krishna Murthy, V. [illegible] Reddy and Digumarti Bhaskara Rao (2004). *Vidya Manovignana Sastra Adharalu* (Foundations of Educational Psychology). Guntur: Sri Nagarjuna Publishers.

Patil, V. S. Dayakara [illegible] and Digumarti Bhaskara Rao (2011). *Vidya [illegible]* (Foundations of Education). Guntur: Sri Nagarjuna Publishers.

Reddy, G.S. [illegible] Narayana, authors, Bhaskara Rao Digumarti, editor (2009). *Sanghika Sastra Bodhana Paddhatulu* (Methods of Teaching Social Studies). Guntur: Sri Nagarjuna Publishers.

Subba Rao, K.P. [illegible] Ayodhya and Digumarti Bhaskara Rao (2011). *Pathasala Nirvahana – Vidya Vyavasthalu* (School Management and Systems of Education). Guntur: Sri Nagarjuna Publishers.

Sudhakar, V. B. [illegible] Babu, D. [illegible] and Digumarti Bhaskara Rao (2004). *Vidya Sankethika Sastram – Computer Vidya* (Educational Technology and Computer Education). Guntur: Sri Nagarjuna Publishers.

Index